Perspectives on Communication

Louis Forsdale
TEACHERS COLLEGE
COLUMBIA UNIVERSITY

McGraw-Hill, Inc.
New York   St. Louis   San Francisco   Auckland   Bogotá   Caracas   Lisbon
London   Madrid   Mexico City   Milan   Montreal   New Delhi
San Juan   Singapore   Sydney   Tokyo   Toronto

PERSPECTIVES ON COMMUNICATION

Unless otherwise credited, photographs are by Louis Forsdale

Library of Congress Cataloging in Publication Data

Forsdale, Louis.
  Perspectives on communication.

  Bibliography: p.
  Includes index.
  1. Communication. I. Title
P90.F657   001.51   80-16616
ISBN 0-07-554858-5

First Edition
10 11 12 13 14 15 MAL MAL 9 9 8 7 6 5 4 3

Copyright ©1981 by McGraw-Hill, Inc.
All rights reserved. Printed in the United States of America. Except as permitted under the United States Copyright Act of 1976, no part of this publication may be reproduced or distributed in any form or by any means, or stored in a data base or retrieval system, without the prior written permission of the publisher.

For Lynn and John

Preface

Despite our awareness that we live in an Age of Communication, we frequently fail to convey to our students a sense of the magnitude, wonder, and fertility of that great intellectual terrain.

Certain aspects of communication, of course, receive considerable attention in our colleges. Almost every student, regardless of major, is asked to gain greater control over one or more of the verbal skills—reading, writing, speaking. Some colleges offer their students courses in interpersonal and small group communication. More and more are offering courses in the media of public communication, in order to prepare their students for careers in such fields as journalism, broadcasting, business, or public relations. These approaches to communication—through personal and work-related skills—are necessary but not sufficient. They are necessary because skill in communicating is central to success in any aspect of life. The learning of skills is not sufficient, however, because skills alone do not ply the intellect with challenges to seek beyond mere competency. Indeed, they more often hide the "beyond" from view.

Yet beyond the teaching and learning of communication skills, there is a vast array of ideas, facts, speculations, and hypotheses about communication that can and should be studied in and for themselves, in the enduring tradition of the liberal arts. These ideas are valuable for their potential to open doors in students' minds, for their beauty, daring, and richness. While they are often useful and practical ideas, they also reach much deeper, into the heart of an individual's awareness and sensibility.

While students who major in communication are often given the opportunity to confront some of these more far-reaching theories in their upper-level courses, the breadth of ideas currently alive among scholars in the field is rarely made accessible to beginning students. This is understandable, since the topography is so vast and varied. How can we examine it in less than a lifetime, let alone in a semester or so? We can't, of course. What does seem possible, however, is to view the terrain from a select number of stimulating perspectives.

But what perspectives? Let me affirm at the outset that the choice of scenic overviews in this text is mine. Topics have been selected for interest, salience, and variety, and the selection is necessarily incomplete. (The dynamic nature of the subject makes a Grand Tour unlikely at any future time, doesn't it?) But if the choice of perspectives is mine, I have been guided by others—those whose function has been to map out largely uncharted regions. There is an abundance of material in the literature, therefore, about every topic touched upon between these covers. It is, then, an underlying purpose of this text to send students (and the rest of us as well) out to scout whatever in that literature is appealing, and in particular, to point out significant directions that students might not otherwise encounter.

The skills that our students need are inseparable from ideas. If the ideas are generative, and if they are consistently linked with stimulating assignments or activities that reinforce both ideas and skills, then gains are made on both fronts. Out of fertile ideas, skills can take root. Further, we have no greater gift to offer our students of communication skills than a large-scale map of the terrain of thought, over which they can wander as independent observers, making discoveries for the rest of their lives.

My sustaining hope in writing this book, therefore, is that students reading it will encounter the scope and vitality of the present field of communication. I hope the text will reveal the sense of excitement that is deeply inherent in the study of communication, so that students will continue their personal interest and involvement long after this volume has been put aside.

I have consequently tried to make this book both readable and provocative. The writing is frequently personal and accented with anecdotes. Photographs and other graphics expand upon text and illustrate specific points. I have avoided statistics, which are not everybody's native or even second language. Readings and suggested activities point toward a variety of student interests. Many others are in the Teacher's Manual. Quotations of three kinds are used to acquaint students with a range of authorities and change the voice from my own. Most quotations are embedded directly into the text. "Head quotations" used at the beginning of chapters help set a tone. And I use "parallel quotes," which appear in distinctive type, set off from the body of the text by heavy horizontal lines, as momentary asides, making a point similar to that in the text, but adding another dimension.

I thank several persons for their help. I am grateful to Damon Gardner for early faith, Brian Walker for continuing faith, C. David Mortenson for gentle but persistent insistence that I do my best, a handful of critics, anonymous to me, who criticized drafts of the manuscript along the way, and Carol A. Spencer for her skilled editiorial work. On my home academic ground, I am grateful to Janet Skupien, Larry Weiss, Betsy Currier, Clifford Hill, Charles Bird, Albert Scheflen, Leslie Beebe, Jonathan Lovell, Peggy Wells, Bob Schuessler, and Christine Guralny for affirmation and research aid of various kinds; Paul Byers for help with a definition; Gabriella Oldham for typing—often under considerable pressure—of the last several drafts; Jane Casselman and Mary L. Allison for encouragement and crucial help in the final stages; and a bundle of students, colleagues, and other friends for patience at times when this work dampened or extinguished my good humor and good manners. I especially thank my son and my daughter, John and Lynn, who knew that my heart was with them even when my head was gyrating in the wild gray elsewhere.

New York City
January 1981

L.F.

Contents

INTRODUCTION 1

    Goals, Attitudes, and Strategies 2
        A broad view of communication is desirable 2
        Human beings are part of nature 2
        Human beings are intimately bound with technology 2
        Many disciplines are used in the study of communication 2
        A book to sharpen critical insights about communication 3
        Personal communication skills will increase through multiperspective study 4

    How Each Chapter Is Organized 4
    The Photographs 4

CHAPTER 1   **WHAT IS COMMUNICATION?** 5

    The Two Ways of Making Definitions 6
        The lexicographer's way 6
        The specialist's way 6

	Five Sample Definitions	8
	Hovland, Janis, and Kelley's definition	8
	Weaver's definition	9
	Wilson's definition	10
	Morris's definition	11
	Cherry's definition	11
	A Definition for This Book	12
	Qualities of this definition	12
	This Chapter in Perspective	14
	Extensions	14
	Reading you might enjoy	14
	Ponderings and projects	15
CHAPTER 2	**MODELS OF COMMUNICATION**	**17**
	Communication Involves Many Variables	17
	What Are Models?	18
	The Hypodermic Needle Model	19
	The Lasswell Model: A Classic Checklist Approach	19
	Who?	20
	Says What?	20
	To whom?	21
	Through what medium?	22
	With what effect?	23
	The Shannon Model: An Influential Engineering View	24
	Information source	25
	Transmitter	25
	Message encoding	25
	Receiver and message decoding	26
	Noise source	26
	The problem of one-way flow in the Shannon diagram	28
	Barnlund's Models: A Sophisticated Dynamic View	29
	Barnlund's intrapersonal model	29
	Barnlund's interpersonal model	33
	A General System Model	35

	System defined	36
	The distinction between a closed and an open system	36
	A diagram of an open system communication model	37
	This Chapter in Perspective	40
	Extensions	41
	Reading you might enjoy	41
	Pondering and projects	42
CHAPTER 3	**A HISTORY OF COMMUNICATION**	**43**
	The Three Revolutions in the History of Human Communication	44
	Undatable Starting Points: Nonverbal Communication and Speech	44
	Oral Cultures and Literate Cultures	46
	Two General Forms of Writing	49
	Sound writing	49
	Sign writing	49
	The Problem of Writing Surfaces	50
	Early Forms of Writing	51
	Sumerian pictographs	51
	Cuneiform writing	52
	Egyptian hieroglyphs	52
	Breakthrough to an alphabet	53
	Writing was not universally regarded as a blessing	56
	Writing has great advantages, too	57
	The Mechanization of Writing	58
	The Importance of Gutenberg's Concept of Mass-produced Type	58
	An important lesson: invention encourages invention	59
	The implications of new communication technology are not always clear at the outset	60
	What was the world of print like before Gutenberg?	60

The Electrochemical Revolution of the Past Century and a Half	62
The difficulty of dating inventions	62
Communication Instruments as Mass Media and as Personal Media	66
All new media begin in the hands of the few and end in the hands of the many	67
Private, public, and medio communication	68
We Are Not at the End of the Odyssey	68
When Did the Systematic Study of Communication Begin?	69
This Chapter in Perspective	71
Extensions	71
Reading you might enjoy	72
Ponderings and projects	73

CHAPTER 4   THE CULTURAL CONTEXT OF COMMUNICATION   75

Communication Habits Are Learned in a Culture	75
A Definition of Culture	76
The concept of being culture-bound	76
What members of a culture share	77
A culture is not necessarily the same as a nation	77
Subcultures	79
Culture as a system	82
Cultural Habits, Including Communication, Are Learned	82
Learning to shift communication behavior according to situations	83
Most of Our Communicative Behavior Is Learned Out-of-Awareness	85
An example of out-of-awareness learning: walking	85
In-Awareness Learning	86
A Culture's Expectations Are Strict	87

The Question of Being Bicultural or Multicultural	89
The Deep and Lasting Effects of Culture	90
Every Culture Has a Complete and Adequate Communication System	90
The Major Communication Problem Is Crossing Lines	91
Three Conversations about Cross-Cultural Communication	93
Intercultural communmication barriers	93
Conversation with Eric Bateson	94
Conversation with Sister Joanna Chan	98
Conversation with Bourama Soumaoro	102
This Chapter in Perspective	104
Extensions	105
Reading you might enjoy	105
Ponderings and projects	106

CHAPTER 5   THE PERSONAL CONTEXT OF COMMUNICATION   109

Each of Us Is a Unique Individual	109
The Individual as an Open System	110
Information input and output	110
Each Individual Is Unique	111
Our Guiding Images	111
The Selective Processes	113
Selective Attention	114
Selective attention to environmental cues	114
Selective attention to communication signals	115
The personal cost of selective attention	116
The personal rewards of selective attention	117
Selective Perception	117
Beliefs shape our perceptions	117
Offbeat perceptions	120
Seeing matters from dramatically new perspectives	123
Other ways of achieving alternate perceptual states	125
Psi	127

Selective Memory		128
We remember what serves and doesn't threaten		128
Memory can also distort		130
So What?		130
This Chapter in Perspective		132
Extensions		133
Reading you might enjoy		133
Ponderings and projects		134

CHAPTER 6   TWO KINDS OF INTELLIGENCE: THE BRAIN HEMISPHERES   137

The Danger of Considering the Brain Outside Its Relationship with Other Body Organs	138
The Two Brain Hemispheres	138
Left-Hemisphere Intelligence or Information Processing	139
Right-Hemisphere Intelligence or Information Processing	139
Proof of Lateralization from Brain-damaged Persons	142
Cultures Apparently Reinforce Hemisphere Development	142
An Example of Right-Hemisphere Development: The Eskimos	143
Julian Jaynes's Historical Theory	146
Doubts about the Two-Intelligence Theory	147
The So What for Communication	147
This Chapter in Perspective	149
Extensions	150
Reading you might enjoy	150
Ponderings and projects	151

CHAPTER 7   OUR MANY CODES   153

We Communicate with Many Signaling Systems	154
Biological and Cultural Codes	154
The Genetic Code	154

Cultural Codes	156
Digital and Analogic Codes	156
Digital codes	157
Analogic codes	160
Digital/Analogic "Illiteracy"	163
Art as Analogic Communication	166
Codification: The Means of Thought as Well as Communication	168
The Sapir-Whorf Hypothesis	168
We apparently think in nonlinguistic ways, too	172
Rhythm and Synchrony in Codification	174
Multiple Messages	175
Metacommunication	176
This Chapter in Perspective	177
Extensions	178
Reading you might enjoy	178
Ponderings and projects	178

CHAPTER 8 NONVERBAL COMMUNICATION 181

What Is Nonverbal Communication?	181
The Importance of Nonverbal Communication in Human Interaction	182
Touch (Haptics, Tacesics)	183
Odor (Olfaction, Smell)	184
Body Movement (Kinesics)	186
Shifts in Body Color	188
Eyes (Gaze, Oculusics)	188
Eye Pupil Size (Pupilometrics)	190
Interpersonal Space (Proxemics)	191
Environmental Communication	192
Body Orientation	194
Posture	196
Rate	197
Clothing and Possessions (Objectics)	197
Time (Chronometrics)	200
Nonverbal Communication and Words	201
This Chapter in Perspective	201

Extensions 202
    Reading you might enjoy 202
    Ponderings and projects 203

CHAPTER 9 THE MEDIUM IS THE MESSAGE 205

Marshall McLuhan's Insight 206
McLuhan's Approach Is Like the Approach of Sapir and Whorf 206
Oral and Print Cultures Again 208
Some Effects of Mechanized Type 208
    Increase in the importance of privacy and of individualism 208
    Emphasis on the visual 209
    Lineal thought habits 209

The "Eye World" and the "Ear World" 210
The Global Village 211
Shifting Media Change People 212
Human-Machine Communication Systems 213
People Can Get Lost in Human-Machine Systems 214
A Counterview 216
Final Thoughts on Our Communication Extensions 218
This Chapter in Perspective 220
Extensions 220
    Reading you might enjoy 220
    Ponderings and projects 221

CHAPTER 10 OTHER CREATURES COMMUNICATE 223

All Species Communicate 223
Intraspecies Communication 225
Interspecies Communication 225
Communication among Honeybees: An Important Discovery 226
    The bees' basic system: dance 227
    A qualitative or quantitative difference from human language? 229

The Difference between Signs and Symbols in Communication 230

Signs	230
Symbols	230
The Argument that Human Beings Are the Only Language-using Creatures	231
Communicating with Chimpanzees: Important Cross-Species Studies	232
A Great Hope: Understanding the Cetacea	235
Cetacean intelligence	237
Cetacean acoustical powers	238
We May Be Caught in a Bind of Assumptions	239
The Effects of Environment on Other Creatures	240
Extraterrestrial Communication	241
This Chapter in Perspective	242
Extensions	242
Reading you might enjoy	242
Ponderings and projects	243

CHAPTER 11 LEARNING TO OBSERVE COMMUNICATION IN ACTION — 247

Observation Leads to Generalization	248
You Have to Be Curious	248
Learning Book Rules Alone Will Not Do the Job	248
The Goal Is to Increase Your Alternatives	249
Emphasis on Naturalistic Observation	249
What Is It to Be Scientific?	250
A crucial test is to try to disprove your theory or hunch	251
How much falsification is necessary to disprove a theory?	251
How to Go About Observing	252
Four tips from anthropology	253
The Use of Informants	254
The Use of Recording Instruments	255
Four Mini–Case Studies in Observing	256
A street sign	256
A numbering system	258

xviii CONTENTS

        Another sign   260
        A backward limousine   261

Observations Are Seldom Earthshaking   263
Improve Your Writing by Observing   263
Spotting Long-range Trends   265
        Added access to television signals   266
        Video discs or tapes   266
        Automated and/or electronic postal systems   266
        Holography   267
        Physical transport systems   267
        Cross-species communication   267
        The crisis in knowledge   268

The Passing Parade of Language   268
This Has Been Only a Beginning   269
This Chapter in Perspective   269
Extensions   269
        Reading you might enjoy   269
        Ponderings and projects   271

POSTSCRIPT   273

NOTES ABOUT THE ILLUSTRATIONS IN THIS BOOK   277

REFERENCES   281

NAME INDEX   291

SUBJECT INDEX   295

Introduction

Welcome to the forest.

In Colorado, where I grew up, there is forest country in the mountains that is kept as wilderness area. The forest rangers build a few trails and put up a minimum number of directional signs, but otherwise they simply patrol to watch for fires and keep fools out of trouble and maintain a watchful eye to see that the natural quality of the land is preserved.

The study of communication is like exploring those wilderness areas—an adventure in the tangled underbrush of ideas and thickets of conflicting opinions, with only a few clearly marked pathways indicating how to get from here to there. It is also exciting, pushing through exhilarating country, discovering wondrous little pockets of beauty or mystery, looking out suddenly over glorious vistas.

You may be surprised to read that someone finds communication a delightful wilderness area, that the study of communication is filled with surprises, is a source of excitement. Isn't communication so old, so trampled by now, as to be a lifeless field over which we have all marched every year of our lives, so that the approach to it might better be viewed with a ho-hum of "not again"?

I hope we will agree by the time you have finished this book that there is nothing ho-humish about communication, an exciting and complex field about which too little is known yet.

GOALS, ATTITUDES, AND STRATEGIES

There are several points of view, goals, and procedures that you will find in the book. These are some of the major ones.

A Broad View of Communication Is Desirable

We will take a broad view of communication in the book, attempting to see large expanses of the whole scene from on high. The study of communication is frequently fragmented so that language ends up here, nonverbal communication is pigeonholed there, the arts end up somewhere else, and so forth. They all come together in our lives, however, so we will try to examine many of them in this book.

Human Beings Are Part of Nature

Too frequently men and women are sharply set apart from other creatures and organisms that share the planet with us. For that reason we will occasionally consider communication systems of other creatures and will always regard people as part of nature. Lewis Thomas, a physician and writer, puts the idea nicely:

> *Modern Man . . . has been trying to detach himself from nature. He sits in the topmost tiers of polymer, glass, and steel, dangling his pulsing legs, surveying at a distance the writhing life of the planet. . . . Nor is it a new thing for man to invent an existence that he imagines to be above the rest of life; this has been his most consistent intellectual exertion down the millennia. As illusion, it has never worked out to his satisfaction in the past, any more than it does today. Man is embedded in nature.* (1974, p. 1)

Human Beings Are Intimately Bound with Technology

Men and women are also embedded in technology of their own making, which has long been part of our environment. Much of it is intimately related to communication. It influences everything on the planet (and beyond, these days) and changes us in the process. A good deal will be said in this book about the relationship between us and our communication tools.

Many Disciplines Are Used in the Study of Communication

A number of disciplines and fields of study—communication theory, anthropology, psychology, rhetoric, psychiatry, biology, linguistics, history, the

GOALS, ATTITUDES, AND STRATEGIES 3

Illustration I.1 We are embedded in nature. (Photo: Lynn Forsdale)

arts—will be drawn upon in this book. There is danger in that approach because nobody knows everything about all those fields. Nobody knows everything about any *one* of them. We must be cautious, then, hoping not to pose as universal experts and trying not to distort material from various disciplines, which we are all likely to do on occasion.

Still, the world has become so specialized that it urgently needs generalists, even if we make mistakes now and again. Without accepting that risk, we run the larger danger of censorship by specialization—that is, of failing to say something because it is outside of our fields of greatest qualification. As students of communication, we must still walk a cafeteria line of disciplines, choosing a tidbit from here, a morsel from there.

A Book to Sharpen Critical Insights about Communication

This is a book, then, that is designed to sharpen insights about communication. The perspectives that are drawn upon here all contribute to that goal. In a sense, in this book we'll walk around the field—communication—viewing it from many angles. Some of the vantage points may reveal aspects of the subject that you have not considered before; others may beam new light on a familiar scene but shift your perception a bit.

4   INTRODUCTION

Personal Communication Skills Will Increase through Multiperspective Study

This many-sided look at communication will help you develop communication skills, too. A knowledge of several ways of looking at the field—some old, some new—will give cues about what aspects of communication are worth focusing on. We are past the point of being able to list more than a few hard and fast rules to follow in effective communication; situations vary too much, and communication is simply too complex for that approach. This is why we must perfect the most useful of all skills: learning to be continuous observers of communiction, every day, in its many facets, and drawing our own generalizations from those observations.

HOW EACH CHAPTER IS ORGANIZED

Each chapter begins with an overview of what is to come and ends with a summary, called "This Chapter in Perspective." At the end of each chapter you will also find a list of additional readings that may interest you and a section called "Ponderings and Projects"—questions and suggestions for activities—which are designed to stimulate your thinking and help develop your ability to apply the matters under discussion to your personal lives. A full list of all references used appears at the end of the book.

THE PHOTOGRAPHS

The photographs in this book come from many different cultures and many different situations. Sometimes the location of the photograph will be identified or will be obvious; at other times it will not be. Since the book is directed in large measure to helping you learn skills of attentive observation of communication, you may want to guess what culture is represented and what situation is pictured in unidentified photos. For example, are there clues in the first photograph in the book that suggest where it was taken and in what the participants are involved? This is a difficult—perhaps impossible—question to answer fully, if only because still photographs freeze a fraction of a second of action and because many of the photographs—like the first one—do not show much context.

Location and context of the photographs are noted at the end of the book when those matters are not clear in the text. I have taken all photographs not otherwise credited.

I hope what follows will be an adventure for you. Learning is increased by pleasure; may you have some.

What Is Communication?

1

Any definition is controversial and already embodies a philosophical attitude.

Bertrand Russell

A quick way of launching our multiperspective look at communication is to ask what the term means. We will soon see that it means many things to many people.

In this short chapter we will consider two basic ways of arriving at definitions and examine five definitions of communication that have been used by respected scholars. Finally, we will settle on one definition for our purposes in this book.

We will also ponder the question of why students of communication create different definitions. (There is one book in print that contains 126 definitions of the term, and it is incomplete!) Why don't they simply agree on one?

One answer to that question, to get us underway, is that no term that names a complex phenomenon such as communication is easy to define. How would you define *love*, for example, to name another familiar but elusive concept.

THE TWO WAYS OF MAKING DEFINITIONS

There are two ways of arriving at definitions of words. The most common one is the way of the lexicographer (dictionary maker). The other, and much less common, way is that of the specialist in the field in which the term is used.

The Lexicographer's Way

Lexicographers behave descriptively. That is, they listen to people in various walks of life, they read books, magazines, and newspapers; they study the history of the language. As a result of tuning in to the use of language, they describe the way terms are being used at a given time in history and the way they have been used in the past. Since words change their meanings with time, dictionaries have to be revised to be up-to-date.

> The responsibility of a dictionary is to record the language, not set its style. For us [lexicographers] to attempt to prescribe the language would be like Life [magazine] reporting the news as its editors would prefer it to happen.
>
> Philip B. Gove (1962, p. 92)

Lexicographers have several ways of listing the meanings of words. Since most words have multiple meanings, they may list these meanings in an arrangement that moves from the most commonly used sense of the word at the time the dictionary is compiled to the least commonly used meaning. Or the lexicographer may use an etymological technique, in which the words are listed according to their historical meanings, often with the oldest meaning first, followed by later meanings. In addition, dictionaries indicate the roots from which the word comes. The word *communication*, for example, comes from the Latin *communicatus*, which means "shared."

A relevant portion of a contemporary dictionary entry for *communication*, chosen randomly from many available American desk dictionaries (this from the 1977 edition of *Webster's New Collegiate Dictionary*), reads:

> [Communication is] *a process by which information is exchanged between individuals through a common system of symbols, signs, or behavior.*

The Specialist's Way

Specialists in a particular field may discover that the dictionary meanings of critical terms, such as the preceding one, frequently are not adequate for their purposes. So they write more precise definitions. In this approach, the specialist says, "I choose to use the term this way." Sometimes these definitions are so far removed from everyday usage that the layperson would not even recognize them.

Why do specialists make up new definitions? Why do they depart from the dictionary? Generally because they are acutely aware of particular problems that are not important in common usage.

Communication scholars may be interested in problems such as the following because the way they do their research (conduct experiments or otherwise seek information) may depend on the answer to these and many other questions:

- Is communication a process or a thing?
- When thinking about communication, are we concerned only about human beings or should the term include other organisms?
- Do participants in communication need to be aware of their intentions, or may communication occur unconsciously?
- Do machines (like computers) communicate? Can they sensibly be thought of as part of a human/machine system?
- Can communication occur through the arts—painting, music, dance, and so on—or should the term be restricted to such modes as language and mathematics?
- Must communication occur between people or other organisms or can it also occur *within* single individuals?

Creating new definitions is a perfectly legitimate—even necessary—way to proceed. As Humpty Dumpty said in Lewis Carroll's *Through the Looking Glass*, "When *I* use a word . . . it means just what I choose it to mean—neither more nor less." Alice replies, "The question is . . . whether you *can* make words mean so many different things." Humpty Dumpty, having the last word, says, "The question is . . . which is to be master—that's all."

Words do not have only one meaning: indeed, in a sense they do not have meaning in their own right at all, but only in so far as people use them in different ways.

John Wilson (1963, p. 10)

There is a requirement, however, that specialists have in departing from the normal dictionary definition of a term. They must advise readers or companions in conversation of the way they intend to use the term, and then be *consistent* in its use. They cannot slip from one usage to another and expect to be followed. And, of course, if the standard dictionary definition does the job, there is no reason to create a new one.

FIVE SAMPLE DEFINITIONS

To illustrate Bertrand Russell's point that all definitions contain points of view or attitudes, let us examine briefly five definitions which have served scholars well. None of these is right or wrong. They are only more or less useful in focusing the studies of their creators. The analyses following each definition are intended to suggest how the terms serve us less well than they did their originators for our multiperspective study of communication. The definitions come from different disciplines, illustrating the widespread relevance of communication.

Hovland, Janis, and Kelley's Definition

Let us begin with a definition used by three American sociologists, Carl I. Hovland, Irving L. Janis, and Harold H. Kelley:

> [*Communication is*] *the process by which an individual (the communicator) transmits stimuli (usually verbal) to modify the behavior of other individuals (the audience).* (1953, p. 12)

What can we find in this definition with a little probing? A complete analysis could take a chapter, but here are some of the implications of the definition.

The authors say here that communication is a process, not a thing. This means that it is constantly shifting and changing, that there are many things to consider when communicating. This is compatible with the view we will be taking.

The phrase "individual (the communicator)" suggests that communication occurs only among people. This creates a problem. Animals, insects, and slime mold also communicate. The authors *could* mean, of course, an individual wolf or an individual ant, but it seems unlikely. And clearly they rule out the notion of communication between machines (as between computers), which some scholars like to regard as a form of communication. Similarly, they appear to rule out internal body communication (if you touch your finger on a hot stove a signal is sent to the brain and central nervous system that calls for the muscular reaction of withdrawing the finger).

The phrase "(usually verbal)" says flat out that most communication occurs through words. That slights many other signaling systems, such as gesture, movement of the body, distancing between persons in a face-to-face conversation, or pictures. Communication among people is probably *not* "usually verbal" at all. The verbal component of our communication is quite possibly less important, in frequency at least, than the nonverbal.

"To modify" seems to suggest a *conscious* attempt on the part of the communicator to do something, in this case to "modify the behavior of other individuals." However, we are not as aware of our intentions in communication as most of us believe. That is, the *unconscious* in us plays an extraordinarily important role in communication behavior, as in all other forms of behavior.

These are some of the philosophical attitudes in this definition, some of which suit our purposes, some of which do not.

Weaver's Definition

Warren Weaver, an American mathematician and writer on science subjects, has used the following definition:

> [Communication is] all of the procedures by which one mind can affect another. (1949, p. 95)

What is to found in Weaver's definition?

Weaver wants broadness with respect to signaling systems. Thus he uses the phrase "all of the procedures," thereby not restricting the phenomenon to language, as do Hovland, Janis, and Kelley.

The word "mind" can be limiting, however. There are endless debates about what "mind" means, and it is not universally accepted as a quality possessed by social creatures such as honeybees, a restriction that reduces its usefulness for our purposes. For most users the definition also excludes the concept of signaling between computers, a phenomenon useful to consider as an instance of communication. Nor would Weaver's definition include, say, the transmission of genetic characteristics from parents to child, because presumably such transmission is not controlled by "mind." While we will spend only a minor amount of time with genetic communication, we need a definition permitting that.

On the other hand, the presence of "mind" in Weaver's definition does not necessarily suggest a *conscious* intent on the part of the communicator. "Mind" can quite easily be interpreted as including both the conscious and the unconscious. This interpretation has value for us, since the unconscious is so heavily involved in communication.

Wilson's Definition

The following definition is from a biologist, Edward O. Wilson:

> *Biological communication is the action on the part of one organism (or cell) that alters the probability pattern of behavior in another organism (or cell) in a fashion adaptive to either one or both of the participants.* (1975, p. 176)

What are some of the assumptions in Wilson's definition?

First, he specifically restricts the definition to biological communication, thus ruling out, for example, machine-to-machine communication. He is, after all, a biologist. But the definition does include *all* organisms, ranging in size and complexity from a single cell (an amoeba, for instance) to the primates (monkeys, chimpanzees, apes, and human beings). Thus with Wilson's definition one can easily talk about insect communication, the communication of dolphins, or the communication of that upright two-legged animal, *Homo sapiens*. But his exclusion of machines in the system reduces the usefulness of the definition to us.

Wilson's definition is all-embracing about signaling systems, however. "Biological communication is the action . . ." says, in effect, "I want to include every means of communication that organisms use without listing them all. Besides, I do not know what all of them are—nobody does. So I'll leave myself room to incorporate sounds, chemical action (as in smell), touch, body motion, and so forth."

The phrase "alters the probability pattern of behavior in another organism . . ." means that Wilson's crucial test of communication comes when he detects a shift in behavior that probably would not occur if the organism weren't influenced by a signal. You cannot ask a flea what it is thinking about or why it is reacting as it is. All you can do is observe it. (Incidentally, some students of communication feel that people aren't much better sources of information about themselves than fleas are. You can ask people what they feel, or how they react to various stimuli, including communication, but because of the monumental role of the unconscious in all of us, frequently we cannot respond with much accuracy.)

"Adaptive" in Wilson's definition means that the organisms are able to use and respond to similar signaling systems. For example, humans have not yet been able to establish an advanced communication system with dolphins—another species—which are widely regarded as extremely intelligent creatures. Oh, trainers at amusement parks are able to train dolphins to respond to certain signals, like the word "jump," which imples some adaptation, but many scientists feel that if dolphins and people could get on the same signaling

Morris's Definition

Here is a definition of communication by American philosopher Charles Morris:

> The term "communication," when widely used, covers any instance of the establishment of a commage, that is, the making common of some property to a number of things. In this sense a radiator "communicates" its heat to surrounding bodies, and whatever medium serves this process of making common is a means of communication (the air, a road, a telegraph system, a language). (1946, p. 118)

This is a very broad definition. It covers all that we will consider as communication in this book—people talking, people using body language, communication of characteristics by means of genes, insect communication, the use of various media, the sharing of feeling, and the like. Morris also skillfully escapes the problem of dealing with conscious or unconscious motivations. On the other hand, Morris embraces more in his definition than will be useful to us. While we will include signaling machines (and perhaps other inanimate objects) in thinking about communication, Morris introduces a diverting complexity when he includes the example of a radiator communicating heat to the environment.

Cherry's Definition

Consider a final definition, one proposed by Colin Cherry, a British professor of telecommunication:

> [Communication is] that which links any organism together. (1966, p. 36)

Cherry's definition has admirable breadth, including all signaling systems, human beings, and other creatures. He also avoids the problems of consciousness and unconsciousness and of intent. By stretching the meaning of the word "organism" the definition can also include machines used for communication purposes. One matter is troublesome in the definition, however. The notion of linkage could include, say, a leash held by a person, restraining a dog. The leash links them together, and by a considerable leap of imagination the two might be considered an organism. In general, however, it seems desirable for our purposes to restrict the "linking" mechanisms to signals or messages.

We will now attempt to create a definition using the useful points from the above definitions and dismissing those points that seem less useful for our purposes.

A DEFINITION FOR THIS BOOK

We will use the following definition of communication in this book.

> *Communication is the process by which a system is established, maintained, and altered by means of shared signals that operate according to rules.*

Like the other definitions, this one is neither right nor wrong. It also carries its freight of attitudes. Let us look explicitly at seven qualities of this definition and how they will serve us in our deliberations.

Qualities of This Definition

1. It includes all living creatures. "System" is used to refer to the societal ways of, say, bees, as well as human beings. It also permits including machines, which are so frequently components in human social systems today.

2. It permits including all signaling modes (words, nonverbal behavior, genes, punched holes in a card, and so forth). As Russell predicts, considering the communication of bodily characteristics through genes as being anything like, say, words, will be controversial. Aren't genes, which carry information from parent to offspring chemically, too "automatic," too outside "intentional control," to be placed in the same bag as other means of signaling? Yet, the fact is that *most* of our communication operates outside consciousness. Indeed, there are some who argue that consciousness is not in the least necessary for any communication (Jaynes, 1977) and is at best a relatively small component in all communication. In any event, we will deal with genetic communication only enough to invite attention to an important phenomenon recognized in contemporary biology.

3. It permits thinking of both conscious intent and lack of conscious intent on the part of the involved individuals or groups, since the matter of intent is never raised.

4. It permits drawing upon many fields of inquiry that contribute to the broad subject of communication, since no discipline is identified as the parent.

5. It permits consideration of intrapersonal communication (internal dialogue, for example), interpersonal communication (exchanges among a small

number of individuals), interspecies communication (communication between chimpanzees and people, for instance), and mass communication, since the phrase "system" can include all of these.

6. It emphasizes the importance of signals that operate according to rules, that is, according to orderly, repeatable, ultimately describable sets of principles. Every language, for example, follows a set of rules. This is not to say, however, that the users of that language—or any other signaling system—can necessarily state what those rules are, because for the most part we simply dredge them up from our unconscious, having learned them by living in a system in which they are continuously applied.

7. It *excludes* certain phenomena. This is a critical problem in definition making. With a subject as complex as communication, definitions can be so broad that they make it difficult to say what is *not* included. Broad as the present definition is, it does exclude (a) systems or structures held together with other than signals (by steel, for example, as in a building) and (b) aggregates of people, animals, and machines so disassociated from each other that they cannot be thought of as a recognizable system.

Why use so broad a definition of communication? The primary reason is to enhance the possibility of noticing important relationships. It is probably best to begin your study broadly, and then, if you want to, focus more narrowly later. We should try to see at least glimpses of the whole forest as best we can in this book. You can carve your initials on individual trees later if you wish. Learning about communication among bees, for instance, is interesting in itself, but it may also help us understand human communication better. Thinking of the transmission of body characteristics through the genes as a communication process is also worth doing for its own sake, but it, too, may help us learn more about *all* communication processes. Thinking about communicating machines may be illuminating in the same way.

In a book called *The Sea of Cortez* the American novelist, and amateur biologist, John Steinbeck, made a similar point about viewing a subject broadly and being open to all possibilities. Over thirty years ago, Steinbeck and a professional biologist, E. F. Ricketts, made a trip into the Gulf of Mexico, the older name of which is the Sea of Cortez. Their purpose was to observe and classify the invertebrates (creatures without vertebrae) in that body of water. Steinbeck wrote lyrically about the two-man expedition:

> *And if we [Steinbeck and Ricketts] seem a small factor in a huge pattern, nevertheless it is of relative importance. We take a tiny colony of soft corals from a rock in a little water world. And that isn't terribly important to the tide pool. Fifty miles away . . . shrimp boats are dredging with overlapping scoops, bringing up tons of*

shrimps, rapidly destroying the species so that it may never come back, and with the species destroying the ecological balance of the whole region. That isn't very important in the world. And thousands of miles away the great bombs are falling and the stars are not moved thereby. None of it is important or all of it is. (1951, pp. 3-4)

In the same spirit let us approach the study of communication, seeking breadth, ferreting out relationships.

THIS CHAPTER IN PERSPECTIVE

In this chapter we have considered the question of how our central term, *communication*, might be defined. We have noted two ways of making definitions—the lexicographer's way, which describes how terms are used, and the specialist's way, which proposes definitions to fit the particular purposes of the scholar. The scholar's definitions are neither right nor wrong; they simply direct attention to matters that their makers want to emphasize. In so doing they always reveal attitudes or biases. We examined five definitions by respected scholars from different disciplines and considered the philosophical positions suggested by each one. Finally, we settled upon a definition for this book. While broader in scope than many scholars would like (and narrower than others would like), it permits us to examine communication as a comprehensive phenomenon, a useful strategy for inexperienced students of the subject to adopt at the outset.

What's in a name? that which we call a rose
By any other name would smell as sweet.

William Shakespeare

EXTENSIONS

Reading You Might Enjoy

1. Dance, Frank E. X., and Carl E. Larson. *The Functions of Human Communication: A Theoretical Approach.* New York: Holt, Rinehart and Winston, 1976.

This book contains 126 definitions of communication. Stalking definitions is not everybody's favorite sport, of course, but this is a good book for those who would like to know about that intellectual enterprise.

2. Murray, K. M. Elisabeth. *Caught in the Web of Words: James A. H. Murray and the Oxford English Dictionary.* New Haven, Conn.: Yale University Press, 1977.

The most comprehensive dictionary of the English language ever compiled is the *Oxford English Dictionary*, familiarly known as the O.E.D. *Caught in the Web of Words* is a biography of Sir James Murray, editor of the dictionary for over a quarter of a century, during the time the gigantic work was being developed. The biography, by Murray's granddaughter, gives great insight into the problems, often monumental, faced by the dictionary maker.

3. Lipton, James. *An Exaltation of Larks or, The Venereal Game.* New York: Penguin Books, 1977.

Lipton plays with words, respectfully but delightfully, in this book. One of the archaic meanings of *venery* is "pertaining to the chase or hunt." In hunting, one frequently needs to use collective nouns in referring to the object of the hunt ("a gaggle of geese," "a pride of lions," "a rafter of turkeys"). This book is about such collective nouns, offering a number of established ones — that are hardly known — but also quickly moving to the invention of new ones ("a liter of chemists," "a plot of playwrights"). Making up new collective nouns is great fun and doing it well requires considerable skill. What's a good collective noun for a group of communicators? A confusion of communicators?

Ponderings and Projects

1. Look up the word *communication* in several modern dictionaries and see if their definitions of the term are similar to or different from the ones we have seen in this chapter. Check etymology and usage through time. A comprehensive dictionary like the O.E.D. (*Oxford English Dictionary*) would be particularly good to use.

2. Pick a subject in which you are interested and consider yourself most expert. It can be anything: a sport, a hobby, a school subject. See how a standard contemporary dictionary defines the term and then create a more precise definition in accordance with your understanding of the subject.

3. In the fourteenth century a Franciscan philosopher, William of Occam, argued a point of view that has come to be known as "Occam's Razor." While Occam was not talking about definitions, the notion still applies here. In an encyclopedia or history of science or philosophy, see what Occam had to say about simplicity, and consider how it applies to definition.

4. Make a list of about twenty-five specialized dictionaries you can find. Before starting on the project, make a guess about how many dictionaries would be in a complete list. Library reference rooms are the best beginning point.

5. In 1978 *The Random House Dictionary* was published. As with all new dictionaries, its editors sought to improve upon the works of their competitors. One of the features they speak of in the Preface is this: "We have tried to free our definitions of sexism, racism, and other prejudices. We believe that we have done so more thoroughly than ever before in lexicographic history." Take the issue of sexism, which is deeply built into the English language, and see how well, in your opinion, they have succeeded. You can check a large number of words, perhaps beginning with such words as *chairman, mankind, cameraman, Ms.* As you consider the validity of their claim, remember that they are obligated to report on usage, that is, how words are actually used, not on their preferences.

Models of Communication

2

Man is the model-making organism par exellence.

Edward T. Hall

Although definitions are helpful in understanding what a field of study is like, they generally do not do the whole job. A second useful step is to develop models—analogies, in a sense—that say a good deal more about the subject than do definitions, although still not all. As there are many definitions of communication, so there are many models, and like definitions, they represent different ways of seeing the field. In this chapter we will consider several models of communication, some old, some new. While examining these models we will also have the opportunity of seeing some of the basic precepts that apply to communication.

As in the first chapter on definitions, we are still engaged in a form of intellectual eavesdropping in which we have a chance to hear specialists say, "Well, I like to think that communication works this way . . ." And, as with all eavesdropping, it is fair for you to agree or disagree.

COMMUNICATION INVOLVES MANY VARIABLES

Communication is a process that involves many variables, many factors, to consider. Generally we do not think consciously about these factors because communication is so much a part of us. We do not remember a time when we did not communicate. We were born into it.

But a commonplace activity like communication often needs detailed analysis, if you strive for special skill or understanding. And analysis, when you get down to fundamentals, depends on knowing when to pay attention. It depends on seeing important *variable factors* (different aspects) in the process and then making decisions about how to work with those variables.

WHAT ARE MODELS?

The key word in this chapter is *models*, but the term is used in a special way. These models neither compete for nor win prizes as Mr. or Ms. Universe, nor do they show off clothes, nor are they meticulous, small renderings of cars or ships or planes.

Rather, models as used here are intellectual devices, frequently but not always graphic, that depict a number of factors that need to be considered in analyzing or describing a process or phenomenon, often showing how the factors relate to each other.

Models are like maps. They show key points and linkups, but as semanticist Alfred Korzybski pointed out, "A map is *not* the territory it represents" (1941, p. 58). There are models of the universe, of the human brain, of economic systems, of social organizations, of communication, and so on. Generally speaking, models, like definitions, are not right or wrong. They are simply more or less useful in helping you think through a problem. Some are more complex than others. Some go out of date and are replaced by newer ones as new observations and discoveries are made.

The history of science is cluttered with the relics of conceptual schemes that were once fervently believed and that have since been replaced.... There is no way of proving that a conceptual scheme is final.

Thomas S. Kuhn (1959, p. 39)

The important question to ask of all models, including the ones about communication that follow, is not whether they are true or false, but whether they help us think, whether they arouse our curiosity, whether they nudge our thinking in new ways. The search for unchanging truths is naive, if not dangerous.

Throughout the rest of this chapter we will consider several models that have been developed to help explain the nature of communication. As with definitions, there are dozens of models of communication. We are merely sampling.

> Doubt is not a very agreeable status, but certainty is a ridiculous one.
>
> Voltaire

THE HYPODERMIC NEEDLE MODEL

Let us begin with perhaps the simplest model of communication. It is frequently referred to as the "hypodermic needle model." The notion here is that we "inject" ideas or messages or values into people, and that all we need is the proper "injection" technique to make the process work. This is close to saying, "If I pound hard enough the idea will get through."

The model's major weakness is a failure to recognize that the organism (human being or other creature) is not passive in the act of communication. We actively, although not necessarily consciously, filter ideas so that they fit our assumptions, our needs, our personal value systems. You might say that we frequently reject attempts at "injected" communication, just as injected medication often does not work as anticipated because our bodies react unexpectedly to it. So some messages are psychologically unacceptable and are rejected. On the other hand, messages matching our assumptions may be accepted quite directly, rather like a successful medical injection. The process is seldom that simple, however.

THE LASSWELL MODEL: A CLASSIC CHECKLIST APPROACH

A second model, an old but still useful one for certain purposes, was suggested by Harold Lasswell (1948, p. 37), a political scientist at Yale University. Applying primarily to human communication, it calls for asking, and answering, five questions. It is a checklist of sorts and is most valuable for early systematic thinking for beginning students. More advanced scholars find it of only modest theoretical value. The five questions posed are these:

> *Who?*
> *Says What?*
> *In Which Medium?*
> *To Whom?*
> *With What Effect??*

Like many models of communication, it is helpful in analyzing a wide range of communication acts, from two people speaking face-to-face to 100 million people watching a telecast of the Super Bowl.

Let us reflect briefly on each of Lasswell's five questions.

Who?

When thinking about the first question, you ask: "Who is the person initiating the communication and what difference does that make? Is the person known to the audience in any way? If so, is the audience likely to have any kind of predisposition toward the communicator—friendliness, animosity, receptivity? Is the communicator known to be, or thought to be, knowledgeable or to have particular qualifications to talk on or write about or make a film on a particular subject? What symbolic qualities are embraced in this person?" Communication specialists refer to these matters as *source credibility*.

The "who" can be you, if you use the model to think about yourself as a communicator. None of us is as simple to analyze as might appear at first glance. Each of us is made up of many parts, and we play many roles in our day-to-day social relationships. We shift, for example, in our behavior from the self who primps for a special date to the casual one-of-the-gang-on-a-picnic self. At the deepest level each of our personalities has considerable consistency. While we remain loyal (generally without being aware of it) to certain beliefs, values, and ideals, we do adapt to a variety of social situations and display flexibility in so doing. We also appear in different lights to different people—to our parents, our teachers, our employers, our close friends, ourselves.

The originator of communication may also be a group, such as a company or a political party. We all know the importance that the name and reputation of an organization may have in making communication from that source more or less creditable. The concept of brand names in advertising depends on the assumption that people believe it makes a difference which company makes a product. And of course we *do* believe that, sometimes for rational reasons, sometimes not.

Says What?

Lasswell's second question, "Says what?" relates to the *content* of the communication. This is the point at which one asks, and answers, the question: "What am I trying to say?" or "What is (are) the person (persons) who originated this message trying to say?" Generally, we ask this question very early in our thinking about an act of communication. Such professional communicators as advertisers, politicians, or television programmers may spend agonizingly long periods of time thinking through their content.

For many people content is the *only* concern in the communication process. This is an unfortunate limitation because it ignores other important variables in the communication process. Still, it is true that the well-turned phrase—certainly part of the content—is an aspect of communication that calls attention to itself. How memorable is Hamlet's "To be or not to be," or

United States General Anthony C. McAuliffe's defiant reply, "Nuts," to the German surrender request at Bastogne, Belgium, during the decisive Battle of the Bulge in World War II. What power Marshall McLuhan's phrase, "The medium is the mesage," has for many people. What hope Dr. Martin Luther King's "I have a dream" had, and has, for millions of people. How striking is Muhammad Ali's "Float like a butterfly, sting like a bee."

Some subjects simply are complex. For example, it is difficult to communicate intelligently about Einstein's theory of relativity, probably not so much because people are reluctant to listen, read, and believe, but because the ideas are tough for most of us.

On the other hand, some subjects are difficult to communicate about because of the predisposition of audiences. For example, it is often extremely difficult to talk about abortion, for or against, not merely because the subject is hard to analyze and organize into sensible terms—medically, morally, ethically, and theologically—but also because people often feel very strongly about it. It is probable that any subject you name will meet with some audience resistance somewhere. The term *audience*, by the way, is used in the field of communication to mean one person or a million people.

At still other times the content of material may be intelligible only to certain audiences for reasons of economy. Every profession—medicine, law, architecture, physics, mathematics—has special jargon that makes communication easier for persons trained in the field. Physicists and mathematicians can read Einstein's formula $E = mc^2$ and find in it what a volume of standard writing could not communicate as well for you and me. Sometimes, unfortunately, communicators hide their own indecision or ignorance by using language, or other modes, that seem impressive but that on close analysis are meaningless to both specialist and layperson.

To Whom?

Let us consider now the factor of audience, the "to whom?" Richard Harrington, a Canadian documentary photographer who spent much time among Eskimos, once wrote of this amusing case of failing to match content with audience:

> I myself had sometimes been guilty of using senseless phrases when talking to Eskimos. For instance, I once caught myself saying something like this: "Look through this view finder. See: the image is reversed. Don't drop it, the thing cost a hell of a lot of money and money doesn't grow on trees . . ." This, to someone who had never studied optics, never seen a real tree, and never handled money in his life! (1952, p. 53)

This story illustrates a profound communication principle: People understand what their experience permits them to understand. To a degree, everybody understands this principle, as we will agree by reflecting on the fact that we talk in a special way to children, recognizing that they have not had certain kinds of experience and consequently lack vocabulary or other appropriate communication codes. Nor do we speak in the same way to all children, because we know that their experiences differ greatly. We might have difficulty in talking with a city child about a chicken brooder, and a farm child would be equally hard pressed to get a clear impression of a subway turnstile.

So it is with all audiences. Because of cultural and personality differences, because of such differences as age, sex, national background, religious training, professional preparation, and educational level, all audiences must be treated as special cases.

Through What Medium?

The question "Through what medium?" is extraordinarily difficult to analyze, and is growing more difficult by the day, if only because we have more means of communication than we once did.

Medium, in communication terminology, refers to the means of communication: speech, gesture, body motion, eye contact, touch, radio, television, film, debate, letter, essay, novel, poem, painting, cartoon, poster, sky writing, or the like. Now and again we will use the term *communication mode* as a synonym for medium.

The question of medium can be divided somewhat artificially for analysis into two parts. First, there is the question of what media* different groups of people generally pay attention to. For example, if you were an advertiser who wanted to sell expensive yachts, you would use a medium—a magazine, for example—that was read by people with enough money to buy yachts. As a result of careful research a great deal is known about the media preference of

---

Each medium, if its bias is properly exploited, reveals and communicates a unique aspect of reality, of truth. Each offers a different perspective, a way of seeing an otherwise hidden dimension of reality.

Edmund Carpenter (1957, p. 14)

---

* A word about the difference between the words *medium* and *media*. The first is singular. Thus, "Television is a medium of communication." The second is plural. Thus, "Television, radio, and newspapers are media of communication."

audiences of different ages, levels of education, income, religion, professional backgrounds, hobby interests, sex, and so forth.

Second, there is the question of whether one medium, because of its nature, is better suited for a job than another medium. Is film, because it can show motion, close-ups, and the like, better to use when teaching how to operate a complicated machine than a written essay? Sometimes yes, but unbending answers about this sort of question are impossible. Too many factors are involved. There are questions, for example, of taste or aesthetic feeling, of personal biases and prejudices, of the quality of the work. Although many people have tried to make hierarchies of media from most effective to least effective, no medium has been shown to always be better than any other medium for every purpose, every audience, every subject, every intended purpose.

The old saying, "A picture is worth a thousand words," either has become misunderstood or was foolishly formulated. What picture? What thousand words? Some pictures—some contemporary art, for instance—are not only meaningless but also repellent to some people. And some words are so complex as to be meaningless.

Reading an image, like the reception of any other message, is dependent on prior knowledge of possibilities; we can only recognize what we know.

E. H. Gombrich (1972, p. 92)

With What Effect?

The payoff question in communication work is, "With what effect?" More time, anxiety, money, talent, and energy have been spent on this question than on any other aspect of communication.

The advertiser wants to know: "Did people buy my client's car as a result of our advertising campaign?" The elementary school teacher asks: "Did my students learn to brush their teeth because of my demonstration?" The sociologist asks: "Do children learn antisocial behavior when reading comic books, watching television programs, reading novels, going to the movies?" The campaigning politician wonders: "Did I get my votes more as a result of that television speech or more because of my handshaking efforts?" The public health nurse asks: "Will that family get chest X rays as a result of our conversation?" A mother worries: "How much good did that talk with Miranda do?" A preacher ponders: "Did my sermon this morning convince anyone?" The propagandist asks: "Is this series of international broadcasts having any effect

24 MODELS OF COMMUNICATION

in the countries I want to influence?" The lover worries: "Will my letter let him know how much I care?" The student wonders: "Will my papers be convincing?"

The difficult question, "With what effect?" can be asked at two points in the communication process. First, it may be asked when a person *contemplates* an act of communication. Here you say: "What do I want to achieve as a result of this communication?" Second, the question may be asked when a person *evaluates* the completed act of communication. Here you ask: "What was achieved?" And the only way any of these questions can be answered with a degree of certainty is the pragmatic one of seeing what behavior actually results, what people do, as a result of communication. And even then you cannot be certain in most cases whether a specific act of communication has caused the behavior or whether other factors have been at work as well. Proving cause-to-effect relationships is one of the most difficult problems any researcher has.

THE SHANNON MODEL: AN INFLUENTIAL ENGINEERING VIEW

Another widely used model of communication is that of Claude Shannon, then of the Bell Telephone Laboratories, now of Massachusetts Institute of Technology. It was first proposed as a means of analyzing the amount of information that could be handled on a given channel, such as the telephone. Warren Weaver interpreted Shannon's difficult mathematical statement into less technical language, and for that reason it is often known as the Shannon-Weaver model.

In fairness, you should know that the interpretation of Shannon's concept here verges on being *dangerously simplistic for the purposes Shannon had in mind.* Our analysis not only bypasses Shannon's mathematical sophistication; it also further condenses Weaver's analysis. Still, it serves to illuminate communication in a way that differs from Lasswell's approach.

The model, represented in diagrammatic form, is shown in Fig. 2.1.

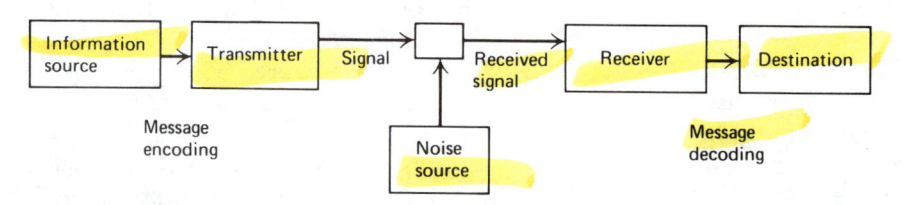

Information source → Transmitter → Signal → [ ] → Received signal → Receiver → Destination

Message encoding   Noise source   Message decoding

Fig. 2.1 Schematic diagram of a general communication system. From C. Shannon and W. Weaver, *The Mathematical Theory of Communication*, Urbana, University of Illinois Press, 1949. Copyright © 1949 by The University of Illinois Press.)

THE SHANNON MODEL: AN INFLUENTIAL ENGINEERING VIEW

Information Source

We move from left to right in the model, beginning with "information source." In human communication or other animal communication (which Shannon and Weaver do not consider), the information source is a brain, and the brain is filled with an infinite number of possible messages. Have you ever paused to "listen" to your own brain in its gyrations? If you are attuned to its complexity of associations, to the extraneous thoughts that sneak in, to the associations that it makes, the memories, the irrelevancies, you know of the millions of possible thoughts in your brain at any moment.

In this model, then, the first task is for the brain to come up with a mesage, or a small set of messages, from those millions of messages available. Often this is a fairly simple task because of social custom. In the United States, if you meet a friend coming down the street, our cultural ways have narrowed the message repertoire to, for example: "Hi!" "How's it goin'?" "What's the story?" "How are you?" "What's happening?" In more complex matters—giving a speech, writing a term paper, explaining a difficult decision to a parent—there are more possible messages to consider. In any event, the brain selects a message appropriate to the situation. This selection process, more often than not, is an unconscious action.

Transmitter

The second step—symbolized by the second box in the model—is choosing a "transmitter." Let us separate here two kinds of communication: (1) face-to-face communication (or interpersonal communication) and (2) machine-interposed communication.

In *face-to-face communication*, the transmitters are vocal cords and associated speech apparatus and the musculature and organs involved in nonverbal body language.

Machine-interposed communication means communication in which a device like a telephone, a radio, a book, a writing pad, a television set, a photograph, or a film serves as a transmitter between the communicating parties or is used in addition to the simple body apparatus of participants in face-to-face communication.

Message Encoding

"Message encoding" is required to change the idea in the brain, which is an electrical impulse, into a code appropriate to the transmitter. That is, the electrical impulse in the brain is not simply transmitted directly from one brain to another, although some scientists believe that this may some day be possible (one brain connected directly to another brain by wire, say). Meanwhile, we change the electrical impulses into a signal that can be transmitted. In face-to-face communication the signal suited to the vocal apparatus is speech; the signals suited to body musculature and senses include gesture, touch, spacing between communicating parties, odor, and eye contact.

In machine-interposed communication—in which tools are employed as extensions of the senses—message encoding also originates with the body but is extended over greater distances by the transmitters. All communication devices, or tools, extend our bodies: radio extends the voice, television extends the eyes, print extends the eyes.

Now obviously, you must know the signals that the other person uses. If you speak English but not Swahili and someone speaks to you in Swahili, then the communication breaks instantly, unless of course you understand something of the other codes used—the gestures, the body movements, the eye contact.

We will ignore for a moment the center portion of Shannon's diagram—the part called "noise source"—returning to it shortly. Meanwhile, we move to the terms on the right—"receiver," "message decoding," and "destination."

Receiver and Message Decoding

Shannon's terms "receiver" and "mesage decoding" are to be taken as mirror opposites of his terms "transmitter" and "message encoding." In face-to-face communication, recall that the possible transmitters for encoded messages are vocal apparatus and body musculature. The receiver in such cases is simply an organ of the body that is capable of perceiving the signals. The ear receives and decodes speech, the eye receives and decodes body movement and gestures, the eye sees and decodes the glint in other eyes, and so forth. Clearly, if one of the persons in the face-to-face communication is deficient in one or more of the body's receiving organs—eyes, ears, fingers, sense of smell—then a breakdown of some degree will occur in the communication.

Finally comes Shannon's right-hand box, "destination." This is another human brain, filled with its own particular mass of details, or memories, of conflicting thoughts, of possible messages. The receiver has simply gained access to the signal—heard it, seen it, felt it, and so on. The signal is then decoded, that is, interpreted by the destination (brain). The chances of *identical* interpretation (called "isomorphism") between the information source (one brain) and the destination (another brain) are almost nil with complex communication. (Notice the word was *identical*, not *close* or *similar*.)

Noise Source

Let us skip back to the middle of Shannon's diagram to the term "noise source," which impinges on the box "signal." Here he suggests the crucial idea

THE SHANNON MODEL: AN INFLUENTIAL ENGINEERING VIEW 27

that in every transmission of communication signals there is outside interference. He calls this interference "noise" or "noise in the channel."

If you are talking with someone on a street, for example, a horn may honk in the background, distracting you for a split second. But in this model, an expanded definition of *noise* is used, so that it is *anything* that might be distracting to the clear transmission of the signal, whether it is auditory or not. Thus a flickering flourescent light in a library while you were reading would be distracting, too, and would be *noise*, even if the distraction were visual, not auditory. For a blind person reading Braille by touch, a page of tissue covering the raised dots would be distracting and, while tactile, would still be *noise* in Shannon's usage. How can he distort the term *noise* that way? Simply because he chooses to expand the normal meaning and gives the reader fair warning about the new usage.

Shannon assumes that noise *always* exists to some degree in every communication act, that distractions are *always* at work. Thus we should always be prepared to counteract noise, never surprised by its presence.

How can we counteract noise? Essentially in four ways, as follows:

1. *Increase the power of the signal.* On the busy street if the horn honks during your conversation, you talk louder. If static interferes in machine-interposed communication, say with a radio signal, boost the power of the radio signal. If you are touching someone's hand while guiding the person through a crowd and if noise in the form of shoving people becomes a problem, clutch the hand more securely, thus increasing the power of that particular signal. Obviously the power of the signal can become so loud as to counteract its purpose. Increased volume in conversation, for example, can become an annoying scream.

2. *Direct the signal more precisely.* If during the street conversation, the honking horn becomes interfering noise, another tactic of countering the noise is to lean closer to the other person, speaking more directly into the person's ear—that is, beaming the signal more precisely. If the radio signal is obscured by static, the signal can be directed more accurately to the receivers, thus countering the noise. The touch on the hand of the person you are helping through the crowd might be more delicately arranged, more precisely adjusted.

3. *Use other signals in addition to the basic one(s).* When the honking horn on the street creates noise during your conversation, a third countering tactic is to reinforce the message with other signals—such as a gesture, a touch, or a shift in body position. If a radio signal is overcome by static, it may be technically possible to shift to a completely different signaling mode—semaphore signs in the instance of ships at sea, for example. If the clutched hands of the couple moving through the crowd are interrupted by the noise of pushing and hauling, the two might talk with each other as well: "Let's head for that exit and meet there if we get separated," thus introducing a second signaling system.

4. *Be redundant*. Redundancy is normally thought of as bad practice. Students who write papers and say the same thing excessively may receive the nasty marginal comment from the teacher: "Redundant." But noise—those external matters that interfere with effective transmission of the signal—can often be counteracted by the positive use of redundancy. During the street conversation, where the honking horn is noise, the obscured statement can be repeated. Key words in the statement can be said again and again to help make the message clear. Redundancy in this situation is a gain, not a loss. If static interferes with the radio signal, as it sometimes does when aircraft in flight communicate with ground control stations, the statement can be repeated, as it frequently is a matter of predetermined practice. In the case of the grasped hand, redundancy might call for holding both hands, or for putting a second hand on a shoulder.

The Problem of One-Way Flow in the Shannon Diagram

Many scholars object to the fact that in the Shannon diagram communication flows in only one direction, from the left box, "information source," to the right box, "destination." These scholars argue that communication should always be thought of as a two-way process, always involving not merely delivery of a message but response to that message as well. It is possible to accommodate that objection in the Shannon diagram merely by assuming that the destination can instantly become the information source simply by flipping the diagram over. The most severe critics of the diagram, and other analyses like it, refer to this flip-flopping as the "ping-pong theory of communication," which is described by Albert Scheflen, a neurologist, psychiatrist, and communication theorist, as a situation in which

> *you talk about what Smith does to Jones and what Jones does to Smith and what Smith then does. . . . The ball goes across the net to the left, to the right, to the left. Smith says something; Jones responds to Smith; Smith responds to Jones.* (Quoted in Forsdale 1974, p. 73)

What is misleading about the ping-pong theory? Mostly the fact that in practice we do not take discrete turns in our communication behavior. Everyday communication is not like the verbal script of a play in which character A says her lines, followed by character B's response. We all communicate all the time.

BARNLUND'S MODELS: A SOPHISTICATED DYNAMIC VIEW

Dean C. Barnlund, an American communication theorist, has proposed two experimental models of communication (1968, 1970) quite different from those we have examined so far. They suggest ways of thinking about *intrapersonal* and *interpersonal* communication.

Barnlund's Intrapersonal Model

Definition of intrapersonal communication *Intrapersonal communication* generally means communication within an individual. In everyday use, when we speak of communication we mean establishing and maintaining with signals some kind of relationship with other people or animals or machines, depending on the breadth of the definition. Yet there is also a kind of communication that each individual does alone. It can be thinking, in which language and images seem to zip around our brains and nervous systems. It might be the internal chemical signaling that unceasingly links body organs.

In analyzing intrapersonal communication, we should begin by recalling two commonsense propositions. First, we all bring to intrapersonal communication, as to all communication, our own accumulation of experiences. Second, each instance of intrapersonal communication occurs within a context, a particular situation, as does all communication.

Against that background, let us look at Barnlund's pilot model of intrapersonal communication, which is shown in diagrammatic form in Fig. 2.2.

Person: P Begin with the gray circle just left of center. It is labeled at the top P_1, for person. (Barnlund limits his scope here to humans.) The subscript 1 indicates that this is a particular person, you for example. Another person might be labeled P_2.

Public cues or stimuli There are three kinds of stimuli, or cues, in the diagram. The cues at the bottom of the diagram are all marked C_{pu}, which means that they are *public cues*. Public cues can be of two kinds—those that are part of the natural environment and those that have been created by people. We have no immediate control over either kind in Barnlund's usage. In the diagram, lines go to only two public cues, although there are more cues there. This is simply meant to suggest that in a given situation we attend to less than the total number of cues available. The wiggly lines ( ) indicate that the number of cues is probably endless.

Let us invent an example. You are studying. You are aware that the sky outside is gray and overcast. It is also windy, and your vision keeps returning to a flapping canvas store awning across the street that may or may not

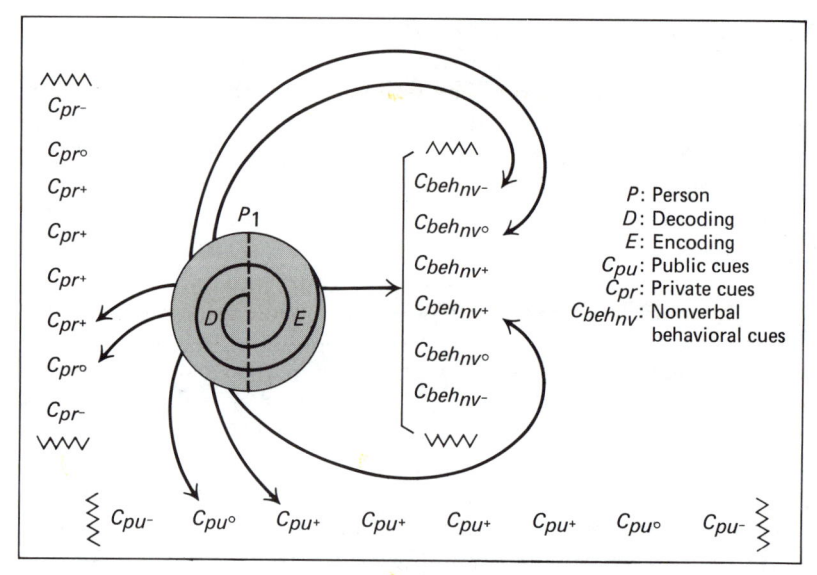

Fig. 2.2 Barnlund's pilot model of intrapersonal communication. (Reprinted from Barnlund, 1970, p. 95, with permission of Mouton Publishers.)

eventually collapse. There are many more public cues of which you are aware (and very many of which you are not), but we'll let the sky and the awning represent two public cues for the moment.

Now, notice that the arrows in the diagram go from the person, you, pointing to the cue. Does that seem strange? Wouldn't it make more sense if the arrows pointed toward the person, indicating meaning flowing from the cues to the perceiver, you? No, it wouldn't, and this is an extremely important point, namely, that the meaning of those cues is assigned, consciously or unconsciously, by the person perceiving them. They have no meaning in and of themselves. If another person were aware of these same two public cues they might mean something quite different to him or her. Perhaps the gray sky evokes a vague feeling of sadness in you, as nearly as you can tell. On the other hand, it might make another person happy, perhaps because that person lives in a place that badly needs rain at the moment, perhaps because it makes that person feel good about being inside and protected. The flapping awning across the street is annoying to you because it is distracting. In addition, perhaps you know and like the woman who owns the store and hope she doesn't lose the awning. For someone else, the windblown awning might be a source of excitement, maybe even joy, for reasons which we'll invent: dislike of the colored stripes, accompanied by the hope that it will come crashing down; dislike of the store owner; the desire to be distracted to avoid an onerous task.

Valence: +, −, 0 In our reactions to the cues lies the meaning of the "+," "−," and "0" after C_{pu}. These symbols are intended to indicate the importance or power of the cue to the perceiver. The technical term that communication specialists often use to describe the importance of cues—positive, negative, or neutral—is *valence*. The plus sign (+) means that the cue is interpreted in a positive sense; the negative sign (−) means that is taken in a negative sense; and the zero (0) means that it is without perceived value one way or another. If the overcast sky in the preceding example makes you feel sad, it has negative value and would be indicated $C_{pu}-$. The person who reacted with pleasure to that same sky would have coded it $C_{pu}+$. A public cue of no particular significance one way or the other in present perception might be some apartment buildings across the street. As public cues they would be noted $C_{pu}0$.

Private cues or stimuli Along the left side of the diagram are cues marked C_{pr}, which means *private cues*. These are not necessarily available to other persons, and they are under control of the perceiver. They also have value (+, −, 0), as do the public cues.

For example (if you will permit me to be personal), I have just eaten a coconut macaroon cookie, and the taste lingers in my mouth. It is a pleasant taste, so I would designate it $C_{pr}+$. I am also typing on an electric portable machine, and one key occasionally sticks. It is distinctly annoying, so I would indicate it as $C_{pr}-$. As I search around for a private cue that is neutral, I notice the jacket I am wearing. In color, weight, fit, and so forth, it means nothing special to me. These same private cues, should you experience them, might have different valences. You might not like the taste of coconut macaroon cookies; the typewriter key might not stick for you (it doesn't seem to upset my daughter when she uses the machine); my sport jacket might be too heavy or too light or of an unpleasant color to you. Again, the wiggly lines suggest an infinite number of private cues available at any given moment.

Nonverbal behavior cues Off to the right in the diagram, the curved lines go to cues marked C_{behnv}, standing for *behavior cues that are nonverbal*. They are cues of our own manufacture that we react to, still with +, −, or 0 valence value. I am aware, for example, of a nervous mannerism in which I run my tongue around inside my mouth. I do that sometimes when I am thinking. That behavior bothers me when I am aware of it, hence it would be assigned a $C_{behnv}-$. And I'm aware of my behavior with respect to the sticking typewriter key! It makes me angry; I pull back the top of the typewriter and vigorously separate the offending keys. I also add a verbal comment now and again, which I react toward. (That may be a minor defect in Barnlund's model, by the way. Even when alone, some of us occasionally talk aloud and then react to that behavior.) In any event, my reaction to the sticking key is a $C_{behnv}-$.

Decoding and encoding Back again the the gray circle representing the individual. Notice that it is vertically divided into two hemispheres, one labeled *D* and the other labeled *E*. *D* stands for *decoding*, which means, roughly, assigning meaning (consciously or unconsciously) to a cue. *Encoding*, which is in the other half of the circle, means creating signals that are detectable to me, and if someone else were present, possibly to that person.

Four additional qualities in the model There are other aspects to the model that are not clear without further explanation. Four characteristics of communication are implied in the curved lines and in the spiral shape of the line within the gray circle. These characteristics or qualities are as follows:

1. *Communication is continuous, without cease.* Communication is not turned off and on at will. We are constantly communicating, awake or asleep, aware of it or not.

2. *"Communication is circular,"* to use Barnlund's phrase. It is not linear, as the Shannon model, for example, might suggest, starting with a sender and ending with a receiver. Even the flip-flopping of the Shannon diagram, which satisfies some, does not quite imply the unending flow of signals in and among the communicating entities in a circular, unbroken fashion.

3. *Communication is not repeatable*, at least in creatures as opposed to machines. That is, we never engage in precisely the same act of communication (or any form of behavior) twice in exactly the same way. Note carefully the word *exactly*. This is true even in repeating a memorized message. We may come close to duplicating the contours of an earlier communication incident, but there are always minor differences. (That may well be true of machine communication, too, if one inspects their workings with sensitivity, but of course Barnlund is not concerned here with machines.)

4. *Communication is irreversible*, at least in living organisms. Life only moves forward (even though we talk about regressing to childhood); our experience grows and cannot be erased, except through some such psychological means as amnesia or selective memory. At the simplest level, you can say or do something, regret it a moment later, and say, "I'm sorry; I take that back." Obviously you *can't* take it back, not totally at least. You can only move forward, trying to modify what you regretted doing, proving the sincerity of your regret through later action. Similarly, every time a judge says to a jury, "You will ignore the testimony just given," it can't be done, except in a rather clumsy way of consciously saying, "Well, I can't consider that evidence." But the testimony generally lingers. As a matter of fact, the judge's statement often simply stresses the testimony, thus going counter to the intent of the order.

Barnlund's Interpersonal Model

Definition of interpersonal communication If intrapersonal communication means communicating within oneself, interpersonal communication means communicating with others. It frequently but by no means always implies face-to-face situations. A device such as a telephone may be employed. It generally does not include mass communication (such as radio or television), however, which implies a large, anonymous audience. In Barnlund's usage, interpersonal communication consists of "relatively informal social situations in which persons in face-to-face encounters sustain a focused interaction through the reciprocal exchange of verbal and nonverbal cues" (1968, p. 10).

Barnlund's pilot model of interpersonal communication facilitates fascinating exploration of this problem (see Fig. 2.3).

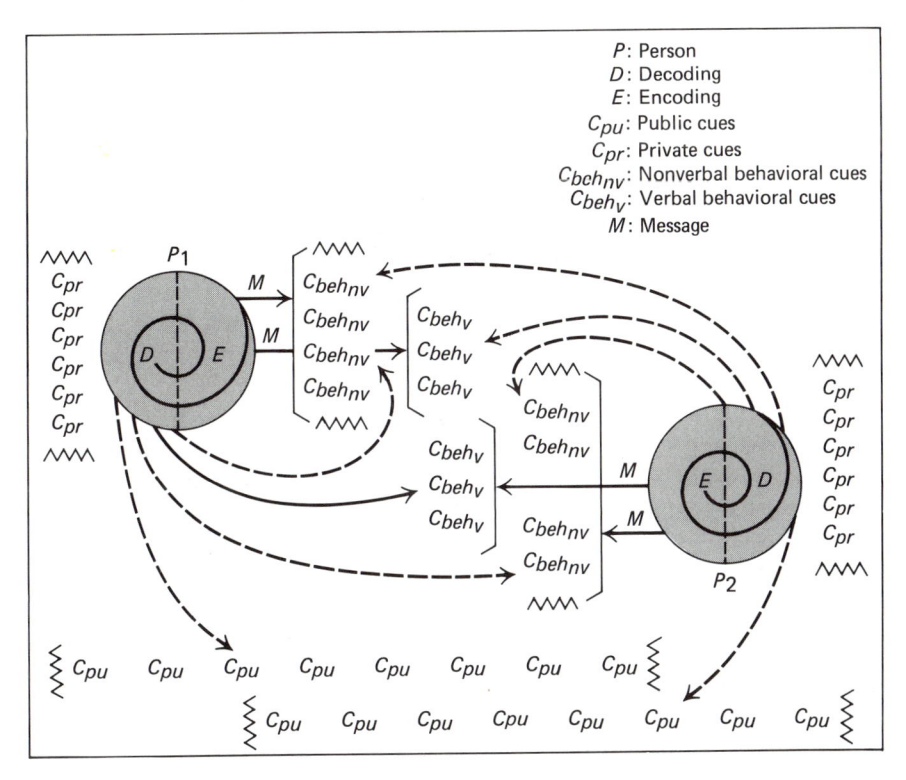

Fig. 2.3 Barnlund's pilot model of interpersonal communication. (Reprinted from Barnlund, 1970, p. 99, with permission of Mouton Publishers.)

Persons: P_1, P_2 In examining Fig. 2.3 you will immediately recognize similarities to Barnlund's pilot intrapersonal model. There is P_1, the person. And now there is also P_2, a second person. One could add P_3, P_4, and so forth. The fact that only two persons appear here is for convenience in understanding. The complexity of the diagram increases rapidly as more persons are added.

Public, private, and nonverbal cues Public cues, (C_{pu}) are along the bottom, one row for each participant to indicate that the two might not note the same cues. They might, but they also might not.

The private cues are there (C_{pr}), standing close to each participant as they always must. Barnlund deemphasizes them here (by omitting the connecting lines), shifting attention to other points in the transaction of the two people in their setting.

Notice as well that the nonverbal behavior cues ($C_{beh_{nv}}$) are still there and that each participant reacts to his or her own personal nonverbal behavior cues.

Message and verbal interaction Two elements besides the additional person are added in this interpersonal model. One is M, for message, which is the overt behavior of the participant that follows internal manipulation of the public and private cues. The other added element is the subscript v, for verbal, which is almost always an element of interpersonal communication. As noted, Barnlund retains the nonverbal element, both in message and in cues.

In interpersonal communication, as contrasted with intrapersonal communication, the tone of the communication changes dramatically with the addition of a second (or third, or fourth) person in the scene. Each person has a heightened awareness of himself or herself, generally to the point of making quite obvious adjustments in posture and other components of physical manner. Attention to cues, private and public, may shift. And so forth. Let me illustrate this shift in tone by creating a little scene in my study.

Suppose I (P_1) am still at work in my study (C_{pu}), and my daughter (P_2) sticks her head into the room (C_{pu}). That tentative gesture on her part inquires nonverbally ($C_{beh_{nv}}$) if she's interrupting something of great importance. I, in turn, switch off my electric typewriter ($C_{beh_{nv}}$), which makes a slight hum when running, and adjust my posture toward her ($C_{beh_{nv}}$). I smile ($C_{beh_{nv}}$) as a further indication of my pleasure in seeing her. We've logged a lot of time together and can read each other's signals pretty well. I also stop the movement of my tongue in my mouth ($C_{beh_{nv}}$), partly because it is a habit that I indulge in mostly (as far as I know) when I am in deep thought or am anxious and which I don't like, but also because she has on occasion kidded me about it.

My behavior leads her to step into the room ($C_{beh_{nv}}$). She has, after all, received a number of friendly cues. Her posture and half-smile ($C_{beh_{nv}}$) signal was friendly but businesslike. Then she simply asks, "Got any rubber cement?" (C_{beh_v}). I say, "Sure" (C_{beh_v}), rise, go to the shelf where I keep it, says, "Thanks. See ya" (C_{beh_v}). Playfully and confirming the fact that she is aware of me, she notes the eternal confusion of my study (C_{pu}) and exits ($C_{beh_{nv}}$) on the line, "You really gotta clean up this joint some day" (C_{beh_v}). I reflect on our transaction for a split second and smile (C_{pr}) as I turn the typewriter back on, assuming that all's well in our mutual world right now. Outside my study, she walks quickly to her room, eyes squinted a bit in concentration about the job she wants to complete. Note that the little tale is told from my point of view. It could also be told from her point of view, doubtless with variations. To simplify matters, I have not assigned valences, although they would exist, of course.

Barnlund's intrapersonal and interpersonal models are both complicated. They must be, even though we are seldom aware of those complexities when engaged in the process. And, of course, if anybody ever did raise all of these elements of the communication process to a conscious level, considering them with deep deliberation before reacting, all participants would not only be bored, but more likely paralyzed. Still, we process such information, in abundance, and in milliseconds, in every communication reaction.

A GENERAL SYSTEM MODEL

A relatively new way of looking at communication, and other complicated phenomena, is called the *General System Theory*.* Some scholars prefer to use the term *field theory*, meaning much the same thing.

Most models of communication tend to identify various elements in the process that should be attended to—originator, message, medium, and private and public cues. They tend to suggest that if you study these elements separately and in suitable depth, you can come up with an adequate view of the way communication works.

The General System approach suggests, above all, that you cannot look at elements singly and independently with much profit. Many model makers strive to see a whole framework, without singling out individual elements except for momentary convenience. Barnlund's models, and others not mentioned here, point clearly in this direction. The General System theorists are

---

* Some scholars capitalize "General System"; others do not. Some use "systems"; others use "system."

after this, and more. As Everett M. Rogers and Rekhas Agarwala Rogers, experts on communication and the operation of organizations, put it:

> *The central credo of the systems viewpoint is the statement that the whole is more than the sum of its parts. . . . systems theory is holistic. It assumes that the complex interaction among the parts of a given system are destroyed by the dissection of the system through atomistic research procedures.* (1976, p. 49)

System Defined

One of the simplest definitions of a system is offered by Lewis Thomas:

> *A system is a structure of interacting, intercommunicating components that, as a group, act or operate individually and jointly to achieve a common goal through the concerted activity of the individual parts.* (1979, p. 15)

The definition includes a number of possible phenomena, ranging from small to large, living to nonliving (or a combination of those). For example, the human body is a system, every part of which relates to every other part. Fiddling with any organ in the body affects every other organ or body subsystem, however subtly, because they are all interlinked by the body's electrical-chemical communication system. The common goal of the body, of which Thomas speaks, is presumably continued life and growth.

A college is another example of a system. It has interacting and intercommunicating components, some physical, some biological—campus, buildings, equipment, administrators, teachers, students, and so forth. Its goal is to sustain and promote knowledge.

Other systems include a nation, an alliance of nations, a colony of ants, a business, a neighborhood, a football team, a group of friends, a family, an ecological unit in nature. A system is a very general idea.

The Distinction between a Closed System and an Open System

General system theorists make a distinction between closed systems and open systems. A closed system is one that does not exchange energy, materials, or information with its environment. There probably is no perfect closed system, unless it is the universe itself. Other systems approximate being closed. Wristwatches that operate for years on batteries are nearly self-sufficient, at least until the battery has to be replaced. Plug-in electric clocks obviously get energy constantly from an external electric system. Wristwatches that work on solar cells draw energy from external light.

Space vehicles also approximate closed systems. Still, they radiate heat and rely upon solar energy; they are frequently in continuous communication with earth stations; hence they are not closed. They do tend, howver, toward the closed end of the scale, which is maintained in some researchers' thinking as a possibility.

Open systems—those that exchange energy, materials, or information with the environment—abound. The human body is an open system. It takes in all kinds of materials and eliminates other kinds (food, oxygen, water, carbon dioxide, radiation, body excretion). And it forever takes in and sends out communication signals. A community is also an open system, because it exchanges materials and information with the environment. We are concerned here only with open systems.

A Diagram of an Open System Communication Model

Most General System theorists work with mathematical models that few of us can understand. Such models are useful to them because they can be programmed into computers, thus permitting generation of various interpretations of material.

For those of us who are not native speakers of mathematics, verbal and diagrammatic approaches work better. Figure 2.4 borrows heavily on a model proposed by Rogers and Rogers (1976, p. 52). Remember, it is intended to be quite general, applying to many types of systems.

The *large outer circle* in Fig. 2.4 represents the fact that the system has a boundary. An individual of any species is bounded by his/her/its skin or outer covering. A class of students is bounded, say, by the classroom. A community has geographical boundaries. The earth is bounded by its gradually diminishing atmosphere. Machines are bounded by their containers. In many cases, as with a community, for example, the boundary can be drawn in different places, depending on whether you want to take a broad or a narrow view of the system being examined. Dotted lines in the boundary indicate that there is always information exchange with the outside environment.

Subsystems are identifiable components of the larger systems. They are the organs of the body, the students in a class, the neighborhoods in a community, the administrative units in a business, the ecologically related regions of the earth. Lines between the subsystems are intended to indicate a continuous interaction. The wiggly lines (∿∿∿) suggest an infinite number of interactional connections, not merely the two used symbolically between the subsystems here. The heart is never out of touch with the brain, the student is never isolated from other students or the teacher, neighborhoods eternally influence each other in a community, all ecological subsystems influence all others. And we must include all our machines as part of the subsystems, banging signals at each other, in between and among people. The fact that

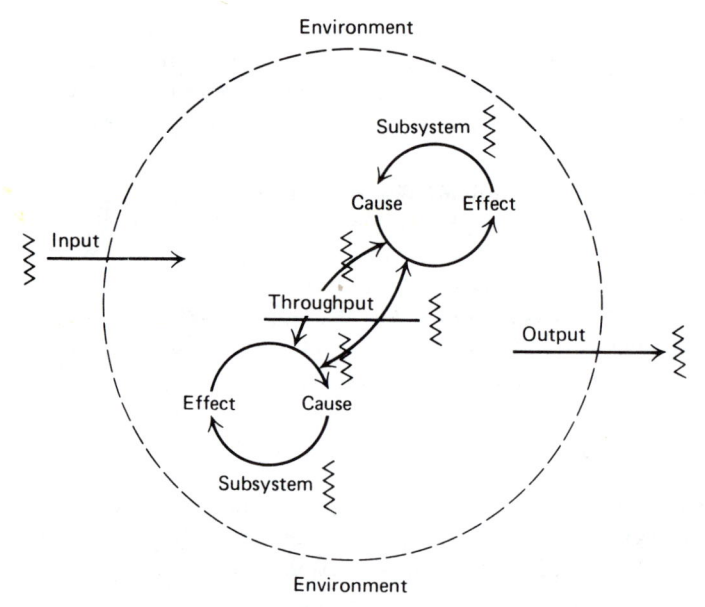

Fig. 2.4 Diagram of factors influencing communication in an open system.

only two subsystems are shown, then, is merely suggestive.

Each subsystem is pictured as following the *circular causality* principle suggested by the biologist and philosopher Ludwig von Bertalanffy. This is an attempt to provide an alternative to the cause-to-effect style of reasoning so dominant in our thinking. Cause-to-effect thinking can be diagrammed this way:

$$\text{cause} \longrightarrow \text{to} \longrightarrow \text{effect}$$

> The idea of cause and effect has taken powerful hold on our minds. We have the greatest difficulty in freeing ourselves from its compulsions.... And unconsciously, we fall back on it at every turn. This has become our natural way of looking at all problems.
>
> J. Bronowski (1953, p. 59)

Thus person A communicates something to person B, who as a result behaves in a certain way. Country X behaves toward country Y in a certain way and country Y responds as a result in such-and-such a way. What's the problem with that type of thinking? It is too simple, too linear. A much more complicated kind of interaction than the *cause* → *to* → *effect* view implies. Bertalanffy (1967, p. 67) suggests that a step toward a more realistic description of how interaction operates in any system would be fostered by adopting the *circular causality idea*, which might be diagrammed as shown in Fig. 2.5.

Continuing the example above, person A communicates something to person B, who reacts, verbally or nonverbally, thus signaling something back to person A, who is influenced in some sense. The signaling interaction continues simultaneously until some kind of behavior results that affects both persons. So with the example of two countries above.

The circular causality principle is also sometimes referred to as a *feedback loop*. A classic example of a feedback loop is a thermostat connected to a furnace. The thermostat is set at a particular temperature. When the temperature in the room drops below the designated point, the thermostat sends an electrical signal to the furnace to light up and start discharging heat. When the proper temperature has been reached, that information is picked up by the thermostat from the thermometer, which reads the air temperature, at which point the thermostat sends another signal to the furnace to shut down. So it goes: each in continuous touch with each other, each supplying information to the other, each influencing the other.

Inputs are information signals or cues from outside the system. Thus the body receives information through the senses, a class in school is influenced by the rest of the school and the community, a community receives its messages from other communities, and so forth. No system can exist without information. Information is a nutrient, like food for a body or fuel for a machine.

Outputs are the signals that the organization feeds to the environment: the individual speaks and signals in nonverbal ways, the business ships its products or its information to the outer environment (the community, the world), schools convey their messages to the community. As with inputs, the wiggly lines (⋀⋀⋀) are intended to suggest an infinite number of both inputs and outputs.

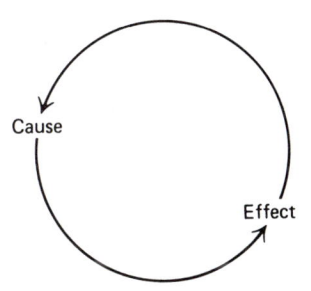

Fig. 2.5 The circular causality idea.

Throughputs, to borrow the definition of Rogers and Rogers, "is the processing of information and materials by a system in which inputs are transformed into outputs" (1976, p. 52). Thus information coming into any one of the systems we have examined is transformed by such factors as psychological states, purposes, assumptions, organizational structure, and environmental conditions, depending on the kind of system we have in mind. No information leaves the system precisely the way it came in; it is *always* altered in some way.

A final word should be said about *environment.* The system represented by the circle is always contained within an environment, a context. To describe precisely the *only* environment is not possible, because there are always many contexts, many environments, within which a system operates. There is always a context beyond the context you are thinking of, an environment beyond the environment you have immediately in mind. Thus, while it is proper to say that the environment of the earth is its complex atmosphere, there is an environment beyond that: the solar system within which the earth operates. And beyond the solar system is our particular galaxy. Beyond our galaxy is the universe. Beyond that, who knows? This principle of a flexible boundary is important for students of communication because we need to remember that a system never has one fixed boundary that one must hold to.

THIS CHAPTER IN PERSPECTIVE

In this chapter we have taken a second step toward understanding what an act of communication is by considering six models of communication among hundreds of available ones. Models, something like maps, identify major features of the terrain they deal with, frequently showing relationships between those features. Like maps, they do not show everything. The six models we have examined ranged from old to new. The hypodermic needle model is too simple for many purposes. The Lasswell model, used today mainly by beginning students, points to five variables (who, says what, to whom, through what medium, with what effect). The Shannon model uses an engineer's approach to describe diagrammatically how an idea gets from one brain to another, going through an appropriate channel, and emphasizes the constant presence of noise, which must always be counteracted. Two models by Dean Barnlund—one of intrapersonal communication (communication within the individual), the other of interpersonal communication (communication among small groups of people generally in close physical proximity)—emphasize a dynamic relationship between communicators and the cues, verbal and nonverbal, with which they interact. The final model a variation on one used by Rogers and Rogers, illustrates the General System theory of an open system.

Such a system draws information from its environment (input), alters it (throughput), and sends out information in a new form (output). The General System theory requires recognition of a continuous intimate relationship between all subsystems within a general system, arguing that altering a subsystem in any way changes all other subsystems and thus the whole. It also rejects our linear cause-to-effect thinking, substituting the notion of circular causality, in which every stimulus (cause) has an effect, which in turn becomes a cause, in a feedback loop. Models, like definitions, are neither absolutely right nor wrong, but rather they serve the person who uses them in varying ways, since we are at various levels of progress in our understanding of a subject. No purely mathematical models were shown in this chapter, since most of us are not able to manipulate them as successfully as we are able to think about verbal or graphic models.

Now, with some background of ways of thinking about communication—although with no firm and final answers—we move onward to a look at the history of communication, for history always illuminates where we stand at the moment and the intricate path that we have followed to get there.

EXTENSIONS

Reading You Might Enjoy

1. Berlo, David K. *The Process of Communication: An Introduction to Theory and Practice.* New York: Holt, Rinehart and Winston, 1960.

Berlo's book is something of a classic in the field of introductory communication texts. In it the author provides not only a useful generalized model of communication but also several other models of different specific aspects of communication.

2. Hawes, Leonard C. *Pragmatics of Analoguing: Theory and Model Construction in Communication.* Reading, Mass.: Addison-Wesley, 1975.

This book is a goldmine with respect to models in communication. Not only does it present a wide variety of models useful in communication, but it also discusses the relationship between theory and models and describes how one can go about judging the adequacy and utility of models. It is fairly difficult at points, but if you are really interested in this aspect of communication research, go quickly to this book.

3. Sereno, Kenneth K., and C. David Mortenson. *Foundations of Communication Theory.* New York: Harper & Row, 1970.

The two dozen essays in this "modest framework of foundational knowledge about the nature of human interaction" cover a considerable range of topics. While several of the articles deal indirectly with models, three provide explicit models—by Westley and MacLean, Dean C. Barnlund, and Frank E. X. Dance. Barnlund's models were used in this chapter.

Ponderings and Projects

1. Communication models are like maps, as noted early in the chapter. Neither maps nor models show the full territory, but both are useful as guides. And various maps, like various models, emphasize different aspects of the subject represented. Study contemporary maps of the world, noting how they differ and in what ways some are better for certain tactical purposes (air travel, for example) than are others. Some of the kinds of maps that you might keep your eye open for are called *Mercator projection*, *central* or *Gnomonic projection*, and *conical projections*. There are many others.

2. Today most people believe that germs and viruses cause certain diseases. This was not always the case. You might be interested in learning by whom, when, and where the germ theory (model) was proposed and what ideological battles its advocates had to fight. By the same token, consider contemporary medical views subscribing to the idea of multiple causality of diseases. For example, many new views (models) of illness associated with germs or viruses add the element of stress as a crucial factor contributing to whether the person is overcome by the disease.

3. Starting with either the Lasswell or the Shannon model, consider whether you would add other elements to it to provide more personally satisfying views of communication. For example, Lasswell lists a minimum of five factors that need to be considered in analyzing an act of communication. Perhaps you feel others should be added.

A History Communication

3

I'm convinced that when historians 100 years from now or 200 years from now try to describe our times, they will say we are living through the third of the great communications revolutions in the history of western civilization.

Lyman Bryson

The history of communication can be approached in many ways, all of them fascinating. In this chapter we will concentrate primarily on one strand of that history and take brief note of another.

Our major focus will be on one of humans' great achievements: the development of new media from the days of cave painting forward. It will become clear that we apparently have an insatiable desire to develop new means of communication, many of which have been among the most revolutionary events in human history. Further, we will see that the rate of development of new media has increased tremendously in recent decades. More new media have been introduced into contemporary technological society in the last hundred years than in all preceding history, and there is no end in sight. We are in the extraordinary position, then, of participating in these new developments and speculating about what they mean, all against some understanding of where we began.

The second strand of history that we will note in this chapter is the manner in which people have studied communication throughout the centuries. For at least two thousand years, some of the world's greatest scholars have

43

clearly felt that communication is near the heart of our lives. But what we study today about communication, while retaining some of the features of what our ancestors studied, has changed radically.

THE THREE REVOLUTIONS IN THE HISTORY OF HUMAN COMMUNICATION

Lyman Bryson, who was an anthropologist, a communication theorist, and a professional moderator on radio discussion programs, speaks in the quotation that introduces this chapter of three revolutions in the history of communication. The figure three could have been four or six just as well. There is value in simplifying complex matters, however, as long as we understand that there is more to the story than one finds in the simplification.

The three revolutions that Bryson considers pivotal came when we: (1) learned to write, thus enabling permanent records to be kept outside human memory; (2) perfected print with movable type, thus making a machine process of what had previously been a handcraft; (3) invented and perfected a whole string of media devices in the last one hundred fifty or so years (Bryson 1954).

Before discussing these three revolutions, however, we need to consider a background problem.

UNDATABLE STARTING POINTS: NONVERBAL COMMUNICATION AND SPEECH

A revolution cannot occur except in relation to, as an extension of, or as a reaction against something else. The most important "something else" is our beginnings in communication.

Probably the earliest clear evidence of our ancestors' communicative facility is found in cave paintings and carved objects in France, Spain, and Africa. These precious remnants date back approximately 35,000 years B.C. There are debates about the function of the paintings and carvings, although they are frequently thought to have ritual or religious significance, perhaps appealing to the gods for protection and assistance. With respect to the paintings, Georges Bataille suggests that with them "*communication between individual minds begins*" (1955, p. 11).

Speech and nonverbal body language probably began long before the time of these cave paintings, but the "clear evidence" noted above with respect to the paintings is simply nonexistent for nonverbal communication and speech. As a matter of fact, widespread interest in the study of nonverbal communication is a relatively recent phenomenon.

UNDATABLE STARTING POINTS 45

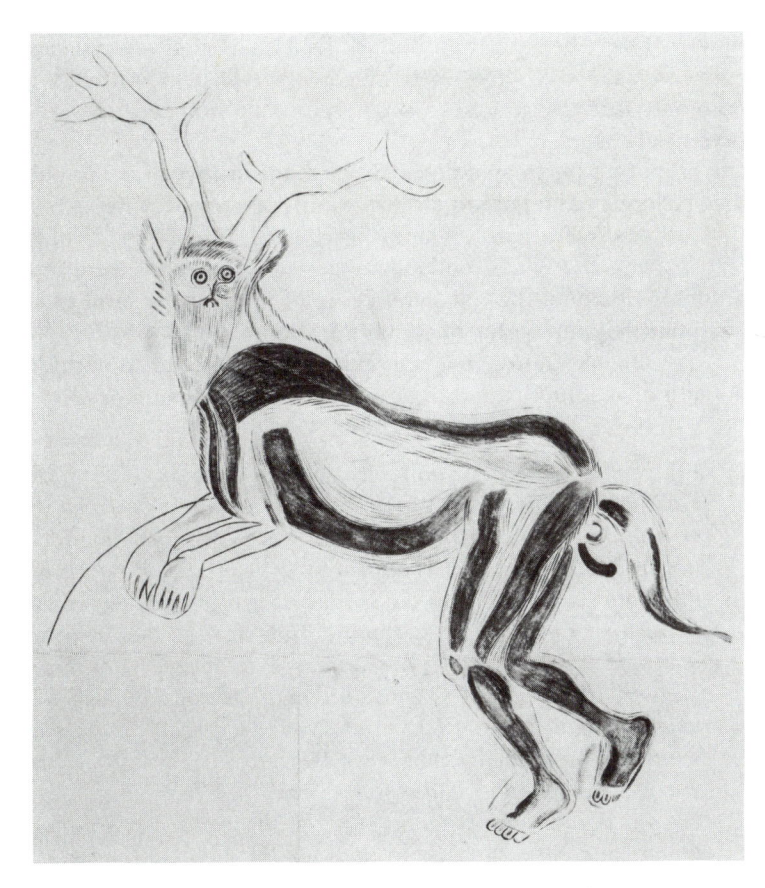

Illustration 3.1 "The Sorcerer," Cave of Trois Frères, France. (Courtesy of the American Museum of Natural History)

Much more attention has been given to speech (language), although its beginnings (like the beginnings of nonverbal communication) can be dated only by indirect evidence, such as observing apparent brain size or making inferences based on probable socialization of our predecessors, such as their ability to cooperate in communal enterprises like hunting.

Undoubtedly speech took a very long time to develop, it not being a gift handed to humans in completed form. Some scholars believe that our hominoid predecessors developed languages in many parts of the world; others believe language sprang from a single area. Some investigators agree that *Homo erectus*, an ancestor who walked the earth approximately a million years ago, may well have been the first humanlike animal to develop speech. Others feel that language was developed much later. There is a maze of conflicting opinions, through which, fortunately, we do not need to find our way for present purposes.

From these estimated dates forward, the history of communication can be viewed largely as an account of the development of further extensions beyond the body itself, for painting and speech extend the body, or of faster ways of transporting the whole body. It is a fascinating adventure in invention, in gradually learning the full significance of innovations, and in gaining public acceptance of new forms of communication.

Speech, like nonverbal communication, is often not thought of as an invention, as John Brockman points out with some humor:

> *I remember a conversation with cultural anthropologist Edward T. Hall, who pointed out to me that the most significant, the most critical inventions of man were not those ever considered to be inventions, but those that appeared to be innate and natural. To illustrate the point, he told a story of a group of cavemen living in prehistoric times. One day, while sitting around the fire, one of the men said, "Guess what? We're talking?" Silence. The others looked at him with suspicion. "What's talking?" one of them asked. "It's what we're all doing. Right now. We're talking!" "You're crazy," another man replied. "Who ever heard of such a thing?" "I'm not crazy," the first man said, "you're crazy. We're talking." And it became a question of "who's crazy?" The group could not see or understand because "talking" was invented by the first man. The moment he said "We're talking" was a moment of great significance in the process of evolution.* (1977, p. 17)

ORAL CULTURES AND LITERATE CULTURES

There was a time when people spoke but did not know how to write. Howard W. Winger of the University of Chicago suggests, tongue in cheek, that this

> *was presumably a happy time. When a wise old man died there were no memoirs to publish, no papers to edit. . . . When the harassed householder tired of paying the rent, there was no lease to make him pay. When the weary breadwinner retired to the lake for a week of fishing and swimming, no letters or directives sought him out to distract his mind from his rustic pleasure.* (1955, p. 293)

You might add that there were no papers to write for school either! Of course the student had to memorize and recite lessons, a skill that most of us have forgotten. If information cannot be preserved in writing (or other means such as photography, television, or audio tapes or records) it has to be memorized and passed on orally from generation to generation.

There are many cultures today on earth that do not have a written language. People are at historically different periods in communication development in different parts of the world at the same moment. Great populations of people today live in *oral cultures,* where transmission of information is done by word of mouth, often by professional storytellers. In such cultures, memory is highly respected, and generations of people can recite word for word the important stories of their culture. In Islamic cultures, for example, the Koran, or portions of it, is memorized by people who can recite it, often for hours at a time, without a single mistake. In the United States and Canada, to cite another instance, a similar tradition continues to exist among some Iroquois Indians who embrace *The Code of Handsome Lake,* a Seneca prophet who told the story of the glories of the Iroquois before their defeat by the white man, how they survived that defeat, and how they revitalized their lives. Anthropologist Anthony F. C. Wallace helps us understand the prodigious feats of memory often found in oral cultures:

Handsome Lake followers hear this Code partially recited twice a year. This "short form," delivered by a local preacher, occupies the first morning of the Midwinter Ceremony in January or February and of the Green Corn Dance in August or September. In the fall of alternate years at each longhouse (except Tonawanda, where it occurs annually, and Sour Springs, which has an irregular schedule) the Code is recited in full by professional speakers at religious "Six Nations Meetings." The full recital occupies the mornings of four days. (1972, p. 8)

A Tibetan Grand Lama once spoke with me about the astonishing duration of their oral tradition. Buddha, the Indian religious leader, generally said to have been born about 550 B.C., took up his religious role when he was thirty or so, gathering disciples to himself. Although much associated with Buddhism is preserved in writing, a good deal of lore, many interpretations, and many stories have been transmitted orally from generation to generation by memory. This adds up to something like twenty-five hundred years of unbroken oral transmission! (The Tibetan lamas are now located in India and other parts of the world, since Tibet was conquered by China in the 1950s, and the Tibetan Buddhist monks were killed, imprisoned, or fled their native land.)

Illustration 3.2 One of the fascinating facts of the contemporary world. Here a scribe writes a letter or fills out a form for an illiterate customer, while in the same city . . .

. . . several blocks away a television program is produced using some of the most modern communication technology available in the world today. Many scholars wonder what the meaning of this phenomenon, repeated in many places, will be. Only time will tell. (Photo courtesy Pakistan Television Corporation)

TWO GENERAL FORMS OF WRITING

There are two general forms of writing. One is "sound writing," the other is "sign writing." Of the two, sound writing, requiring a phonetic alphabet, is more flexible and more important today, although it came later in human development than sign writing.

Sound Writing

In sound writing, the spoken language is represented in a relatively small number of alphabet letters. English, for example, has an alphabet of twenty-six letters. One of the reasons English words are so difficult to spell is that the match between the sounds in our language and the letters in our alphabet is not exact. To do a top-notch job of representing our sounds in writing would require about double the number of alphabet letters we have.

Sign Writing

Sign writing works in a different way. Instead of attempting to assign alphabet letters representing the sound system of their language, peoples who use sign writing, such as the Chinese, have two completely independent systems. Their speech is only indirectly related to their writing. That is, they have thousands of written signs standing for things and ideas, and these are learned independently of the spoken language. It is difficult to memorize these thousands of written signs, of course, and generally speaking, the phonetic alphabet is thought to be a superior means of writing. The oral language is learned first anyway, and then the phonetic marks representing the sounds are learned.

Chinese sign writing, known more technically as ideograms, does have an unexpected advantage over our phonetic alphabet. Some Chinese *speakers* cannot understand each other because their dialects are so different. In mainland China today, for example, speakers of Mandarin Chinese literally do not understand speakers of Cantonese Chinese. Chinese writers and readers use a single system of ideograms, however, which educated Chinese everywhere understand.* That cannot be said for all users of the phonetic alphabet. Even though the French, Spanish, and English use essentially the same alphabet, they do not necessarily understand one another's writing. Nor do they understand one another's speech.

---

* In 1956, the People's Republic of China decided both to simplify its system of calligraphy, that is, its ideograms, and to develop a method of spelling using the Latin alphabet, the one we employ. The alphabet is intended only as a technique for assisting in learning the sound of Chinese, for they apparently do not intend to abandon their ancient system of calligraphy because this would deprive them of a culture, including a literature, that is thirty-five centuries old.

THE PROBLEM OF WRITING SURFACES

The problem of getting suitable material to write on needs to be considered before seeing in greater detail the order in which writing developed. Paper was not discovered lying on the ground, ready to be picked up and used. As a matter of fact, paper as a surface to write on came after writing. Winger observes:

> Man experimented with inscribing . . . signs on almost any surface that would take a mark and with any material that would submit to pen, stylus, or chisel. He tried bark, stone, metal, clay, leather, and payprus. His first written messages tended to be private and commercial in nature. Later, writing went beyond this private, commercial character, and messages were inscribed with the original intent of publication. Public messages were written on cliffs and monuments, over portals and doorways, and on wheat bins, coffins, and other containers. Then came the ultimate refinement. It was found that public messages of considerable length could be put on materials that were light enough and compact enough, when ingeniously arranged, to be carried around conveniently from place to place. This was the book—a graphic record of human speech, so manufactured as to be easily portable and primarily intended to be a vehicle of public communication. (1955, p. 293)

Winger might also have mentioned bamboo, animal bones, large plant leaves, wood, and probably a hundred other materials.

Stone probably was used early in human efforts at writing. It is durable and available, but hard to work with (imagine chiseling a message in stone!) and difficult to transport.

Clay has been used for at least five thousand years as a writing medium, perhaps ten thousand years according to one scholar, Denise Schmandt-Besserat (1977). Clay is inexpensive, and while in a moist state is much easier to work than stone. After being fired, it is also remarkably durable. There are enough ancient clay tablets in excellent condition remaining today to fill dozens of warehouses. Although easier to work than stone, clay does not lend itself to delicate markings such as can be made on papyrus, parchment, or paper.

Papyrus is made of strips of a reed plant that grows in certain parts of the world, notably the Middle East. The papyrus writing surface was made by weaving together strips of the reed that were uniform in width, soaking the woven material, pounding it into a flattish surface, and then further rubbing it down with a polished rock or other suitable device so that a brush or pen

> Clay is practically indestructible. . . . think of it: almost every scrap of writing, even if it was unimportant or discarded, is waiting for us somewhere in the ruins of those ancient cities. Suppose you throw a letter in the wastebasket today. Where will it be tomorrow?
>
> Edward Chiera (1966, pp. 12, 22)

could be used easily on it. Not nearly so durable as stone or clay, papyrus was readily available and was reasonably tough. Perhaps above all, it was light enough to transport.

Parchment is a treated form of animal hide, usually of sheep, goat, or calf. Skins were prepared so that one or both sides could be used. Preparation of a hide involved washing, removing hair, stretching on a frame, scraping, paring down bumps in the surface, and sometimes shaving into material thinner than the original skin. Parchment is much tougher than papyrus, lighter than stone or clay, and easily written upon by pen or brush. It can also be used for printing. Parchment is expensive, both because the process to prepare it is time-consuming and because animals are not as abundant as, say, the reed from which papyrus was made. Curt F. Bühler, historian of the printed book, says:

> *It has been computed that each copy [of Gutenberg's forty-two-line Bible, printed on parchment in the mid-fifteenth century] required 170 calf-skins, with the result that the thirty odd copies believed to have been produced . . . used up the skins of no less than 5,000 calves.* (1960, p. 42.)

EARLY FORMS OF WRITING

Sumerian Pictographs

It is generally believed today that writing began around fifty-five hundred years ago in the valley or delta between the Tigris and Euphrates rivers in what is now known as Iraq. The people, Sumerians, used sign writing (or *pictographs*, a more widely used term) in which they delicately scribed into the surface of moist clay a cartoonlike outline of the thing or idea represented. These pictographs apparently grew naturally from the artistic ability demonstrated by people much earlier, when they created those masterful pictures in caves in France, Spain, and Africa, among other places.

S. H. Hooke, a British scholar of ancient writings, estimates that there were about two thousand picture signs available to the early Sumerians. When you consider that contemporary English has twenty-six letters in the alphabet in writing, two thousand pictographs seems a large number indeed. The Sumerians apparently felt the pressure of that many pictographs, too, for the thrust of their writing development was in the direction of simplification. This they did by introducing early in their history a number of phonetic signs, that is, signs standing for sounds in the language, like the letters in our alphabet. Thus Hooke (1954, p. 749) observes that by around 3000 B.C. the Sumerians had reduced their signs to about five hundred to six hundred, including about one hundred phonetic signs.

Cuneiform Writing

The Sumerians shortly moved in the direction of a form of writing known as *cuneiform*, meaning "wedgelike in form." The reason for developing the cuneiform technique was the difficulty of making delicate pictographs in moist clay. In cuneiform writing, a wedgelike instrument was simply pushed into the clay in a variety of quite abstract marks. (The payprus reed was not easily grown in the Tigris-Euphrates delta, where the Sumerians lived, as it was in Egypt, for example.)

The development toward abstract cuneiform writing proceeded in the following manner. The original pictograph standing for "head," say, looked very much like a modern cartoon of a human head in profile, with nose, mouth, chin, and eyes shown simply. (These pictographs were something like the contemporary ones shown in Illustration 3.3.) As the simplification process proceeded over many decades the head became less and less recognizable, until it was finally totally unrecognizable—a series of short wedge-shaped marks arranged geometrically which the reader had to memorize. Although the Sumerians invented cuneiform writing, the style was carried on and further developed by the Babylonians, an empire that flourished from approximately 2000 to 1000 B.C., also in the Tigris-Euphrates valley.

Egyptian Hieroglyphs

While it is impossible in the space at hand to describe all the various early writing systems that were developed around the world, mention should be made of the famous Egyptian hieroglyphic system. Hieroglyphs, which developed a bit later than the Sumerian pictographic system (and which many think were borrowed, in some measure at least, from the Sumerians), were largely pictographic, inscribed first on stone surfaces and later on papyrus. The Egyptian hieroglyphic system was both pictographic and ideographic. As time passed, a cursive form of hieroglyphics was developed. "Cursive" means simply that the signs became more flowing and were frequently connected, as

EARLY FORMS OF WRITING   53

Illustration 3.3 Modern pictographs. We still use pictographs, both with and without words. The simple outline drawings of people, airplanes, a suitcase, fire, and arrows are as simple and stylized as were their ancient predecessors.

in the handwriting we use today. The availability of papyrus was important to development of the cursive script. It is hard to write with a flowing hand on either stone or moist clay.

Egyptian hieroglyphs were not understood in the Western world for centuries after their initial use. The mystery of their meaning was solved largely by discovery of the Rosetta stone, shown in Illustration 3.5.

Breakthrough to an Alphabet

While writing began as basically separate from the speech process—recording simplified representations of things (pictographs) or ideas (ideograms)—there were, as noted earlier, minor elements of sound writing in both the early

Illustration 3.4 A cuneiform tablet from Babylonia. These marks look like a jumble to us. They looked like a jumble to most Babylonians, too, for only a small percentage of the population—businesspeople, scribes, priests, and scholars—could read cuneiform marks. (Courtesy The Pierpont Morgan Library)

Sumerian and Egyptian writing styles, not to mention the dozens of other early writing techniques that for reasons of space are not discussed here. The big leap in writing, however, was the development of a true alphabet, in which visual signs were made to represent sounds in the language. Hindsight makes this seem a less monumental accomplishment than it was, but it was an astonishing advance. An improbable commentator on the subject, Abraham Lincoln, once talked about the alphabet in a lecture, "Discoveries and Inventions," that he made before various groups before becoming president:

> When we remember that spoken words are sounds merely, we shall conclude that the idea of representing those sounds by marks, so that whoever should at any time after see the marks and understand what sounds they meant, was a bold and ingenious conception, not likely to occur to one man in a million in the run of a thousand years. (Quoted in Sandburg, 1949, p. 78)

As with all complex inventions, this one did not appear in a single place at a single time. The alphabet that you and I use had its roots in an alphabet consisting of twenty-two letters that was shaped by the Phoenicians, a people living in Syria, perhaps between 1700 B.C. and 1500 B.C. It spread gradually in the Middle East, then to the Mediterranean, including Greece. The Greek alphabet almost certainly drew upon this Phoenician start, and in 350 B.C. or so a standard Greek alphabet employing twenty-four letters was in use. Skipping many stages, the Latin (Roman) alphabet built on the Greek one, with minor adaptations. Gradually, additional letters were added to make up the twenty-six in our English alphabet.

Illustration 3.5 The Rosetta stone. This black basalt stone, just under four feet in length and just over two feet in width, is one of the most remarkable discoveries in the history of communication. It was found in July 1799 by a French solider, serving under Napoleon, near a branch of the Nile river called the Rosetta, in Egypt. What is remarkable about it is that it contains the same message in three forms of writing: Egyptian hieroglyphics, a later cursive Egyptian form known as Demotic, and finally, Greek. Greek could be read by scholars, but the other two codes had not been broken. The Rosetta stone served as the key to breaking the other codes. The story of the decipherment is one of the best detective stories in history. The original Rosetta stone is in the British Museum in London. (Photo: British Museum)

Writing Was Not Universally Regarded as a Blessing

You may be surprised to learn that writing has been regarded as a mixed blessing by many people, including some observers at the time it was being introduced. The most notable on-the-spot critic of writing was doubtless the Greek philosopher Socrates, who is quoted by Plato as believing that

> [writing] will create forgetfulness in the learners' souls, because they will not use their memories: they will trust to the external written characters and not remember of themselves.... [Writing] is an aid not to memory but to reminiscence, and you give your disciples not truth, but only the semblance of truth; they will be hearers of many things and will have learned nothing; they will appear to be omniscient and will generally know nothing; they will be tiresome company, having the show of wisdom without the reality. (Jowett, 1952, pp. 138-139)

Was Socrates' worry merely the foolish folly of a man who had difficulty facing up to progress? Not necessarily. Writing has its pluses and minuses. Let's start with the minuses, including Socrates' perception. Socrates was an oral man, a citizen of an oral culture. Oral peoples have extraordinary memories, as we have noted. They have to, obviously. What you and I can look up in an encyclopedia or on a scrap of paper in a notebook, they must carry in their heads. There are many more tales of the prodigious memory feats of people in oral cultures than were related a few pages earlier.

Ashokh was the name given everywhere in Asia and the Balkan peninsula to the local bards, who composed, recited or sang poems, songs, legends, folktales, and all sort of stories.

In spite of the fact that these people of the past . . . were in most cases illiterate . . . they possessed such a memory and such alertness of mind as would now be considered remarkable and even phenomenal.

G. I. Gurjieff (1969, p. 32)

Still, while the development of memory can be an important asset, perhaps keeping one's memory sharp may not be the most important attribute of being in an oral culture. Perhaps a more important quality of oral people, a quality that is modified by writing, is that they are always dealing directly with other human beings. This may be an invaluable aid for keeping in touch with the feelings of others. Want a story in an oral culture? Go hear it told, or tell it yourself. When it gets written down, you can go into your room, close the door, and become completely isolated from other human beings, except as you might *imagine* the author behind those marks on the page. But that's a good distance from actually being in close proximity to the storyteller. And, of course, when Socrates speaks of getting from reading "not truth, but only the semblance of truth," he suggests that the *process* of active thinking, which comes from live dialogue, from working through matters aloud, is lost in reading. Yes, obviously, reading is a different dialogue.

Writing Has Great Advantages, Too

There's another side to the invention of writing, of course. (More likely, there are a hundred other sides, as in all matters of such importance.) To counter the idea of missing the "breath of life" that is present in the oral culture, writing helps us to learn things about other people and other places and times. Writing is a great and reasonably economical storehouse of information. (The "reasonably" appears in the foregoing sentence because print on pages, bound in books, is rapidly becoming an uneconomical way, in terms of both space and money, for storing the enormous amount of information with which we must now deal. Still, writing is not in danger of dying; it is simply being moved into new containers on new surfaces: computers, microfilm, microfiche, and so on.)

Writing also helps us keep in touch with people at a distance, both friends and members of social, political, and cultural groups. Further, writing is a fine analytical tool. When you write something it generally takes a great deal more time than saying it. Writing literally requires slowing down the processes of the mind and can help us study carefully what we are thinking. Some writers do not recognize this truth, but every writer of good material wrestles with the slowed-down ideas. Every good writer knows that he or she has to go over the text again and again until it is satisfactory. A first draft of writing often looks utterly stupid. Most teachers, for example, work much harder at getting their thoughts properly organized when writing for publication than when lecturing or conducting a class discussion.

Written language . . . is an instrument of great power. . . . it is the development of this explicit formal system which accounts for the predominant features of Western culture.

David R. Olson (1977, p. 24)

58 A HISTORY OF COMMUNICATION

We will return later in the book to this question of what writing and reading does to people. For now let us remember that the invention of writing was probably not a clear-cut blessing or a clear-cut evil. No medium of communication is. But, like ice cream and taxes, we've got it, and it is convenient to think of it as the first great communication revolution. Now to Bryson's second revolution.

THE MECHANIZATION OF WRITING

In the middle of the fifteenth century there came a second critical turning point in the history of communication. A printing press that used movable type cast from metal was invented and introduced into Western society. Similar inventions had been made far earlier in China (about 1040, using clay type) and Korea (about 1403, using metal type), but the information about these Eastern inventions apparently was not known, in detail at least, to the craftspeople who were striving to develop systems of "artificial script," as they were sometimes called, in Europe.

There is some debate, as there is about many inventions, concerning printing with movable type in Europe, but the major early contributions are most frequently attributed today to Johann Gutenberg (1396-1468), a German goldsmith. The first major work of printing Gutenberg did, and the one that symbolizes the invention of printing with movable type today, is the famous "Forty-two Line Bible," printed about 1453, a page of which is shown in Illustration 3.6.

A Gutenberg Bible, the most coveted book of all books and one of the rarest in the world, has been sold . . . for $1.8 million [in 1978].

Rita Reif (1978, p. C30)

THE IMPORTANCE OF GUTENBERG'S CONCEPT OF MASS-PRODUCED TYPE

Johann Gutenberg perfected a means of *mass production of type*, which required a way of making hundreds of duplicates of the same letter—*a, b, c, d,* and so on—so that the printer could reach into the type container and pull out any one of a certain letter and it would be like any other one, similar to reaching into a box of screws of a certain size, confident that all the screws in the container will be identical. Some think this was the first clear example of mass production, which always requires identical interchangeable parts. You cannot

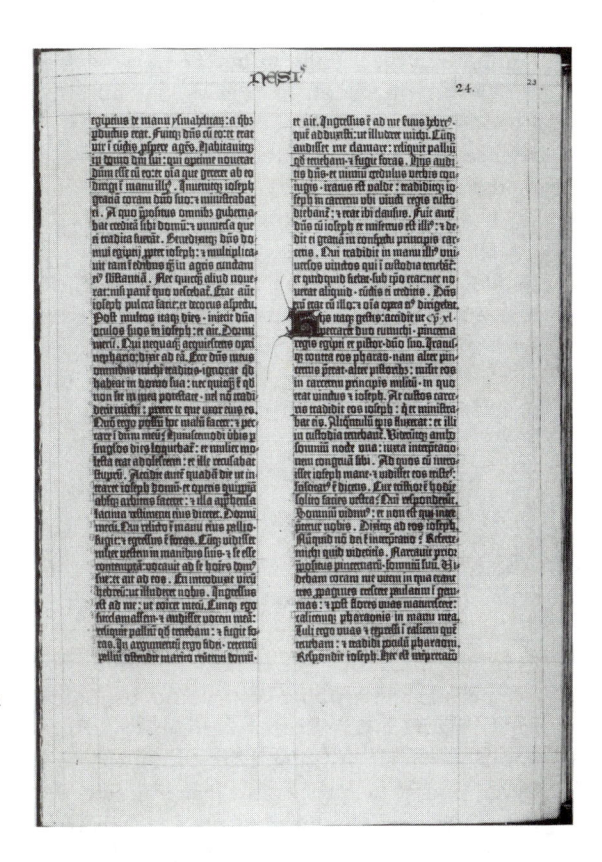

Illustration 3.6 A page from Johann Gutenberg's Forty-two line Bible. (Courtesy The Pierpont Morgan Library)

mass produce watches or automobiles or sewing machines or cameras—you name it—without having a stock of identical parts. That conception, then, was a major intellectual feat.

Gutenberg also had to develop such other components of the process as new kinds of ink, clamps for holding the type when it was composed, and presses.

An Important Lesson: Invention Encourages Invention

Modern printing was not completed with Gutenberg's contributions. Other technical developments followed; many—like computer-set printing—are still being made today. One lesson learned in studying the development of communication technology is that invention encourages invention; technology builds upon technology. In the field of printing, the invention of movable type was just a beginning. Various typefaces were later designed and cast, and companion pieces of equipment were developed for the production of paper, for power operation of presses, for automatic setting of type, and the like. Even today, as noted, technical processes involved in printing are being refined in a number of ways. One can never safely conclude, then, that we are at the end of the line in *any* communication technology. Everybody knows, for example, that our current color television sets are not as good as they will be in ten years. Each year bigger screens with more accurate color are available. Some manufacturers already market home television projectors that show images up to four feet in the diagonal dimension. One of the great frustrations of living in a technological society is that what is up-to-date today is out-of-date tomorrow. If you are a photographic hobbyist, or a stereo bug, or a computer enthusiast, you know how quickly obsolesence occurs.

The Implications of New Communication Technology Are Not Always Clear at the Outset

Another lesson that can be learned from the invention of print with movable type and that applies to all communication technology is that the meaning to society of new technology often emerges very slowly. All of the implications of a new medium are generally not understood at the outset. For example, an inexpensive newspaper that could be bought by every citizen took almost four hundred years after Gutenberg's time to develop. In part, this mass application of printing had to await perfection of such other technical developments as processes for manufacturing paper and application of power to presses. But the inexpensive newspaper also had to await the birth of the *idea* of a cheap mass newspaper as well as the technology. In the final analysis, of course, the technology and the idea of its use cannot be separated, but it is important to consider the fact that the mere presence of a technical capability does not mean that people will sense in what direction to turn that capability. A good contemporary example of the availability of technology that people do not yet seem ready for is the picture phone (the combination of telephone and television), which has been technically possible for decades but which hasn't found a large market yet.

What Was the World of Print Like before Gutenberg?

It is difficult even for the most imaginative reader to conceive of what the world was like before this second revolution in the history of communication — the invention of "mechanical writing," as print with movable type has been called. Those were the times of the scribes, who wrote out manuscripts copy by copy, one by one, slowly and laboriously, making private versions and interpretations, frequently shifting words and punctuation as they worked.

Scribes were craftspeople, like excellent carpenters or tailors, using expensive materials, and only the rich could afford their products. The resulting books were so precious that they were guarded. In monasteries, where collections were frequently kept, manuscript copies were often *chained* down to keep them safe.

And, because handmade books were so expensive, very few people could read. How could one expect them to? You can't learn to play the violin without a violin; you can't learn to read without a book. Some time ago I saw the film *Robin and Marian*, which is based on the notion that Robin Hood and his companion Little John had gone off to the Crusades in the Middle East and were now going home twenty years later. They arrive in England and head back into their beloved Sherwood Forest, their middle-aged bones creaking. Skipping details to get to the point, at one moment in the film Robin Hood—this competent leader—is scolded by Marian, the woman he left behind two decades before. "You never wrote," she says. "I can't write," says Robin Hood, matter-of-factly. I was shocked for a second, although I've been a student of communication most of my adult life. Then I realized how deeply embedded in me is the notion that everybody who is anybody writes and reads, and always has. Even if one has intellectual knowledge of something, it does not fix it in the gut, in the reflexes of thinking. Maybe that is partly what Socrates was talking about, too, when he said the alphabet would give us only the "semblance of truth."

Beatrice Warde, a British scholar, wrote eloquently about the meaning of print with movable type. She said:

These were the five hundred years of the Printer. These were the centuries in which there was his way, but no other way, of broadcasting identical messages to a thousand or more people, a thousand or more miles apart. This was the epoch that we have been calling "modern times."

We gave it that name because we have imagined ourselves as standing on this side of the deep cleft-in-history that opened up midway of the fifteenth century; the cleft into which Johann Gutenberg and his followers drove those leaden wedges that are called printing type, and split us clean away from that almost inconceivable world in which there was no such thing as printing. (1955, p. 7)

Yes, that world of the scribe is hard to imagine. It would be like a world today in which a wealthy person wanted a copy of a book, and instead of going to a bookstore or library to get it, or better yet, going to the corner drugstore and buying it in paperback, he or she hired a scribe to make a

> A copyist [scribe] turning over the leaves of the 42-line Bible must have been shocked to realize that his occupation had slipped away from under him, now that it was possible... to produce mechanically as much reading matter in a day as one man's pen could manage in a year.
>
> Victor Scholderer (1970, p. 23)

personal copy, haggling over price, binding, decoration, and perhaps above all delivery date.

Today, of course, print is found everywhere in industrial societies. It has almost created a crisis in some countries, like the United States, where the mails are at times clogged nearly to the point of standstill by the abundance of print moved, much of it annoying "junk mail." A huge percentage of our population is involved in the creation and movement of the printed word. We often seem to be drowning in it. Yet, here I sit writing a book, and there you sit reading! And we still respect certain overwhelming advantages of print—its relative inexpensiveness, its portability, and the fact that we can go back repeatedly to study material recorded in this form.

THE ELECTROCHEMICAL REVOLUTION OF THE PAST CENTURY AND A HALF

Warde continues the previous quotation by asking the provocative question: "But what if another such cleft proves to have been opening just behind us, in this very century?"

She asks, of course, if the recent string of media changes are as important as Gutenberg's "leaden wedges." (Gutenberg's pieces of type were made of lead.) The answer seems clear: There's no question that they are.

Referring to Bryson's third revolution in communication as "the electrochemical revolution of the past century and a half" is unwieldly. The phrase simply means that the almost continuous string of media inventions rocking industrial societies today can best be dated from photography, which has a huge chemical component. Most media developments following photography have shifted and are partially or wholly electrical in character. Still, whatever we call it, we are in a new age of communication, and it appears to be just as powerful in its social impact as the Gutenberg era was.

The Difficulty of Dating Inventions

It is difficult to date inventions exactly and to attribute them to particular people, partly because of a repeated phenomenon in which nearly equivalent inventions occur simultaneously in different parts of the world. The components seem to be "in the air," ready to come together. Another reason for the difficulty of dating and attributing inventions is that new ideas build on older ideas, and who is to say when the climax (the invention) has occurred? Photography, for example, is frequently dated from 1839, when the French painter Louis Daguerre announced his Daguerrotype process. Still, the insights that contributed to photography began much earlier. That astonishing universal genius, Leonardo da Vinci, described the *camera obscura* ("dark room") in his notebooks five centuries ago by noting that "light entering a minute hole in the wall of a darkened room forms on the opposite wall an inverted image of whatever lies outside" (quoted in MacCurdy, 1958, p. 227). The first "camera," then, was literally a windowless room that one walked into. On one side was a tiny hole, and on the opposite wall the awestruck spectator saw an upside-down version of the view outside the room. In 1727 a German physicist, Johann Heinrich Schulze, made the crucial discovery that certain silver salts turned black when struck by light. This was a necessary forerunner of photographs on glass, metal, or paper surfaces. By 1826 the Frenchman Nicéphore Nièpce produced a faint photographic image on a piece of polished pewter plate. His process was not of widespread usefulness, however, and Daguerre perfected it. The point of this brief history of photography is merely to emphasize the difficulty of determining precisely when something was invented, and by whom. Being duly warned about the necessity of caution along the way, let us nevertheless proceed, since pinpoint exactness is not as much our need as a sweeping look.

Let us accept 1839, the date when Louis Daguerre announced his invention, as the birth of *photography*.

The next important medium to be perfected, the *telegraph*, was the product of the fertile brain of a famous American painter, Samuel F. B. Morse. Morse's telegraph won an award of $30,000 from the United States government when, in the words of Carroll W. Pursell, Jr.:

> On May 24, 1844, . . . [a] wire from the railroad depot in Baltimore to the Supreme Court in the Capital [Washington, D.C.] was ready. Morse sat quietly in Washington and began sending with his new transmitting key: "dot dash dash — dot dot dot dot — dot dash — dash — . . ." Forty-one miles away Vail [his assistant] decoded the message: "What hath God wrought?" The telegraph was a proven success. (1971, p. 103)

Although the telegraph today seems rather primitive to many of us, its impact is difficult to overstate. The nineteenth-century American poet William Cullen Bryant said, with appropriate eloquence, that Morse had "annihilated both space and time in the transmission of intelligence" (quoted in Pursell,

1971, p. 106). Not only did the telegraph help open up the American West—so vast a continent to span without the ability to keep in touch somehow—it also revolutionized journalism by making news available at electric speed and eventually created a network of wires that interlinked nations.

C. L. Sholes, a Wisconsin printer, after years of work patented a *typewriter* in 1867. According to novelist, physicist, and inventor Mitchell Wilson: "The machine was first offered to ministers and authors without too much success. No one thought of its office possibilities" (1954, p. 252). In 1875, Mark Twain, who loved gadgets, wrote this witty testimonial, which was quoted in ads for the instrument:

> *Gentlemen: Please do not use my name in any way. Please do not even divulge the fact that I own a machine. I have entirely stopped using the Type-Writer, for the reason that I never could write a letter with it to anybody without receiving a request by return mail that I would not only describe the machine, but state what progress I had made in the use of it, etc., etc. I don't like to write letters, and so I don't want people to know I own this curiosity-breeding little joker.*

Although he joked about the machine, Mark Twain is regarded as the first major author to type his manuscripts.

Alexander Graham Bell's *telephone*, which became the backbone of the world's largest corporation, American Telephone and Telegraph (AT&T), was patented in 1876. The instrument, which was to transform nearly every aspect of social and business practice in industrialized countries, was not easily explained in its first advertisement, quoted by historian John Brooks:

> *The proprietors of the Telephone . . . are now prepared to furnish Telephones for the transmission of articulate speech through instruments not more than twenty miles apart. Conversation can easily be carried on after slight practice and with occasional repetition of a word or sentence. On first listening to the Telephone, though the sound is perfectly audible, the articulation seems to be indistinct; but after a few trials the ear becomes accustomed to the peculiar sound.* (1976, p. 60)

Thomas Edison's *phonograph* swiftly followed the telegraph. In 1877 Edison, while attempting to make a machine enabling high-speed transmission of telegraphic signals, stumbled accidentally on the fact that telegraphers' signals sounded something like speech when sped up on his recording cylinders. Reporter Hans Fantel writes:

> It was December 6, 1877, that Edison first conversed with his new invention about Mary's little lamb. [He recited "Mary had a little lamb..."] When the machine recognizably reproduced Edison's voice, Kruesi [a Swiss watchmaker who built the machine for Edison] turned pale and invoked the protection of the Holy Ghost in German.
> Edison himself was dumbfounded. "I was never so taken aback in all my life," he later admitted. (1977, p. D31)

Inventions continued to tumble into our lives like boulders in a rock slide. Edison's motion picture was shown in 1891. Guglielmo Marconi sent his first wireless telegraph signals in 1895. The earliest known public radio broadcast in the United States was a brief Christmas Eve "program" in 1906, presented by an experimenter, R. A. Fessenden of Brant Rock, Massachusetts. The beginning of modern commercial radio broadcasting in the United States is generally said to be the 1920 presidential election returns from station KDKA in Pittsburgh. Vladimir Zworkin patented the first television system in 1928, although television did not become popular until after World War II, in the 1950s. ENIAC, the prototype of modern electronic computers, was put into operation in 1946. Gordon Gould invented the laser, a communication device of enormous importance, in 1958, although a patent was not granted to him until 1978. The first commercial communications satellite, Telestar I, was launched in 1962. Dennis Gabor, a Hungarian engineer, invented the hologram, a three-dimensional pictorial technique, in 1947, receiving the Nobel Prize for it in 1971 (see Illustration 3.7).

If you want to count transportation of the whole human body as communication (some do; some don't), then we must include at least the motor car, the airplane, and the rocket as monumental advances.

The recent explosion of communication tools has been incredible. It has made the world close to a "global village," to use Canadian philosopher of communication Marshall McLuhan's phrase, a planet around which information travels at the speed of light, around which we have placed, so to speak, "our own nervous system" in the form of electric technology. As this technological "nervous system" accelerates communication, so it apparently accelerates changes in nations, in alignments of political groups, perhaps in global anxiety. While change is natural, the recent rhythm of change in communication means has been like a throbbing tympani roll building to a climax such as we have never before witnessed.

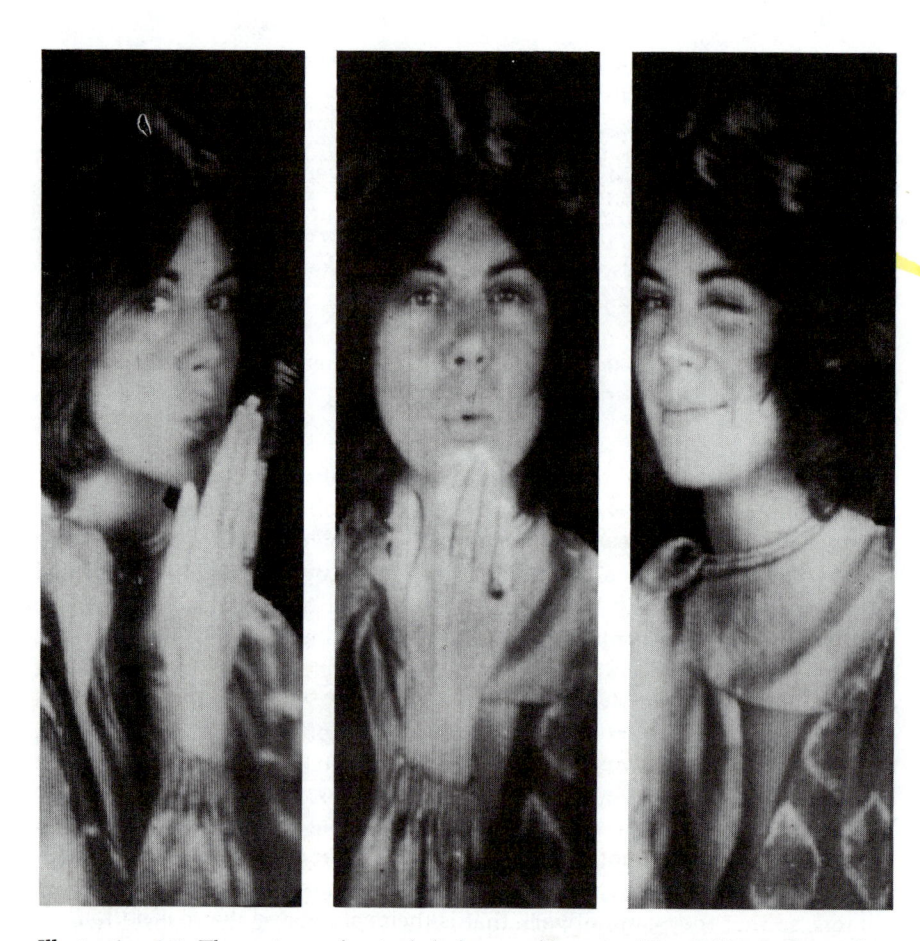

Illustration 3.7 Three views of a single hologram filmstrip, "Kiss II." R. F. Shepard writes: "Holography is a form of picture-taking that uses no camera but harnesses laser beams to make images that are seen in three dimensions with startling clarity. Holograms seem to float in mid-space and can often be eyed from perspectives that make them move; indeed, there are holographic films that are moving pictures" (1976, p. 16). "Kiss II" is by Lloyd Cross, inventor of the holographic movie process. (Photo by Daniel Quat. © Museum of Holography)

COMMUNICATION INSTRUMENTS AS MASS MEDIA AND AS PERSONAL MEDIA

All media of communication extend the human body, as McLuhan (1964) pointed out. They have traditionally been called *mass media*. Sometimes they have this mass quality, however, and sometimes they don't. Radio, for example, is certainly a mass medium when 100 million people listen to the same program. Television is a mass medium when a satellite broadcast reaches a billion people simultaneously around the world. Print is a mass medium when millions of people read a newspaper. But there is also a seductive booby trap involved in referring to all technological communication tools as mass media, for there frequently is no mass audience at all, only a single person at the receiving end of the technology. A large audience is always implied in the term "mass media."

All New Media Begin in the Hands of the Few and End in the Hands of the Many

There is no communication technology that, because of its complexity and expense of operation and maintenance, does not begin in the hands of the few and end up in the hands of the many. Name any medium you want to. Motion pictures? The original cameras and projectors were so expensive and so difficult to operate that millions of people couldn't own them, and good-sized audiences were needed to pay the production and distribution costs of films. But today millions of people do own motion picture cameras and projectors and they both take and show motion pictures for their own personal pleasure and the pleasure (or punishment—depending on the quality of the material) of their friends or captive audiences. Incidentally, the equipment that those millions can afford today is also technically better than the original equipment. Television? That, too, obviously began in the hands of the few who had the huge sums of money required to set up television stations and handle the programming and promotion. Today more and more individuals have television cameras and videotape recorders, either personally or available in their schools, so that they can do work that is theirs alone and that has nothing to do with masses of people. Newspapers? Sure, it takes millions of dollars to set up the machinery and hire employees for a major newspaper. But there are also mimeograph machines, ditto machines, Xerox and similar duplicating systems, which, if we don't own personally, are available for use by almost everybody in our technological societies at a cost that most of us can afford.

There is a general principle involved here. The technological tools of communication first begin in the hands of the few and then gradually "democratize" themselves and end up in the hands of the many. Can you think of an exception? Computers? Although you can buy or build efficient mini-computers for a few hundred dollars today, they will inevitably follow the course of hand calculators, which are mini-computers of sorts, and will be priced one day so that computer terminals, if not the full computers themselves, will be available to all of us. When the newest forms of communication technology get swinging—laser beam transmission and holographs, for example—they, too, will follow the course of every communication technology that has preceded them. They are expensive now, but the price will tumble quickly.

This is not to say, of course, that big producers will cease to exist. We still go to commercial films, even though most of us own or have access to simple, relatively inexpensive motion picture cameras.

Private, Public, and Medio Communication

Because the new media are sometimes used with masses and sometimes by individuals or small groups, some scholars prefer to make distinctions by using terms like *public media* and *private media* or *mass media* and *personal media*. A third term—*medio communication* (*medio* is from Latin, meaning "middle")—has arisen to refer to the use of technical devices in interpersonal or small group settings. Home movies, unless they happen to be good enough to show on a local television station, are examples of private, personal, or medio communication.

WE ARE NOT AT THE END OF THE ODYSSEY

Several lessons suggest themselves when considering the history of communication, even as briefly as we have done it here. An obvious one is that we frequently have no idea where new media technology will take us when it is introduced. A second is that communication technology is accelerating at a tremendous rate. A third, and corollary lesson, is that we have an insatiable desire for speeding up means of communication with one another and for making information more and more accessible.

For anyone who has the impression that there can't be many more advances in media technology, relax. The development of satellites alone has tremendously increased the capacity for worldwide communication; and we have just begun to fling our satellites into space. When near space has been filled with satellites we may indeed have fully achieved the external electronic nervous system around the globe that Marshall McLuhan speculated about when thinking of the global village. The number of interconnecting signals (via telephone or videophone, for example) that now are available will be increased many times over when fiber optic technology begins to replace in large scale the increasingly clumsy and costly system of copper wire lines used in the telephone, telegraphy, cable television, and the like. The union of computers, satellites, and cable television—a process already underway—will probably be one of the most explosive developments in the history of communication.

When the world is indeed a global village in communication terms, it seems inevitable to many observers that we will then turn our attention to space. Debates already sizzle around the issues of colonizing near and outer

THE SYSTEMATIC STUDY OF COMMUNICATION 69

space. It is useful to remember that if and when we colonize space, then our present global village will be one way station among many possibilities for us. Perhaps your grandchildren will regard the whole solar system as their global village. Their grandchildren may expand the vision to our galaxy.

As Arthur C. Clarke, a British scientist and writer of science fiction, has pointed out, when that day comes (he doesn't doubt that it will), then we will begin anew with isolated pockets of people here and there in space, just as similar pockets once dotted the earth. There could be such pockets of people in artificial space stations, on the moon, on various planets, all separate and developing spatially removed from Mother Earth. We'll be able to sustain communication, of course, doubtless using laser beams, which have a remarkable capacity for carrying information tremendous distances.

Our insatiable desire for information has led Clarke to say:

For we can now say, in the widest possible meaning of the phrase, that the purpose of human life is information processing. . . . And therefore the real value of all the devices such as discussed here is that they have the potential for immensely enriching and enlarging life, by giving us more information to process—up to the maximum number of bits per second that the human brain can absorb. (1977, p. 265)

Clarke is wise enough to know that he has opened up a bottomless philosophical pit when speaking of "the purpose of human life," a fact that he acknowledges. But if we leave out the word "purpose," it still seems clear that we have a monomaniacal drive for more information about more things processed at greater and greater speed.

Information is becoming America's most consumed product. Already 50 percent of our gross national product is bound up with information activity. Nearly half of our labor force earns it living by creating, transferring, processing, or evaluating information.

Charles D. Ferris (1978, p. 22)

WHEN DID THE SYSTEMATIC STUDY OF COMMUNICATION BEGIN?

So far this chapter has focused on a single dimension of communication history: how new media have entered our world and changed our lives. It is useful, however, to also ask whether communication has been studied before our time, for if it has been studied previously, then people before us have recognized its importance.

And, yes, communication has been studied systematically in the West for well over two thousand years.

We know about the beginnings of communication study only since the advent of writing. Would you guess that those cave painters in Spain, France, and Africa taught one another tricks of the trade, or even held their version of master classes in proper execution of the craft? Would you guess that speakers before the time of writing argued about the best way of making a point? Probably, but we have no way of knowing for sure, because our knowledge of what our ancestors thought about communication comes to us through written documents, beginning with the Greeks and their remarkable phonetic alphabet. The Greeks, and the Romans, did think communication was one of the processes at the heart of our lives.

We do not have the space in this book to treat the many ways in which communication has been studied throughout the ages. We will, however, look at one of the major themes of the study of communication, *rhetoric*. Rhetoric meant, and still means, different things to different people. At base, however, it has been considered the study of language (sometimes only spoken, sometimes both spoken and written) as a means of persuasion. The Greeks were concerned mostly with speaking, that is to say, oratory, since writing had not yet caught on strongly.

Undoubtedly the most famous name from those beginning days is Aristotle (384-322 B.C.), who was an encyclopedic scholar, turning his attention in a scientific way to such subjects as physics, botany and biology, physiology, logic, ethics, and rhetoric. His *Rhetoric*, a massive work, is a towering landmark in that subject, as are his *Ethics*, *Logic*, and *Poetics*, all works concerned with communication through language. His procedure was one of systematic analysis and classification, and no student of rhetoric today should be without knowledge of this great philosopher's work.

Aristotle's teacher, Plato (428-348 B.C.), while his contributions to the study of rhetoric are not as central to the world today as are Aristotle's, was also concerned with communication, and he too wrote about it. In turn, Plato gave us knowledge of his teacher, Socrates (469-399 B.C.), a renowned teacher who gathered youth around him to engage in reasoned consideration of all manner of issues. It is from Plato's writing that we learn of Socrates' deep uneasiness about what impact the invention of writing would have on the world of the mind. Hating the prospect of "frozen thought," Socrates preferred the live give-and-take of learners involved in continuing dialogue.

The Greek tradition, as symbolized (inadequately) by the preceding names, was carried forward by the Romans. At least two names should be mentioned here. Cicero (106-43 B.C.) was a renowned Roman orator, a teacher of oratory, and a writer on the subject of rhetoric. His speeches are still studied today as models of structuring words toward persuasive ends. Quintilian (A.D. 35-c.97), also a trained orator and teacher of oratory, wrote a larger body of literature on the subject of rhetoric than did Cicero. The author of twelve books on rhetoric, he used Cicero, the elegant craftsman with words, as a major example.

Rhetoric, and its sibling subjects, grammar and logic, have always flourished in education in the West, drawing heavily on Greek and Roman beginnings. In the Middle Ages seven subjects, known as the liberal arts, were the curriculum. Grammar, rhetoric, and logic, known as the *trivium*, were three of the essential subjects. The other four, known as the *quadrivium*, were music, arithmetic, geometry, and astronomy.

Even today we doubtless spend more time and money in formal education on communication than on any other subject. Our approach has changed, however. Few modern books on communication are mere updatings of what the ancients studied. Part of the reason for this is the rise of new media of communication. Part comes from the contributions of new disciplines, such as anthropology, neurology, sociology, and the like. The word, spoken and written, has also taken on a new position in our lives, although the impact of electronic media is changing so rapidly that it is not precisely clear what that position is.

The printing press doubtless reduced the role of the orator, at least a bit. On the other hand, television has brought back the central position of rhetoric—but with a new look—to our political and other social affairs. Dozens of authors address themselves today to those matters.

Still, there were giants in those days—Aristotle, Cicero, and Quintilian, for example—and in many ways their basic analyses have never been surpassed. Times have changed, however, and our study has changed with those times.

THIS CHAPTER IN PERSPECTIVE

In this chapter we have briefly surveyed one aspect of the history of human communication: the development of new media. While the oldest remaining indications of human interest in communication and ability to communicate are found today in cave paintings, our ancestors doubtless began to speak and signal nonverbally long before they created those notable underground works of art. But no one can say when speech and nonverbal communication began.

The first revolution in communication came when humans began to make written records, at least five thousand and possibly ten thousand years ago. Our ancestors developed two general writing systems—sign writing, in which hundreds of signs standing for objects and ideas were used, and phonetic writing, in which a few signs (letters) stood for sounds in languages.

The second revolution in communication came when writing was mechanized by print with movable type. Gutenberg perfected his process around 1450, although similar processes had been developed earlier in China and Korea. Printing was the dominant medium of written communication until the third revolution of the past century and a half, beginning in 1839, when photography was introduced. This was followed rapidly by the telegraph, the typewriter, the telephone, the phonograph, motion pictures, wireless telegraphy, radio, television, the electronic computer, the laser, the communication satellite, the hologram, and the many means of transporting the whole human body. We have seen more changes in communication in the last century and a half than in all previous human history. And we are not at the end of our communication inventions. If our current media now serve to make the world a global village, tomorrow may find us in a neighborhood planetary system. Information explodes around us and all signs point to vastly expanded and accelerated information systems.

Further, we have clear evidence that the study of communication, particularly rhetoric—the art of persuading through language—has been of central concern at least since the beginning of writing. People of dedication and genius developed analyses of the communication process that stand as monuments today. They were concerned with morals almost exclusively, but that is where the primary communication action was in those days. Times change, media change, possibilities, problems, and points of view change.

EXTENSIONS

Reading You Might Enjoy

1. Carter, Thomas Francis. *The Invention of Print with Movable Type in China and Its Spread Westward.* 2nd ed. New York: Ronald Press, 1955.

An excellent work about movable type, the invention that battered our thinking about media first and longest in the pre-electric days.

2. Harper, Nancy. *Human Communication Theory: The History of a Paradigm.* Rochelle Park, N.J.: Hayden Book Co., 1979.

This book is about the manner in which communication has been studied in the West for twenty-five centuries. It is an excellent account of the development of theories of human communication, emphasizing the fact that, as with so many matters, we should feel humility on understanding that scholars long before our day had profound insights into the nature of communication.

3. Hogben, Lancelot. *From Cave Painting to Comic Strip: A Kaleidoscope of Human Communication.* New York: Chanticleer Press, 1949.

Hogben's book is a short (287-page) work on the history of communication from the cave paintings to television. Although somewhat dated, it is a highly readable book about the history of many forms of communication.

4. Ivins, William M., Jr. *Prints and Visual Communication.* Cambridge, Mass.: Harvard University Press, 1953.

Long before photography was perfected, identical copies of drawings could be made. They were called prints. Ivins tells the story of this important breakthrough in the history of communication—the equivalent for pictures of Gutenberg's invention of print with movable type.

5. McLuhan, Marshall, and Quentin Fiore. *War and Peace in the Global Village.* New York: Bantam Books, 1968.

The first title in this book, predictive of its provocative content, is "An inventory of some of the current spastic situations that could be eliminated by more feedforward." Filled with quotations, photographs, and drawings, this book offers a look at where we stand now with our electronic communication and where we are likely to be tomorrow.

Ponderings and Projects

1. Take a tough-minded view of the importance of writing. As noted in the chapter, humans have not always been able to write, and even today there are peoples on earth who cannot write. Prepare "pro" and "con" lists about the role of writing in your personal world or in the world at large. That is, continue the discussion of the advantages and disadvantages of writing.

2. Should schools and colleges accept *all* communication media as equally valid in their work? Should the time-honored term paper or critical essay be replaced or augmented by audio essays made by students? By picture essays? By student-produced videotapes?

3. Marshall McLuhan has suggested that the flow of information outside the classroom has for a long time been greater than the flow inside the classroom. He attributes this to the growth of such media as film, television, and radio and suggests, for example, that the average child in a technological society with a television set learns more about space travel from television than from school. Do you think this is true? If so, what does it mean about the role of schools in the future?

4. Henry David Thoreau, the important nineteenth-century American author, wrote in *Walden* that:

> *We are in great haste to construct a magnetic telegraph from Maine to Texas; but Maine and Texas, it may be, have nothing important to communicate.... We are eager to tunnel under the Atlantic and bring the Old World some weeks nearer to the New; but perchance the first news that will leak through into the broad, flapping American ear will be that Princess Adelaide has the whooping cough.*

you react to Thoreau's observation that sped-up communication might not be all that useful to the world?

5. The energy crisis we are in might conceivably effect further profound changes in the traveling behavior of people, with resulting increases in the development of electronic forms of communication. It is less consuming of energy, for example, to stay in touch with an office thirty miles away from home by two-way (interactive) television than it is to transport a person to and from that office. Since this is not in the least a remote possibility, it could be both interesting and instructive to imagine what such a world would be like.

The Cultural Context of Communication

4

The life history of the individual is first and foremost an accommodation to the patterns and standards traditionally handed down in his community.

Ruth Benedict

Communication always occurs within a *context*—a setting or a system. Studying communication outside of a context can lead to inadequate conclusions. Culture is a major context within which communication occurs. Further, culture is a large enough context to permit a wide-angle view, yet it is not too broad to be comprehended. This chapter will help us understand what a culture is and will offer some examples of different communication habits, rules, and attitudes that have evolved in different cultures. The importance for us of understanding cultural differences is that effective intercultural communication is not merely a question of understanding language and nonverbal communication, for example; it also requires sensing and respecting the convictions that people of a culture hold. We can use the same words and still not understand one another except in the most superficial way.

COMMUNICATION HABITS ARE LEARNED IN A CULTURE

You and I are born into a world filled with rigorous, complicated, and generally unstated communication habits. Everybody is born into such a world. We are dropped into a particular culture, which is like a river, with its confining banks, its currents, its still waters and rapids, that has been flowing for a very long time. We are pebbles in the river, and we flow with it. We are shaped by the river, tumbled and smoothed as we flow its course. Yet most of us change the river very little during our lifetimes. That is, the ways we communicate are taught within our cultures. Such is the power of culture, the prime context within which communication occurs.

A DEFINITION OF CULTURE

A culture is a way of life of a group of people, the behaviors and beliefs that they accept, generally without thinking about them, and that are passed along by communication and imitation from one generation to the next. The term *culture* is sometimes applied to creatures other than humans, but generally it refers to people. *Culture* used in this sense does not refer to that other meaning of the term: refinement or appreciation of the "better" things of life.

The Concept of Being Culture-Bound

From the day each of us is born into a culture, that ongoing river, we begin to learn its ways. We are, to use the technical term, *culture-bound.* That is, we are shaped, formed, molded, by the culture. As Ruth Benedict, a respected American anthropologist, said, expanding on the statement that begins this chapter:

> *The life history of the individual is first and foremost an accommodation to the patterns and standards traditionally handed down in his community. From the moment of birth the customs into which he is born shape his experience and behaviour. By the time he can talk, he is a little creature of his culture, and by the time he is grown and able to take part in its activities, its habits are his habits, its beliefs his beliefs, its impossibilities his impossibilities.* (1946, p. 2)

In traditional Arab society, a man and his wife would never dream of walking together in the street, side by side, let alone arm in arm or hand in hand. Such behavior would be considered an indecent public display of intimacy.

Raphael Patai (1976, p. 131)

What Members of a Culture Share

What are the qualities that a culture shapes us to accept and emulate? There are many, some more important than others. But the habits, rules, outlooks, and values that are formed by the culture into which we are born include the language we speak, the nonverbal rules we follow, the system of family arrangements we accept, the goals we think are worthy or unworthy, our attitudes about how men, women, and children should behave, our feelings about time and space, our notions about our personal roles in the world, our assumptions about life after death, our feelings about the importance of individuals as contrasted with the community, and the significance that we attach to material things. Some of these learnings are precisely habits of communication; all emerge in communication.

A Culture Is Not Necessarily the Same as a Nation

We should clear up a possible source of confusion early in our thinking about cultures: A culture is frequently not the same as a nation. The political entity known as a nation may contain different cultures within it. In an opposite manner, several nations can be thought of as belonging to the same general culture.

An example of a nation containing within it quite different cultures is illustrated dramatically by the Philippines. A tribe called the Tasaday was "discovered" by the Philippine government in 1971. Following leads, Manuel Elizalade, Jr., Presidential Assistant on National Minorities, flew by helicopter to the jungle area where the "new" tribe lived. Journalist John Nance dramatically described the first reaction of these isolated forest people as the helicopter descended, hovering above the ground:

> *The forest men cowered and threw their arms over their heads. Then one leaped to his feet, eyes wide with terror. He tried to turn toward the forest. Hesitated. Froze. Shuddered and plunged forward, sprawling face down on the wet earth.* (1975, p. 11)

After meeting members of the tribe, Elizalade, who was not an anthropologist, radioed with urgent excitement the question of what to look for to confirm whether or not the tribe was a legitimate discovery, whether they were indeed an isolated pocket of people—a separate culture—who had not been influenced by the outside world. The reply, cryptically stated and punctuated for telegraphic purposes, suggested what an anthropologist would look for in determining whether the group should be considered a separate culture:

> *If they are truly food gatherers with no agriculture [they are] among worlds rarest people. Two most widely diffused articles in modern times since Age of Discovery 15th Century A.D. are tobacco and sweet potato. If they know tobacco incredible discovery . . . If Ubu, Tboli, Tirruray, Blaan [other persons with Elizalade] cannot speak easily with them a new language is likely and highly possible. Obtain estimated number of families. Check marriage arrangements and local leadership. . . . Check economic base; what are they living on—wild yams? Pith of palms? Shoots of bamboo and rattan? Ferns? Edible flowers? etc. What proteins—bats? pig? deer? fish? crabs and shrimp? Check type of shelter—caves? Bark of trees? Wild palm leaves? Group's isolation of great interest. Estimate extent and pattern of extra group contacts. Ask them names for other people they have heard of—whites? Chinese? Moros? Tboli? Ubu? etc. What are their basic tools—iron? Stone? Extent of iron tools. Only bolo or others? Do they have bow and arrow complex? Spears? Type of traps? Try to get something on their world view and the world that surrounds them and their relationship with environment.* (Nance, 1975, p. 11)

This example of a spectacular discovery of a group of people heretofore unknown to the mainstream culture makes the obvious point that a nation is not necessarily the same as a culture. Not all Filipinos are Tasaday, yet the Tasaday tribe is located in the Philippines.

Illustrations are almost as obvious in the United States. Although there is a dominant culture (white, English speaking, Christian, oriented toward certain goals and values), there are also groups that depart considerably from these norms: the Amish Dutch, for example, or American Indians living on reservations, or Chicanos in the Southwest, or Cajuns in Louisiana. So, too, can it be argued that American blacks are distinctive in their ways, as are many American Jews, as are Mennonites and Shakers. It is convenient to refer to such groups whenever they are found as subcultures.

Here in the Williamsburgh section of Brooklyn, New York, a single subway stop from Manhattan, children [of Hasidic Jews] learn Yiddish as their native tongue, and rarely if ever see a television show or movie, or read a novel. . . . For here the *mitzvahs*, or commandments, which God on Mount Sinai charged His chosen people to obey, are honored as rules of living with a devotion so vibrant that the tablets of the law might have been carried down by Moses to Lee Avenue this very morning.

Harvey Arden (1975, pp. 276, 298)

Subcultures

Subculture does not mean "inferior." The prefix *sub-* means, in this case, "not the main culture." Thus black ways are efficient and adequate, as are Puerto Rican, Indian, Chicano, Pennsylvania Dutch, or Haitian ways.

When a subculture is geographically embedded in another culture, there is generally some sharing by both groups of similar habits and values. The relationship might be pictured as in Fig. 4.1.

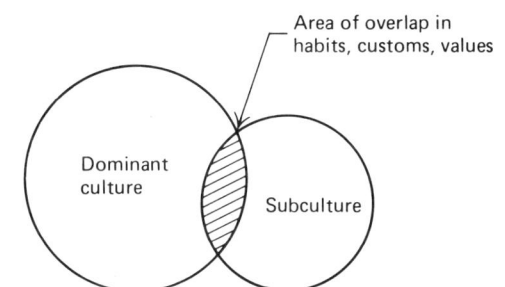

Figure 4.1

How much overlap occurs in that shaded area depends on many matters. For example, some black people in the United States have gradually drifted almost totally into the ways of the dominant white culture, for better or worse. Other blacks, seeking to preserve or to reestablish their own unique heritage, have deliberately sought to rediscover their lost lineage, which often goes back to Africa. Many have adopted African names, African clothing, and even African languages, in particular, Swahili. Among themselves many seek, without the shame that has been imposed on them, to maintain black English, and more and more they use, again without the feelings of guilt that have been imposed by the dominant culture, their black nonverbal habits. The old-fashioned argument that black English represents inferior intellectual potential is accepted by almost no contemporary linguists.

Other minority groups maintain their traditions in similar fashion, while geographically in another dominant culture. Many Jewish families in the United States, for example, send their children to Jewish schools after the regular school day as ended. So too do some Chinese familes, especially those in New York or San Francisco, send their children to Chinese schools.

Actually, Fig. 4.1 simplified matters too much. A more accurate way of picturing subcultural relationships might look like Fig. 4.2, using the United States and only three cultural groups as examples.

The large circles (A, B, C) stand for what we might call *macro* (large or major) cultures, such as the white, black, and hispanic. Let's not concern ourselves for the moment with which is larger or more or less dominant. The

80   THE CULTURAL CONTEXT OF COMMUNICATION

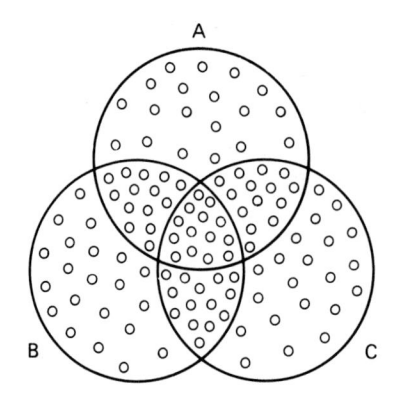

Figure 4.2

three cultures (and many others not shown here) overlap in many ways, as the big circles overlap, and as noted in Fig. 4.1.

The small circles within each big circle represent *micro* (small) cultures or groups to which we all belong. These include churches, schools, clubs, hobby groups, friends. Some of these micro cultures are shared by the macro cultures, and some are not. For example, I am in the same macro culture as my mother and my children. At the same time, we all belong to different micro cultures as well. I teach in a college, something which neither my mother nor my children do. When I am at the college, I behave in accordance with the ways of that group, in terms of communication and all other matters. I drop many of my college communication ways, however, when relaxing at home or when with my children during vacations. Tuned-in observers could instantly detect these shifts. So, even those of us who are "monolinguals," speaking only one language in the general sense of that term, actually shift our communicative behavior dozens of times a day. Each of our cultures is a complex mix of many elements.

The capability of "drifting" in and out of a dominant culture—sharing some qualities, but having some unique ones—is demonstrated dramatically by a practice that the U.S. Marine Corps used in Pacific Ocean island-hopping warfare in World War II. Searching for a code that would be easy to use and difficult to break, the Marines recruited and used American Navajo Indians to send uncoded messages in their own language, on the correct assumption that the language was not known to the Japanese foes. A spokesman for the Navajo group said:

> *Most codes developed by the military are logical codes, developed mechanically. . . . If you can find key words, you can eventually decode it.*

But that is difficult to do with a language that has so many variations, exceptions to the rules. Also, the Navajo language was unwritten [at that time], so you couldn't find a textbook. You had to base it solely on the sounds you were hearing. This made it difficult for the Japanese or for anybody else for that matter. ("Navajo war code," 1979, p. 41)

The code was never broken. Thus the Navajo Indians, who also spoke English, of course, were an integral part of the U.S. Marine culture, but they could break away from that culture, as well as from Navajo culture, at crucial moments and still serve the Marines, to whom they showed great loyalty.

Another striking example of persons in a subculture shifting behavior in the presence of other members of the culture is told by John Baugh:

The scene is a public swimming pool in a black working-class neighborhood in Los Angeles. . . . The staff members, some black and from the local community and some white from other communities, are making and reestablishing acquaintances. In a typical reunion, two black staff members greet each other with dialogue:

Howard: "Hey babe, what's happening? It's been a while."

Douglas: "Well, you know how it is. Always slow and not enough dough."

Howard: "I heard that."

While they talk, Howard and Douglas use the black power handshake, which, in this neighborhood, consists of three separate grasps executed in rapid order.

A white staff member, Dave, then approaches. He lives outside the local community, and neither Howard nor Douglas knows him. [He is, therefore, from another subculture.] They greet each other with some hesitation:

Dave: "Hi, I'm Dave."

Howard: "How you feeling, my man? I'm Howard—and this here is Douglas."

Douglas (nodding toward Dave in recognition): "What's happening?"

Dave: "Not much. Tell me, have you guys ever worked here before?"

Dave offers his hand to Howard for a black power handshake, with his forearm vertical. But Howard raises his arm, with the forearm horizontal, and grasps Dave's hand in the traditional, standard [U.S.] handshake. When they release hands, Dave offers his hand to Douglas at hip level for the standard handshake, which Douglas returns quite naturally. (1978, p. 32)

Culture as a System

A culture is one kind of system, as the term was used in the earlier chapter on models. You may want to look again at Fig. 2.4 for a reminder.

A culture, like the diagram in Fig. 2.4, has a boundary, although the boundary can be quite vague. Within the general (dominant) culture are subsystems, or subcultures, which are in communication with one another in varying degrees. A culture is an open system, so there are continuous *inputs* and *outputs* from and to the surrounding environment. In this case, the environment is not only nature but also other cultures. There is also *throughput*, in the sense that inputs from the outside are altered before they become outputs. Information is transformed by the culture.

In all cultures the boundaries are open, or porous, to a greater or lesser extent; one of the fascinating qualities of cultures is the degree to which they consciously attempt to maintain their boundaries. Some cultures, like the United States—to use a nation as synonymous with a culture for a moment—maintain rather porous boundaries, permitting a fairly free flow of information, people, and goods. Other cultures attempt to maintain relatively nonporous boundaries. The phrase "Iron Curtain" refers to the conscious boundary building at the end of World War II by the U.S.S.R. between itself and most of the rest of the West. Indeed, between East Germany, influenced heavily by the U.S.S.R., and West Germany, influenced heavily by Western Europe and North America, a literal wall, the Berlin wall, was built. People have escaped through, over, and under that wall on many occasions, and electronic communication has leaped the wall with greater ease. Still, the wall represents an attempt at strict boundary maintenance, with the lessened possibility of the introduction of new ideas from the outside than is the case with countries such as the United States or England or Canada or modern Japan, where a much greater porousness of the boundary line is assumed to be desirable.

CULTURAL HABITS, INCLUDING COMMUNICATION, ARE LEARNED

All forms of behavior, including communicative behavior, are learned within a culture. This obviously applies to language, but it also applies to forms of communication that most of us think of as natural to everyone: We must also learn from our culture how to express nonverbally such basic emotions as happiness or sadness or anger or boredom. Within cultures we learn how to meet people, how to operate in groups, how to conduct a love affair. None of these are natural, in the sense that people everywhere do them in precisely the same way, in the same time and place, and with the same meaning.

Albert Scheflen says it well:

*There are rules and laws, traditions [within culture], that govern
how people are supposed to act toward each other in . . .
communication. . . . Let me explain a little more what I mean by
rules: an orchestra assembles to play Beethoven's* Fifth Symphony.
*They have a score, and they follow the score. The violinists play the
violin part, the cellists play the cello part. The conductor helps them
integrate and coordinate all parts. But none of them is composing
Beethoven's* Fifth Symphony. *They're not making it up. True, there
are probably no two violin players who have identical styles, and
each will add his own stylistic variations to playing Beethoven. But
yet they must stick to the score or they will not play in concert.
Similarly, you don't think of yourself as making up bridge when you
play bridge or chess or checkers. You think of yourself as obeying
rules which allow you certain variations. They allow you a certain
number of tactical alternatives. . . . People accept these rules in
regard to rituals or meetings. But when you talk about love affairs
or psychotherapy sessions [which are communication events],
there's a tremendous tendency in America to deny that these interactions have agendas or programs or rules. Each lover thinks he and
his partner are making up the love relationship. I'm saying that
although he may add stylistic variations, he is following rules of
communication. The course of a love affair is probably just as
ritualistically ordered as a church service.* (Quoted in Forsdale, 1974,
p. 72)

Learning to Shift Communication Behavior According to Situations

Furthermore, before we go to school we have begun to learn how our communicative behavior must be changed to fit rules appropriate to various settings or contexts. Depending on our particular subculture, we have learned, for example, what our communication should be like in a Catholic church, or a Jewish synagogue, or an Islamic mosque, or an Indian kiva. We have learned how street communication is generally somewhat different from communication at home. In all of these contexts we will generally behave as society expects us to. Oh, we may rebel sometimes, out of anger or mischievousness or discontent. We may know, for example, that respectful silence is a cultural rule expected of us in some, although not all, churches, but we may decide to kick up a ruckus because we are annoyed on that particular day. But such deliberate misbehavior merely proves that we *do* know the rules. Otherwise we wouldn't know how to violate the expectations so well!

Some people are born into cultures that require more drastic "shifting of communication gears" than those just described. For example, I have an acquaintance who was born in the country of Bangladesh (then called East Pakistan, to the northeast of India). He grew up from childhood speaking three languages quite well and having had some facility in two others.

He lived in the city of Dacca. On the street, with his friends, he spoke mostly Bengali. At home the family spoke Urdu. When the family went to visit his grandparents at a nearby village, everybody spoke Hindustani.

The most fascinating part of the story is that he did not know while learning and using these three languages that they had names like "Bengali," or "Urdu," or "Hindustani." He did not even know at the time that they were different languages. He simply knew that on the street he talked one way, at home another way, and with his grandparents and their friends a third way. For all he knew, these different ways of talking were variations of one language. (The English you speak at home may not be the same English you speak at school.) He also learned to read Arabic, because he was a Moslem by religion, and the Koran, the holy book, is written and recited from memory in Arabic. He also learned some English by reading advertisements and by hearing it at movies.

He also learned dozens of other communication ways appropriate to his culture. I have seen in many parts of India and Pakistan (whose cultures are closely related to the culture of Bangladesh) that in motion picture theaters there is a much more direct, outspoken reaction on the part of the audience to what is happening on the screen than we generally experience in this country. In the United States, except for some audiences at some kinds of films, we tend to be fairly quiet at motion pictures. It is considered discourteous among most North American movie audiences to yell out at actors on the screen. That's one reason young children are not permitted to go alone to many movie theaters in this country. They are segregated, watched by elders, "kept in their place." Otherwise they tend to "bother" the adults who seek silence. Indian/Pakistani/Bangladesh audiences (and many other audiences around the world) frequently get into a give-and-take, hoot-and-holler kind of interaction with characters on the screen. This is true even of well-educated audiences. They clap, whistle, shout encouragement, stamp their feet, call out in approval or disapproval, roar in laughter. They operate with a different set of rules of propriety. To a visitor from another culture it is a strange experience. We sometimes put it down with an air of superiority, as we tend to do with customs that are strange to us. (A Bengali might think of us, for example, as passive or emotionless.) It should be viewed, of course, as a sign of cultural difference, as part of a style of communicative behavior into which people are born. One of the crucial ground rules in viewing different cultures is to do it nonjudgmentally.

MOST OF OUR COMMUNICATIVE BEHAVIOR IS LEARNED OUT-OF-AWARENESS

Most of the communication ways, or rules, that we follow in a culture are not stated anywhere. We learn them by observing and mimicking others around us. As children we are seldom aware of this behavior. Neither are we as adults. Most communicative behavior is learned and practiced unconsciously, or, to use the term many specialists prefer, *out-of-awareness*. Some communicative behavior is taught to us through direct, explicit communication from others who say "Do this," but such instruction is distinctly in the minority.

The notion that most communicative behavior is not stated anywhere may seem odd. After all, there are hundreds of books on grammar, on how to write, on word choice, on speech making, on taking photographs. There are stacks of tools like dictionaries, thesauruses, style manuals, technical journals, all valuable. These tools deal with only a small percentage of our total communicative behavior; a behavior so very complex, particularly if you include the many situations in which we shift our communicative behavior, that the rules governing it are almost countless. Still, there are rules. Communication is not chaotic. We simply come to know most of these rules without being able to state them.

An Example of Out-of-Awareness Learning: Walking

As an example of out-of-awareness learning, consider walking. You do it every day—a hundred times. Yet can you describe precisely the action of the various body parts as you walk? Can you say with confidence (and without watching yourself or someone else walk) such things as what strikes the floor or sidewalk first—the heel, the toe, or the whole foot, whether the knees are bent in walking, whether the ankle configuration is altered in walking, whether the arms swing, and if so, whether the right arm goes out at the same time as the right leg or vice versa, whether the feet are pointed straight forward or pointed out a bit or in a bit, whether the elbows and wrists are bent, approximately how high off the walking surface the feet are lifted?

People who are acutely aware of their bodies and have to control them well—athletes, dancers, models, actors—would have a better chance of answering those questions in some detail than do the rest of us, but even they might be hard pressed to do so.

Have you ever tried to teach a child to walk? You can help a bit with words, but they are almost entirely words of encouragement, not specific instructions about how to place the feet or other body parts. Infants learn that extraordinarily difficult task—and it is one of the most difficult tasks we ever learn—mostly by watching, mimicking, and accepting a helping hand. Walking

Illustration 4.1 A child walks.

is difficult in great measure because it involves our eternal enemy, gravity. Getting up off all fours and standing on our two hind legs is an extraordinary feat. Gravity is forever with us, unless you happen to be an astronaut. No wonder everybody celebrates the auspicious victory of walking!

Part of the reason we can't describe the process of walking very accurately is that we learned the skill when we were very young. But the major reason is that the learning occurred out-of-awareness.

So it is with most of our communicative behavior as well. For example, we may learn to communicate comfort to someone in distress by speaking gently, yet no one has ever told us explicitly to do that. We learn it by observing and mimicking.

IN-AWARENESS LEARNING

There is also in-awareness learning, of course. Let's consider walking again. Some specialists—athletes and dancers, for example—consciously learn that same simple activity, walking, in new ways. Good boxers, for example, may learn to "dance" on the balls of their feet. Similarly, baseball outfielders may learn to run on the balls of their feet while chasing fly balls so that they won't bounce up and down excessively and lose sight of the ball. Dancers in classical ballet also depart—in the extreme—from "natural" walking. (The word *natural* is in quotes because there is no single natural way of walking that applies everywhere in the world. All walking is learned behavior and it varies from place to place.) There are various styles of walking in classical ballet. Some require turning the feet out, others demand that the toes touch the floor before any other part of the foot. These are learned in detail, with instruction, and after exhausting hours of practice. A skateboarder generally gets some conscious instruction, too.

> There are culture-induced *styles of walking.* . . . In my observation, the Bengali walk differently (all elbows and knees, with considerable foot-lifting) from the Punjabi (with a more puppet-like rigidity and verticality), south Chinese very differently from the Singhalese.
>
> Weston LaBarre (1964, p. 195)

Some communication is learned with this kind of formal instruction. Most of us learn to read and write in this way. We also learn to make speeches, construct term papers, take and develop photos, play musical instruments, conduct good group discussions, and do other such tasks in this way. Still, most of what we learn about communicative behavior is done out-of-awareness.

A CULTURE'S EXPECTATIONS ARE STRICT

Every culture's expectations about behavior, communicative and otherwise, are strict and severe. If we don't meet the culture's unwritten rules, we are likely to be penalized heavily—by being doubted, disliked, misunderstood, or mistrusted. Anthropologist Robert G. Edgerton writes, for example, about a form of behavior that follows cultural rules—but the rules vary in different cultures.

> *Suicide in the West is typically thought to be as tragic as it is troublesome. We have civil laws and religious proscriptions against it. If a suicide fails, the result can be a deviant identity; if it succeeds, the survivors must often live with a "taint."* (1976, p. 39)

On the other hand, Edgerton notes:

> *In other societies, suicide may be seen as unfortunate but necessary. Thus, in Highland New Guinea a Bena Bena woman whose husband*

Illustration 4.2 A skateboarder. A skateboarder learning, aware of each action, how to master the feat. She'll soon abandon consciousness of her behavior, of course, or fall flat on her face debating what comes next.

has just died may decide to kill herself rather than be inherited by another man. If this is her decision, she will call upon her brother for assistance. He bends over under a tree limb and she stands on his back while affixing the noose. At her signal he walks away. He may be very fond of his sister, but he sees the decision as hers to make without interference. (1976, p. 38)

While Edgerton's examples here are not about communication, the point remains the same. Those who stray too far from the communicative ways of their society may even be institutionalized as insane. Some scholars define insanity as such a severe departure from the communicative behavior of a culture that other members of the culture cannot accept it because of fear. In another culture the same communicative behavior might merely seem odd, or might even be considered normal.

The Cheyennes [tribe of the United States] abhor anyone forcing his will on others by self display, and this behavior principle must be learned from the outset. Crying babies are not scolded, slapped, or threatened. They are simply taken out on the cradleboard away from the camp and into the brush where they are hung on a bush. There the squalling infant is left alone until it cries itself out.

E. Adamson Hoebel (1960, pp. 91-92)

Being considered insane is an extreme penalty for engaging in communicative behavior outside the prescribed rules. More commonly, the violators of communication rules of a group are simply frowned on or considered obnoxious or are excluded from a good job or from many social settings.

THE QUESTION OF BEING BICULTURAL OR MULTICULTURAL

Some people strive for bicultural or multicultural lives, which they are able to establish and preserve with varying degrees of success. Some cross the lines, adopting two or more forms of communicative behavior, with comparative ease. Others have greater difficulty, for a variety of reasons. And it is probably not possible for anybody to be completely bicultural or multicultural in every detail. Still, being multicultural in some degree is a goal toward which all of us must now strive in a world shrinking daily because of the speed of communication. American anthropologist Edward T. Hall has said that the "greatest . . . feat of all is when one manages to gradually free oneself from the grip of unconscious culture" (1976, p. 211). What Hall urges all of us to learn to see is what our own culture is like and what other cultures are like, and in so doing to make visible that that has formerly been invisible, or unconscious. Only then can understanding of the highest order begin.

What an effort that will take! What a job it will be to maintain your own heritage while learning honestly to believe that your ways, including your ways with communication, are not the only or even necessarily the best ways.

THE DEEP AND LASTING EFFECTS OF CULTURE

You could say that the culture you are born into is a prison from which it is nearly impossible to escape. Or you could say that it is a set of traditions you share with other people and that sharing makes you a part of a great ongoing life process that provides security and order without which you could not exist. It's like the old point made about half a glass of water when viewed by an optimist and a pessimist. The pessimist looks at the glass and says it's half empty. The optimist looks at the glass and says it's half full.

So it can be asked of culture: Do its rules, such as its communication rules, entrap you? Or does understanding of the rules, even out-of-awareness, permit you to act openly and freely with the people around you? The pessimist says yes to the first question; the optimist says yes to the second question. To put it another way, how much fun would it be to play tennis without a net or without white lines around the court? The net and boundaries are like the sets of cultural rules that permit you to "play the game" as other people around you do, leaving you free to be creative within boundaries permitted by the culture.

EVERY CULTURE HAS A COMPLETE AND ADEQUATE COMMUNICATION SYSTEM

It is crucial to understand that every culture in the world operates within a complete and fully appropriate communication system of its own. That is, each culture's sets of rules or values or understandings or ways of behavior are a full and complete system. Each culture's set of communication habits is therefore also a full and adequate system, *for that culture*. While none of us has to admire the ways of every culture, it is naive to assume that any culture's ways are better or worse than those of any other culture. It is, for instance, an unfortunate mistake to assume that the communication habits of a particular group of Nigerians, for example, is better (or worse) than the set of communication habits of middle-class white Protestant Americans living, say, in Iowa. Each system works efficiently, on its own terms.

This concept is frequently referred to as *cultural relativism*. Cultures should be viewed relatively, not against some absolute standard, such as the culture you are part of. Judging another culture in terms of an absolute standard, called *ethnocentrism*, is profoundly damaging to the kind of world view that we must nurture if we are to survive as neighbors in the global village. As with our present next-door neighbors, we don't need to love them, but we do need to accept and respect their (peaceful) ways, which may be different from our own.

THE MAJOR COMMUNICATION PROBLEM IS CROSSING LINES

Because we are born into established cultural systems, some of the communication we do during our lifetime is handled without undue complexity, according to that system. We merely flow with the river of the culture, to call back the earlier analogy.

Problems occur when we attempt to cross over from one culture (or subculture), or one context, to another. Habits clash with habits, and if you have ever been in such a situation, the intellectual knowledge that no set of cultural habits is "better" than any other set helps only a bit. Ways still clash, and it often takes real understanding, patience, good will, and work on the part of everybody to make such crossing of cultural boundaries come off reasonably well in successful communication.

Brushing up against the communicative ways of another group causes tension, because strangeness causes tension. Unexpected responses cause anxiety. To move into a new setting is like the stranger riding into a dust-blown town in an American Western movie. He arrives, tired and hungry, dismounts, ties up his horse, and asks where he can get some grub and bed down for the night. More than likely he gets the response, "You're a stranger in these parts, ain't ya?" "Yup," says the stranger, and he knows—we know—that all eyes are on him. He'd better fit in or suffer the consequences.

If some communication is simple, much is extraordinarily complex. It has to do with crossing barriers or lines. Perhaps the most important of these barriers is our personal identity. This point can be made with another analogy, beginning with a reminder of the widely quoted portion of John Donne's "Meditation XVII," written in 1624:

> No man is an island, entire of itself; every man is a piece of the continent, a part of the main; if a clod be washed away by the sea, Europe is the less, as well as if a promontory were, as well as if a manor of thy friends or thine own were. Any man's death diminishes me, because I am involved in mankind; and therefore never send to know for whom the bell tolls; it tolls for thee.

Donne's point is that we are all part of each other, interdependent, linked together. Few people quarrel with either his concept or his eloquence.

Nevertheless, the passage can be turned upside down, so to speak, to ferret out a new meaning that will serve us well in thinking about communication.

Every person is an island, isolated from all others in his or her self, forever physically separated after the umbilical cord is cut. The anxiety, the loneliness of the isolation moves us to create bridges between our islands. We extend our hands, fingers touching; we span the distance with our eyes. We speak; we smile. Through such strivings we construct transitory bridges, pathways of signals, that carry delicate freight of meaning. In fair weather the bridges hold; in foul weather they collapse. We work a lifetime keeping the bridges open between our personal islands. The tolling bell signals the death of an island, the collapse of a bridge, punctuating the eternal state of isolation that we endure, seeking always to alleviate.

This reworking emphasizes the delicate nature of communication. It suggests the difficulties in communication that arise simply because we are distinct human beings playing unique roles. No two of us are identical.

If our own personal identities represent major barriers to transcend in communication, cultural, class, regional, and linguistic barriers are equally difficult. In some cultures people seldom cross lines, particularly social class lines. They are born into a niche and they stay there. In most modern technological societies, however, particularly those that aspire to democratic ideals, we *must* cross lines in order to achieve the mobility necessary to get into new jobs, into new educational situations, into new settings. When many of us go to college, we have to learn a whole new set of communication habits, which, although they represent a small part of our total communicative behavior, are absolutely crucial in that setting. We may have to learn, for example, how to write documented term papers, something that may not have been dealt with in the high schools we went to.

Babies are longed for [in the Asian Indian village], and greatly loved when they arrive. But the spirit of caste has so permeated their lives that they are indifferent toward children outside their own brotherhood, especially toward the children of untouchables. It still distresses us to see a grandmother of caste suddenly change from proud smiles to vindictive shouts because some untouchable [lowest social status] toddler has innocently ventured near her grandchild.

William Wiser and Charlotte Wiser (1969, p. 75)

For example, I was born into a family that spoke nonstandard, or substandard, English (a term that does *not* mean "bad English" but rather English that isn't used by the major decision makers of the community), and I had to learn standard English. It was like learning what clothes to wear or how to eat "properly." Thousands of us have done that.

To repeat an important point, we learn those things and many others essentially by observing how people around us behave and imitating them. That's the way we learn almost everything. It is probably our best hope in the continuing struggle to become ever more skillful communicators.

THREE CONVERSATIONS ABOUT CROSS-CULTURAL COMMUNICATION

The general theme of this chapter has been that the cultures or subcultures into which we are born are paramount determiners of the values we hold and of the communication systems we must follow. Individual differences are permitted within cultural settings, of course, and the ways of cultures change over time. Still, communicators can never ignore the shaping forces of culture. That becomes clear when one personally crosses cultural lines. We even have a term for it: *culture shock.*

In an effort to make more personal the problems that face persons who cross cultural or subcultural boundaries, I interviewed three young people about their experiences in crossing cultural lines. Our informal conversations follow. These are not conversations with communication scholars but with young people who have felt like, or do feel like, outsiders. The first conversation is with a white American student who lived for a short time in Bali. The second is with a Roman Catholic nun, Chinese by birth, but serving at the time of the conversation in New York City's Chinatown. The third is with a black native of the Republic of Mali in West Africa who came to the United States to attend a university.

Beyond providing brief identifying remarks about each person and clarifying the meaning of certain words, there is one other approach that will enrich the meanings in these conversations.

Intercultural Communication Barriers

Communication specialist LaRay M. Barna (1976) has suggested five points at which communication can go astray between peoples of different cultures. Condensing Barna's views, the stumbling points are:

☐ *Language*—wherein we simply do not know the words or do not use them in the same sense as the other person does.

- *Nonverbal areas* — in which we do not share the same nonverbal signals.
- *Preconceptions and stereotypes* — or the problem of bringing with us to another culture impressions about that culture that may have little truth to them.
- *Tendency to evaluate* — or that all-too-human but troublesome tendency to make approving or disapproving judgments about the ways of another culture.
- *High anxiety* — which we sometimes call culture shock: that uncomfortable feeling that escalates the four preceding qualities when we feel out of place — like strangers among strangers in a strange place.

As you read these conversations, you should repeatedly be able to find points where one or more of these five factors is operating: (1) *language* difficulties, (2) *nonverbal* difficulties, (3) presence of *preconceptions and stereotypes*, (4) a *tendency to evaluate* a culture, and (5) the *high anxiety* of being in a strange setting. The factors may apply to me, as interviewer, or to my companions in conversation.

Conversation with Eric Bateson

Eric Bateson, an American college student, has traveled widely. This conversation is about a visit he made to the island of Bali as part of a round-the-world trip while a junior in college.

ERIC BATESON: I wanted to get close to the culture in Bali in the brief time I had, so, rather than learn Indonesian, the lingua franca, I decided to learn a form of Balinese which would be easiest for me and perhaps give me a little edge in being accepted. Most white people who go there use either their native European tongue or Indonesian, the rudiments of which can be picked up in several days. It helped to know at least something of the local language.

    I was taught by a local schoolmaster, one of our hosts, who was experimenting in teaching Balinese culture. His family unit had abandoned most of their section of the *puri* (compound) and condensed themselves into a room or so, making room for six or eight students. Our hosts, three brothers, and their families, were descendants of the local king — when kings still existed around the turn of the century, before the Dutch took over. (Bali then had probably thirty to forty kingdoms, though most were quite small.) This was a Cassatria caste (warrior-ruling caste) family. Gregory Bateson had studied there from 1936 to 1939 and they welcomed the traveling group, of which he was the leader.

Illustration 4.3 Eric Bateson.

Students in the group went off in different directions, but I studied Balinese with my host for about a week and a half, learning a minimum number of sentences and vocabulary items—elementary stuff, such as, "Where are you going?" "How can I locate so and so?" "Where is the market?" Though I didn't realize it at first, I was being taught the language that lower caste persons use in addressing persons of higher caste. (The caste system of Bali comes from that of India, although it is quite different now.) Being an outcaste by definition, since I was not a member of one of the three upper castes (Brahmana, Cassatria, Uwesia), I couldn't make a mistake in addressing any Balinese person using this form, though members of lower castes might find it strange that I was addressing them in Bali Alus, the "high" form used in speaking to one's social superiors. They wouldn't be offended, however.

At the end of my brief period of language study, I knew about one hundred fifty sentences and could play with a few combinations, having had a chance to practice on our hosts in the *puri*. I then took off on a bicycle, riding around the eastern end of the island, an area which had been hit by the volcanic eruption, mostly of ash.

LOUIS FORSDALE: When was the eruption?

ERIC BATESON: 1963. I pushed hard, riding seventy to seventy-five kilometers a day. I wore the Balinese sarong—a wrap-around piece of clothing—because it suited the heat and seemed to matter to the Balinese with whom I wanted to be on good terms. I spent about seven days on the ride, basically not knowing what I was looking for. As it turned out, the road on the eastern side had never been repaired after the eruption, so the people hadn't seen whites for many years. I kept having flat tires and was forever looking for a pump. Actually, I began to use that as a conversation opener. I might have a flat, see a *warung* (snack stand)—Bali is filled with little places that sell tea and snacks—and I'd ask for a bicycle pump. (The island is also loaded with bicycles.) I'd ask in my Balinese, and, after the initial shock, the questions would fly back: "Why are you here?" "How did you get here?" "Where did you learn Balinese?"

In one instance, I came around a bend in the road and there was a woman sweeping the road in front of her house. A four- or five-year-old child was across the road with a one- or two-year-old baby in her arms. The child saw me before her mother did and stared, petrified, paralyzed. I was concerned, too. This was the first time I really understood that they hadn't seen whites in a while. I kept pedaling, and just as I crossed the line between her and her mother, she darted in front of me, causing me to dump the bicycle. The girl was screaming and yelling something that I think meant "demon." It was quite a scene. There I was, on the ground, the hysterical child clutching her mother, who was rigid with fear herself. So I looked up at the mother and asked, "Do you have a bicycle pump?" In fact, she did have one, and that helped establish contact. We sat and talked, and she told me that the child had never seen a white man before. The mother had, but not recently, and certainly not one riding a bicycle with a flat tire.

L. F.:   And you were speaking the high caste language, I assume. The mother probably wasn't of high caste.

ERIC BATESON: Yes, I was using the only form of the language that I knew. On such brief encounters, I really had no way of discovering what caste people were without asking them directly, which seemed an odd thing for me to do.

L. F.:   Did anyone on your travels ever get offended at your use of the "high caste" language?

ERIC BATESON: I don't think anybody was offended. The unusual thing was that at first, almost always, they apparently didn't hear or understand a word I said. Not a word. Then, after I repeated myself, they understood and would often laugh.

L. F.: Were they playing a game with you?

ERIC BATESON: No. At first they were totally surprised, I think. Then I have a hunch they *did* start to play a game. They would say, "What you just said isn't right. You should have said . . ."

We constantly joked with one another. They used to ask me, for example, how many wives I had, and I would tell them I had twenty wives. They knew I was kidding, but they liked developing a story with me, a stranger, and I welcomed the chance to practice my language. Usually, after this verbal play, people would stop kidding around and try to communicate seriously about other things. They were interested in the outside world that they had heard only bits and pieces about.

When I got back to Batuan from my bicycle trip I became really sick. I hadn't eaten well on the ride, partly because I was embarrassed about spending the money I had for food, because the paper bills I had with me were too large, and I didn't want to separate myself from the people by a display of money. So I didn't eat well, although people were kind about giving me food. Then, too, I know I was exposed to hepatitis. I was pushing myself terribly hard on the bicycle as well. I had lost twenty pounds on the ride. I was so ill when the trip was over that I didn't eat for about eleven days. Constant diarrhea. During this illness I lost another twenty pounds. The *puri* was empty, except for the hosts and one or two students. I knew I was sick as hell. I was in a whitewashed room, which was rather dark (the Balinese tend to have rather small windows, located high on the wall, because of the heat). Every day, around noon, a *barong* figure—just the head—would appear at the door and then move at the same level along the wall, around the room to the right of my bed. It would come to rest on the wall behind me near my head, then turn and go back, the way it had come, and on out the door. This happened once a day for eight days. The *barong* is a dragon in Bali, but not an evil one.

L. F.: Was the *barong* bodiless?

ERIC BATESON: Yes. It was just the head.

L. F.: Were you hallucinating, or was it a real event?

ERIC BATESON: Who knows? It was a real event for me in my state. Oh, I probably was hallucinating, but it is interesting that the form I saw was that of the *barong*. I had seen people perform in these *barong* heads—masks. You see them in Bali. When I first saw it in my room, I thought I was going to die, then I began to regard it as something of a friend. People were leaving me alone, except to be sure I had water. I didn't ask for any help, either; I was so sick I didn't care. Strangely, my experience with the *barong* gave me the greatest comfort I had in Bali. This was a real interaction with a culture of which I wasn't a part.

L. F.: Did you live?

ERIC BATESON: Yes, I'm here.

Conversation with Sister Joanna Chan

Sister Joanna Chan belongs to the Maryknoll Order of the Roman Catholic Church and at the time of this interview worked with youth groups in New York City's Chinatown. She was subsequently assigned to a worldwide audiovisual center operated by her order in Hong Kong but has now returned to the United States.

LOUIS FORSDALE: Tell me about your background.

SISTER JOANNA: First of all, let me make it clear that I do not speak for the eight hundred million Chinese of the world. We are a very diversified

Illustration 4.4 Sister Joanna Chan.

people. Also, I have lost direct touch with much of the old culture. And you must remember that I have followed the course of becoming a Catholic sister. Most Chinese in the world do not, of course, practice Christianity.

L. F.: What was your name in China and Hong Kong?

SISTER JOANNA: Chan, the same as now. That is one of the most common last names in Chinese culture. We have an almost infinite number of first names, more than most peoples. My first name was Wen-Ying, as best I can render the sound in English. Wen means "uprightness." Ying is a kind of jade representing virtues, such as fidelity and perseverance.

L. F.: When you first came to the United States, what were some of the biggest problems which you had in communication, in getting along with people—non-Chinese people, that is?

SISTER JOANNA: I was very shy, very reserved. I had trouble expressing my ideas, and it wasn't only a language problem that got in my way. In the traditional Chinese agricultural society, where I grew up, everyone has a well-defined, well-understood role. There is less need of explaining yourself in such circumstances. I was taught to be an obedient daughter. Even after I had finished college, when I went around with my parents, I didn't talk. And I wasn't frustrated either: I understood and accepted my "place." Adult Chinese women, after marriage, play a stronger role. They decide most family matters, in conversation with the husband, of course. It happens today in Chinatown in New York City. At the PTA meeting, more often than not, the mother represents the family and makes the decisions.

L.F.: Duty is very important for the Chinese woman?

SISTER JOANNA: Not just for women. A sense of duty is a major virtue for everyone. For every well-defined role, there are specific duties that go with it. It follows that there is less need for questioning or explaining than one finds in other cultures.

This poses a serious problem for Chinese immigrants in American urban society. For example, difficult marriage problems result from reassessment of the woman's traditional role as dutiful wife. The men, who often immigrate here much earlier and then send for their wives after they have gotten jobs and made some money, need to spend so much time in their long and arduous jobs that they seldom see much of the rest of the culture. On the other hand, when the wives arrive here they see much more of the new way of life, not being tied to jobs as much as their husbands. In the process they lose some of the older sense of reticence. So do the children.

I'll give you another example of how our understanding of a role can be misinterpreted. In the Philippines, during my first week as a novice, we were eating a meal. My superior, an American who was seated opposite me, offered to pour tea for me. I had just come from Hong Kong, and I followed the ways I learned there. I said, "Thank you very much, I'll pour it myself." What that meant to me was "I'm not worthy to have you pour for me because you are my superior." But my remark meant something else to her, probably that I was refusing her generous gesture. I thought she would throw the teapot at me because I was being so rude. I was so frightened by the experience that it took me about three years to get over it. We're great friends now, and we laugh about that "mistake" in communication. After that I was extremely cautious, however. I observed everybody very carefully to learn the new ways. Only recently have I begun to be more relaxed in this culture.

Another problem had to do with my memory work. Memorization was an important part of our education in China. Once I could memorize great amounts of material. But when I got here, people began to ask my *opinion*, and that was something I didn't understand. It took a long time for me to realize that I might have something to say on my own.

L. F.: I realize that you have gotten away from a lot of the memory work, but when you were good at it, how much could you memorize?

SISTER JOANNA: I'll give you an example. In the Philippines, I played Joan of Arc in Anouilh's play *The Lark*, which runs about three and one-half hours. I memorized all the parts—every character's role—in a week. In Chicago, where I went to college for a while, the professor said that we would be tested on fifty pages of reading, so I memorized every word on all fifty pages, word for word. Of course, when the test came I was thrown into confusion because I didn't have time to put down anywhere near what I had memorized, and I didn't know how to be selective. I don't do much memory work now, although I still respect it more than most native-born Americans do, I suspect.

L. F.: Anthropologists speak about how the importance of being on time for appointments and meetings is different for different cultures. How important is time in Chinese culture?

SISTER JOANNA: Remember, I'm pretty thoroughly Westernized by now in this respect, so I speak from memories. But one thing stands out: in an agricultural society, *clock time* is not nearly as important as it is here. There the important thing is the sun—whether it is up or down. And, in a farming country, there really aren't that many appointments to keep, that many meetings, and so forth.

L. F.: I understand that some young Chinese students in New York's Chinatown, who study in English, also learn Chinese.

SISTER JOANNA: Yes, they go to regular school first, in English. Then, at three in the afternoon, many go to a Chinese school. That creates problems. The Cantonese dialect—which is what adults speak in New York's Chinatown and which is taught in these Chinese afternoon schools—is complicated because it is spoken one way, written another way, and read still another way. (Mandarin Chinese is easier in those respects.) It is an awfully heavy burden, learning all those Chinese writing characters on top of everything else. The result is often that as soon as the child is able to say "no" he stops going to Chinese school. This immensely difficult experience may also impair his future interest in Chinese culture.

I'm for studying and understanding Chinese culture—the great traditions—but I do not favor the terribly difficult task of the learning of a Chinese language in addition to English. It is the respect and appreciation of our culture but not the reading and writing of characters that are important.

L. F.: What do people in Chinatown call white Americans? Do they call them Anglos or what?

SISTER JOANNA: We call them Americans or foreigners. The Cantonese colloquial expression for foreigner was "foreign devils." Maybe at one time it had a bitter meaning, but now I think it is mostly playful.

L. F.: It is often said that Chinese students here are very good in math. Do you think that's so?

SISTER JOANNA: Yes. As a matter of fact, I was talking with someone the other day about why Chinese students tend to be so good in math. Maybe one reason is that in our language we use numbers a lot. For example, we don't say "Monday," "Tuesday," "Wednesday," "Thursday," et cetera. We say, "First Day of the Week," "Second Day of the Week," "Third Day of the Week," and so forth. We also say, "First Moon," "Second Moon," et cetera, for months. We use numbers in our language much more than in English. It is also true that, while China has a great cultural heritage, it was for a long time undeveloped scientifically. That put our country through an unthinkable humiliation some seventy years ago. That has had a tremendous effect upon scientific education. Until this day, the brightest Chinese students often aspire to excel in science subjects, and that involves math, of course. The Chinese are extremely dedicated to education. In China, it was the only way to get ahead. Today, new Chinese immigrants in the United States struggle to put their children through higher education. By the second generation most of them make it into America's white middle-class society.

China has a very strict class system. There are four classes: scholar first, farmer second, working man third, merchant fourth. There is an ancient tradition in China that people sneer at those who work merely to make profit. And notice that military service was not even in the list. In the West a military person can be a great hero. In China, all military heroes were also renowned scholars. So education is the major goal. In the old China I knew—and I think it's still true—a farm child could get to the top through education.

Conversation with Bourama Soumaoro

Bourama Soumaoro is from the village of Kabaya in the Yanfolilia Circle, Republic of Mali, West Africa. Bourama had been in the United States for nine months, attending the University of Indiana, when this interview took place. In Mali, his father, who has since died, was chief of the Numu (blacksmith) caste in Kabaya. In Kabaya blacksmiths perform a wide variety of functions: working in iron in making tools and weapons, farming, performing certain medical functions such as treating stomach ailments and broken bones, and dealing with problems of mental health. They also initiate adolescent boys

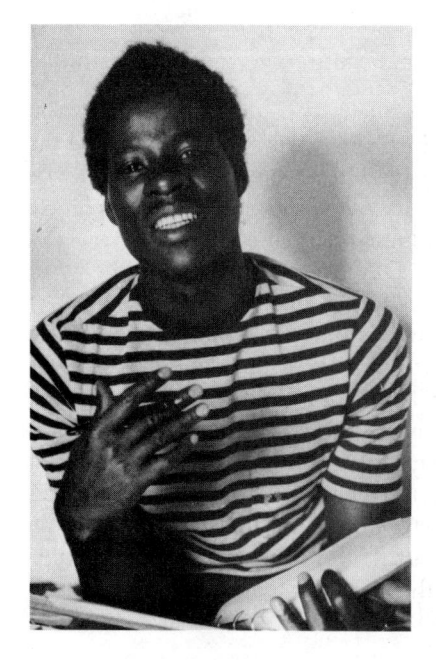

Illustration 4.5 Bourama Soumaoro.

into manhood by passing on crucial instruction and performing circumcision rites. Bourama's native language is Bambara (which has only had a system of writing for half a dozen years), although he speaks, in addition, French and English. His religion is a traditional African one, Komo.

LOUIS FORSDALE: Would you tell us some of the communication problems which you faced when you came to the United States?

BOURAMA SOUMAORO: Sure. In my culture the young people stick together in most of their activities, and, if a stranger comes in, we try to help that person feel comfortable. We try to give ourselves to that person. When I came here I kept looking around for people of my age so that I could communicate with them, make relationships, make friends. For almost two months I had great difficulty finding friends, even on a college campus. People would see that I was a stranger, and that my English wasn't too good, and they seemed to try and protect themselves. I couldn't articulate who I was, or ask for help in the right way. So I had to go to my home and be alone. Here students seem to be worried about being distracted, especially by someone they don't quite understand. The human being often seems like something plastic here.

I was surprised, too, by the university. For example, I needed to take some courses in English. I really needed to ask the teacher questions, but I got the feeling that to ask questions implied that the teacher was bad. It seemed better not to ask questions: If you don't understand something, forget it, otherwise you'll be embarrassed. So I learned to shut up. Young people here in school seem to be controlled by the instructor; competition and discipline seem to be very important. If the learner departs from what the instructor wants, it is not approved. I have the impression also that the student is not allowed to confront things outside the school. It seems to me to be a limited experience.

When I taught younger people at home, I worked differently. I let the children do what they felt like, to try and manage for themselves, to try out different things. I tried not to be too strict until the child began himself to sense his problems and needs.

L. F.: Did you finally get to the point where you were no longer considered a stranger here?

BOURAMA SOUMAORO: Somewhat. But not nearly so much as it would have been among our own people in Africa. In Africa, I would give myself to help make somebody else comfortable. I think it is a duty. People here are able to do it, but they have no time. Rush, rush, rush.

L. F.: Did you find *any* Americans who were able to give up some of their time to make you as a stranger feel welcome?

BOURAMA SOUMAORO: I found some. Generally they were people who had been out of America and had seen other cultures. Because of that, they learned to think about the other person; they began to think about how to be a human being. Here money is very important. Helping yourself is very important. When Americans go outside their culture they can see that you can have a relationship not involved with money, not involved with materialism.

L. F.: Does it frighten you to see Americans as you do, particularly when you think about how powerful a nation the United States is?

BOURAMA SOUMAORO: We say something at home which I think is true: "If your interior politics are bad, your exterior politics can be bad, too." I'm not just talking about political parties and scandals, I hope you understand. The fact that you ask me how I feel about this country is an indication of something. As I see it, nothing goes easy here: everything is complicated. Every day you have to go crazy in this country about something. It seems to me that most Americans think Africa needs help. It's true that we need some mechanical aid which America can help us with. But I don't know now what kind of politics would go with that aid. It *is* true, you know, "If your interior politics are bad, your exterior politics can be bad, too." It would frighten me to live here.

L. F.: Do you see any way out of the problem?

BOURAMA SOUMAORO: It really is a problem of communication. I think we need more cultural exchanges so that young people can have opportunities to learn at first hand about other cultures. Just on television alone here there are so many untruths about Africa. I think also that cultural exchange probably should come when students are young—before college is too far along, when students often begin to struggle so hard for grades and degrees. We need to learn more about each other at a friendly level, before the academic material becomes as important. We need to learn about each other when the interaction can still be very free and open. We need to be friendly, as young people can be, not simply intellectual observers of each other's cultures.

THIS CHAPTER IN PERSPECTIVE

One of the richest settings within which to study communication is culture— the system of habits, rules, assumptions, and beliefs into which each of us is born, by which each of us is shaped. A culture is not easily defined, but it can be identified by a considerable degree of similarity of belief and behavior among its members. We all belong to various subcultures as well. While some subcultural membership is relatively permanent, we all shift as well according to roles that we play at the moment. All behavior, including communication, is learned in a culture, and the ways of one culture should not be judged as superior or inferior to the ways of any other culture. This includes language and nonverbal communication, which are among the most obvious characteristics of every culture. Intercultural (or cross-cultural) communication is difficult, because it is hard to deal with people who operate from sets of assumptions different from ours. Still, intercultural communication is an obligation that we must increasingly accept. Indeed, we probably should strive to recognize and thus learn to modify the ties that bind us so closely, and often exclusively, to our native cultures. Citizens of the world will be able to transcend their own cultures, at least to some degree. Perhaps the accelerated flow of communication in our global village will help reduce the cultural barriers separating us. Perhaps that accelerated flow will also permit us to get at each other's throats more easily. In any event, transcending culture will not be easy. Or will it?

EXTENSIONS

Reading You Might Enjoy

1. Condon, John C., and Fathi S. Yousef. *An Introduction to Intercultural Communication.* Indianapolis: Bobbs-Merrill Educational Publishing, 1977.

Although written by knowledgeable specialists in communication and culture, this book is neither stuffy nor too technical for those of us who seek a beginning knowledge of the field. Loaded with anecdotes from various cultures, the book systematically builds a framework for thinking about the nature of culture and the difficult problem of crossing cultural and subcultural borders through communication. The excellent bibliography will carry you far in exploring other sources.

2. Hall, Edward T. *Beyond Culture.* Garden City, N.Y.: Doubleday, Anchor Books, 1976.

The American anthropologist Edward T. Hall is among the handful of writers who have done most to merge the fields of social anthropology and communication. His earlier books, *The Silent Language* (emphasizing the role of nonverbal communication, particularly time, in various cultures) and *The Hidden Dimension* (emphasizing differences in cultural views and uses of space) are considered classics by many students of communication. *Beyond Culture* continues the tradition, again exploring cultural differences, but urging an attempt to move beyond unconscious allegiance to one's own culture toward genuine acceptance of other cultures as well.

3. Nance, John. *The Gentle Tasaday: A Stone Age People in the Philippine Rain Forest.* New York: Harcourt Brace Jovanovich, 1975.

The spark in this book comes from the fact that it deals with the recent discovery of a group of people—the Tasaday in the Philippines—who have not been in contact with modern societies. Imagine a discovery like this today in a world that has been gone over from top to bottom and from side to side by explorers and travelers! Moreover, the Tasaday are a people who do not understand war and violence, who are peaceful and gentle in everything they do. That takes some imagining, too! Nance is a journalist who writes carefully, well, and above all, interestingly.

4. Samovar, Larry A., and Richard E. Porter, eds. *Intercultural Communication: A Reader.* Belmont, Calif.: Wadsworth, 1976.

This is an anthology of thirty-five essays about various aspects of culture that directly touch upon communication and about problems and successes in verbal and nonverbal communication between cultures. The many authors come from diverse fields, illustrating that those from a wide range of disciplines find the topic interesting. This is an excellent collection of articles for the curious newcomer.

Ponderings and Projects

1. You may have traveled in other cultures, or you may have had the advantage of living in another culture or subculture for some time. If so, what are some of the major communication problems you faced, verbal and nonverbal? What customs surprised you? Did you become accustomed to them? Such a subject might make an interesting report, speech, or audiovisual presentation.

2. Finding identity in a heterogeneous culture such as that of the United States is not always easy. In reviewing N. Scott Momaday's autobiographical account of the search for his own lineage as an American Indian, the novelist Wallace Stegner speaks movingly of this problem:

> *Personal identity is achieved only by affiliation. We are made by the language we speak, the foods we eat, the ceremonies we participate in, the beliefs we acquire, the tools we use. And especially in Western America, affiliation is confusing: our culture is like a field full of junked cars out of which a composite car is being made from cannibalized parts. Origins may be searched out and defined; identity is not a fact but a task.* (1979, p. 7)

Do you know your lineage, your family tree, your cultural identity? Tracing it could be a rewarding venture.

3. The role of black English in the United States is a persistent and difficult subject to explore. For example, should black English be accepted and/or

EXTENSION

taught in schools? Two good scholarly anchors to rely on in exploration of the question are the books by Thomas Kochman (1972, L. Dillard (1973).

4. You might find it very instructive to interview people from other cultures, as I did in this chapter. Perhaps there are students in your school who were born and raised outside the United States. Perhaps others, born here, have spent extended periods of time in other cultures.

The Personal Context of Communication

5

Perhaps the best documented generalization in the field of psychology is that, at any given moment, the behavioral characteristics of any mammal, and especially man, depend upon the previous experience and behavior of that individual.

Gregory Bateson

Although we all live and learn within cultures and subcultures, each of us is a unique individual. Each of us has a different personal background, a different accumulation of experiences, from the next person's. What our senses tell us about ourselves, about each other, and about the world is different for each of us. Members of the same culture or subculture, do, however, tend to see the world in ways closer then do persons from different cultures. Further, we hold tightly to our assumptions and expectations. In this chapter we will explore some of the mechanisms all of us use to let certain messages through and keep others out. We will also consider the manner in which some people expand their horizons—escape their skins, so to speak—and find new views of the world.

EACH OF US IS A UNIQUE INDIVIDUAL

While one useful broad context within which to examine communication is culture, a second useful one is the individual. In thinking about the individual—you or me—it is important to always remember that each of us operates within a larger system, either a culture or a subculture. We are children of culture, of continuous interaction with others. We are also uniquely ourselves.

THE INDIVIDUAL AS AN OPEN SYSTEM

The individual is an open system, involved continuously in input and output with the environment. It is easy to see that the individual cannot exist without input of food and air, for example, from the environment and the subsequent output of such waste products as feces, urine, and carbon dioxide after the body has completed its metabolic processes to provide energy and repair the cells, which are constantly deteriorating. In this inevitable organic exchange mutual benefit generally occurs. If what we take from the environment is done so in moderation, we do not deplete nature. Our body wastes in turn become food for plant life. The technological societies that we have created, however, particularly in the past century, have screamed stridently for greater amounts of material from nature than ever before. In exchange, our industrial establishments often pollute the environment in what has become a kind of normal nightmare.

Information Input and Output

The individual is also constantly involved in information input from the environment, throughput (transformation) of that information in ways that serve the individual, and output of information. The individual also carefully maintains his or her boundaries, keeping the self more or less separate from all other persons, yet all the while interacting with others.

Some communication specialists, Brent D. Ruben (1975), for example, speak of the individual as *metabolizing information* in a way analogous to the body's use of organic materials from the environment. Just as the body cannot live without exchange of material products from the environment, so the individual cannot live without exchange of information. Information is just as essential as food to the life of the individual and to the life of society.

The concept of pollution can be applied to communication as well as to the world of material things. In recent years it has been said frequently, and accurately, that we live in an "age of information," a time of "information explosion," that we may be "drowning in a sea of information." The tidal wave of messages flows from institutions of our creation (television and radio stations, publishing houses, motion picture production companies, advertising agencies, schools, religious and cultural groups), and we thus often contribute to pollution of our communication environment with information that we cannot metabolize, that is, incorporate productively into our lives. Just as we have an ethical responsibility for maintaining a workable ecological balance in the organic world, so also we have a similar obligation in our communication world. Each of us must accept that obligation personally.

EACH INDIVIDUAL IS UNIQUE

Although our personalities are shaped by culture, through communication, we are nevertheless unique individuals. No two persons are precisely the same. Just as we do not metabolize food and other substances in precisely the same way (although the principle may be the same), so we do not metabolize information in precisely the same way, although the overwhelming majority of our meanings are shared in large measure by other members of our culture. Still, there is not exact *isomorphism* (similarity of form or structure) in our personal reactions to signals. This is because, referring to the quotation by Gregory Bateson, an anthropologist, at the beginning of this chapter, our behavior (and communication is a form of behavior) depends upon our previous experience, and that experience is not identical. Thus the meanings that different persons assign to a message or signal are not identical. René Dubos, a biologist, states, "Each human being is unique, unprecedented, unrepeatable" (1968, p. vii).

We cannot escape our own skins, so to speak, any more than we can totally escape our culture. The head of the girl in Illustration 5.1 is covered with a thin stocking, distorting her features, disguising her. We all tend at times to hide our feelings from others. The girl can pull that thin outer mask off, revealing more of her true self, as we can be more open with others if we choose to. But she can never turn herself inside-out, psychologically, to reveal her inner self fully. None of us can. The great American physicist P. W. Bridgman writes that "we never get away from ourselves. Not only do I see that I cannot get away from myself, but I see that you cannot get away from yourself" (1959, p. 6). This seems like a simple enough observation, but for Bridgman, and others who have sought after the elusive goal of objectivity (which means keeping oneself out of the observation and reporting neutrally), the inability to escape one's skin—one's personal background—can be a shattering discovery.

OUR GUIDING IMAGES

The impressions, attitudes, ideas, and concepts we get about everything as we grow up form images that we carry with us at all times and against which we compare all messages. *Image* is Kenneth Boulding's term, about which he wrote a classic little book, *The Image*, in 1956. Boulding, an economist and philosopher, points out that at any given moment he has impressions of where he is located in space and time, what his network of personal relations consists

112 THE PERSONAL CONTEXT OF COMMUNICATION

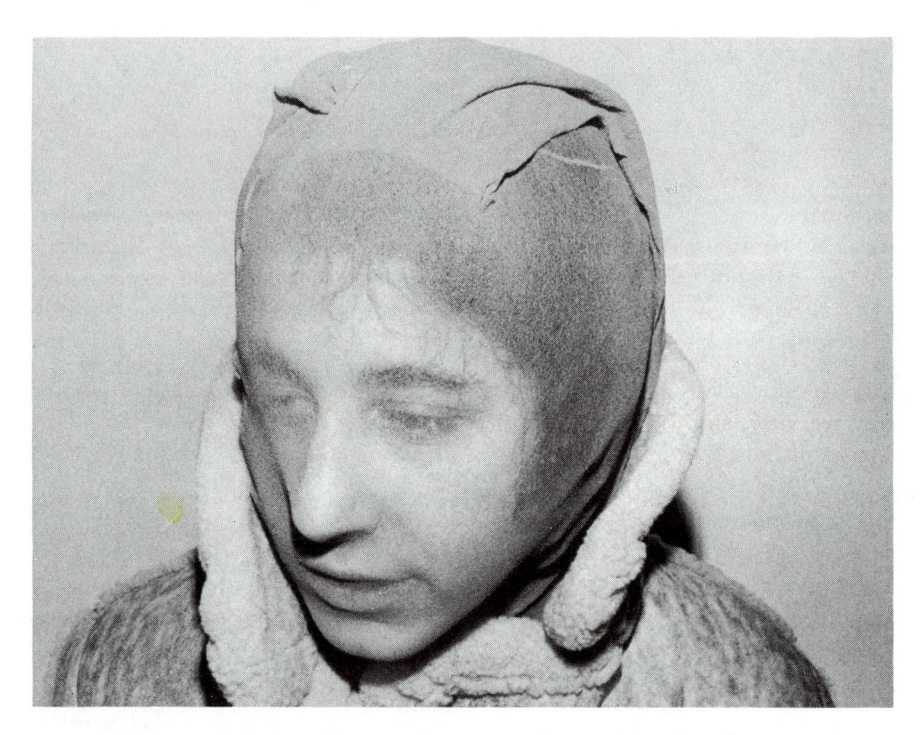

Illustration 5.1 She can remove this thin disguise, as we all can, but she cannot remove her skin. (Photo: Lynn Forsdale)

of, where in nature he fits, and what his emotions and feelings are. We all have these understandings, at least to some degree. Boulding says:

> *What I have been talking about is knowledge. Knowledge, perhaps, is not a good word for this. Perhaps one would rather say my Image of the world. Knowledge has an implication of validity, of truth. What I am talking about is what I believe to be true; my subjective knowledge. It is this Image that largely governs my behavior.* (1956, pp. 5-6)

We begin to form these images of the world the day we are born, or earlier, since there is evidence that we get impressions about many things while still in the womb. Our images grow and change throughout our lives. It is of major importance in the study of communication to understand, however, that we strive—unconsciously, in the main—to keep our images intact rather than to change them. Our basic thrust is to preserve those images that are important to us. Thus you and I cling to the values of the culture in which we are nurtured and hold dearly the personal images that are peculiar to each of us.

> The fundamental motive of human behavior is *not* self-preservation, but the preservation of the symbolic self.
>
> S. I. Hayakawa (1963, p. 37)

We retain some images with greater tenacity than others. For example, the way we subjectively view our parents is likely to change far less easily than the way we view, say, the current governor of the state in which we live. Our images of ourselves are generally less amenable to change than the way we view someone else.

Participating in an act of communication is more likely to reinforce what we already believe than it is to change us radically. Dramatic conversion from one strongly held position to another is perhaps the most unlikely result of an act of communication. This is one of the major reasons why it is so difficult to assess the effects of an act of communication. Discussions about the results of showing violence on television, for example, are extraordinarily difficult to evaluate because people tend to turn communication into something congruent with their personal values and attitudes—their images—and thus find it difficult to believe that other people may be influenced differently.

THE SELECTIVE PROCESSES

There are three related processes constantly at work in communication, around which we can now arrange our discussion. They are sometimes known as the *selective processes*, namely *selective attention, selective perception*, and *selective memory*. They all reflect our cultures and our subcultures. But they also reflect our personalities, our particular nature as individuals, shaped by a thousand factors—family, sex, religion, age, education, and particularly our ongoing interactions with other people.

There are two major theories that explain the workings of the selective processes. The first is generally referred to as the reinforcement theory. Communication scholars W. Phillips Davison, James Boylan, and Frederick T. C. Yu explain it this way:

> *We subconsciously or consciously select from the flow of communications those ideas that fit in with [reinforce] our attitudes, values, and pictures of the world—that are congruent with our existing*

ideas. At the same time, we ignore, dismiss, misunderstand, or forget those communications that would be "dissonant"—that would not fit in. If our beliefs are shaken, but not changed, by a dissonant piece of information, we may seek out other people who share our beliefs to obtain reassurance. (1976, p. 133)

The other major theory is generally referred to as the uses and gratification approach. Davison, Boylan, and Yu summarize this approach:

According to this theory . . . we will attend, perceive, and remember information that is pleasurable, or that will in some way help to satisfy our needs. This information may or may not be in accord with our existing ideas, but we will attend to it if we expect it to be useful or think that it will give us satisfaction. (1976, p. 139)

The difference between the two theories is that the reinforcement theory argues that we seek to preserve our understandings of the way things are, while the uses and gratification approach leaves the way open for greater seeking and accepting of information that is likely to lead to change in our understandings and beliefs, in our images.
The two approaches are not opposed; they merely emphasize different matters. Finally, both theories converge in agreeing that rapid radical change in our views is not likely to result from our communication encounters.

SELECTIVE ATTENTION

Selective attention (or selective exposure, as some call it) simply means that we pay attention to matters that have *salience* (prominence) for us. Consciously or unconsciously we select certain events to focus on and we ignore others.

We are dealing with a tricky point here. Some communication scholars prefer to relate the idea of selective attention only to messages from media or from other persons. It is useful, however, to include as well cues from the natural and the humanmade environment.

It is also frequently difficult, as we will soon see, to distinguish between selective attention and selective perception. It can be argued, in fact, that selective attention is part and parcel of selective perception. While we will separate the two here, recall the possible overlapping.

Selective Attention to Environmental Cues

When you walk down a street in any city, a thousand things compete for your attention every minute. Shop windows, automobiles, traffic lights, pedestrians, planes overhead, cats, dogs, the state of the weather—all are potential stimuli. We do not pay attention to all of these things, of course. Nobody could. In William James's immortal phrase, it is "a vast blooming, buzzing confusion."

In a typical business block there might be twelve or so stores at ground level. If we paused to examine everything in the windows of those stores it would take hours to get to the end of a single block. Literally. If we inspected carefully every item in the window of a drugstore, for example, really *every* one, that might take half an hour. In another culture, if we attended to every event or product in the local bazaar it would take a day. Even dedicated window-shoppers are necessarily highly selective.

Selective Attention to Communication Signals

Now add to the kind of communication stimuli just described from the natural and human environment all of the signals that bombard us through the many media of communication surrounding us. There are dozens of radio stations instantly accessible to most of us in the United States, a handful of television stations available even in the most remote parts of the country, dozens of newspapers, hundreds of magazines and books, floods of motion pictures. Nobody can take them all in.

Illustration 5.2 A "busy" drugstore window.

Illustration 5.3 Nine pairs of eyes, none focused on the same thing: a study in selective attention.

> The function of the brain and nervous system is to protect us from being overwhelmed and confused by this mass of largely useless and irrelevant knowledge, by shutting out most of what we should otherwise perceive or remember at any moment, and leaving only that very small and special selection which is likely to be practically useful.
>
> C. D. Broad, in Aldous Huxley (1970, pp. 22-23)

The Personal Cost of Selective Attention

We pay a price for such selective attention, of course, since it obviously tends to limit the experiences that we gain from a nearly boundless world. If you like rock music, for example, and groove only on its various forms, you may exclude other musical experiences from your world: reggae, for example, or the classical symphony, or country music, or jazz. If you are convinced that the Democratic party is the one you want to support, you may consciously or unconsciously listen to and read material only from Democratic party sources.

If in school you like courses in graphic arts—drawing, painting, and lithography—you may consciously or unconsciously avoid courses from other fields—the sciences for example. That's also a case of selective attention.

The Personal Rewards of Selective Attention

If we restrict our lives by our habits of selective attention, we gain serenity and cohesiveness. We also gain sanity, since a totally unscreened or unselective input of all environmental stimuli would doubtless result in disorientation or insanity.

SELECTIVE PERCEPTION

Once we have attended to an environmental stimulus or an act of communication, we do not all perceive it in identical ways.

Beliefs Shape Our Perceptions

Edmund Carpenter, an anthropologist, writes, "If I hadn't believed it with all my heart, I woudn't have seen it" (1974, p. 18). He refers, of course, to the role of personal beliefs and attitudes in shaping perception. You don't perceive what you don't believe.

> Many people do not seem to realize that very much of our thinking proceeds from assumptions often experienced as fact.
>
> Virginia Satir (1976)

The following anecdotes will illustrate how a profound belief in something, growing from experience, shapes perception. Carpenter says, "I wouldn't have *seen* it" (italics mine), but the incidents below relate to various senses, not merely sight. It doesn't matter, however: the principle is the same.

An example: reactions to "The Exorcist" An example of selective perception can be seen in reactions to the motion picture *The Exorcist* (1973), one of the most widely attended films in the history of the medium. (As you read this, it will probably still be among the twenty-five biggest money-makers in film history.) It is about a young girl who becomes possessed, presumably by the devil. While in this state of possession she uses incredibly foul language, vomits, turns into a monstrous-appearing child, and suffers from an unearthly set of experiences. Finally, the devil is driven out of her in a ritual performed by two priests.

The Exorcist has been interpreted in many ways. Let us consider two extreme reactions of people who enjoyed the film, skipping for convenience reactions of people who disliked it. One group of people who liked it found it to be a powerful and convincing story of how the two faithful and persistent Roman Catholic priests performed an ancient church ritual to rid the child of possession by the devil. These viewers saw the film as a dramatization of literal truth, an account of the power of the devil and the greater power of faith in ridding the child of the devil's evil presence.

Another group of people who enjoyed the film regarded it quite differently, however. They saw it as a horror film that gave them chilling kicks, as a film about vampires or werewolves might. This set of viewers did not believe literally in the devil or in exorcism rituals at all, but they liked to have fulfilled their fantasies about evil, their tenacious and titillating visions of monsters, their convictions that good whips evil — all beliefs, we should note, that our culture tends to perpetuate.

And, of course, there were many groups of viewers between these two extremes.

How each viewer finally reacted to the film (or to any film), then, depended primarily upon his or her background, on the assumptions that he or she brought to the experience. Many staunch Roman Catholics found the film to be false or excessive.

An example: an Oscar incident Shelley Winters, an American actress, tells a story (on a television talk show) about herself and how a strong conviction led her to hear an important announcement totally inaccurately in a setting in which her emotional investment was high.

In 1951 Winters starred in a film called *A Place in the Sun*. It was an excellent film that was well reviewed, and she thought her performance was good enough to win an acting Oscar, for which she was nominated. When the time came for the announcement of that award at the ceremony, Ronald Coleman, a distinguished film actor, walked on stage to open the ceremonial envelope. Winters had worked with Coleman in another film a year earlier, and she persuaded herself further as she sat there waiting hopefully that he had been chosen to announce the award because she would be the winner. He opened the envelope and announced the name of Vivian Leigh, who had played the feminine lead in *A Streetcar Named Desire*, as winner of the award. Winters reports that she distinctly heard her own name, however, and started running up the aisle to receive the award. Her husband caught up with her and held her back, avoiding the ultimate embarrassment. She believed so strongly that she would win that she misheard the announcement. The story is a dramatic one. Similar things have happened to all of us, however, although probably not in such a glamorous setting.

An example: the hole in Adlai Stevenson's shoe Adlai E. Stevenson ran for president of the United States twice, in 1952 and 1956, and lost both times. In each case his opponent was the enormously popular World War II general, Dwight D. Eisenhower.

Although I respected Eisenhower's abilities and qualities of leadership, I preferred Stevenson, and I worked hard to help him. He was an eloquent speaker and a man richly filled with humor, a trait that I admire. I spent a lot of time trying to raise money and votes for Stevenson.

One day the picture shown in Illustration 5.4 appeared in newspapers all over the United States. An alert photographer, William M. Gallagher, of the

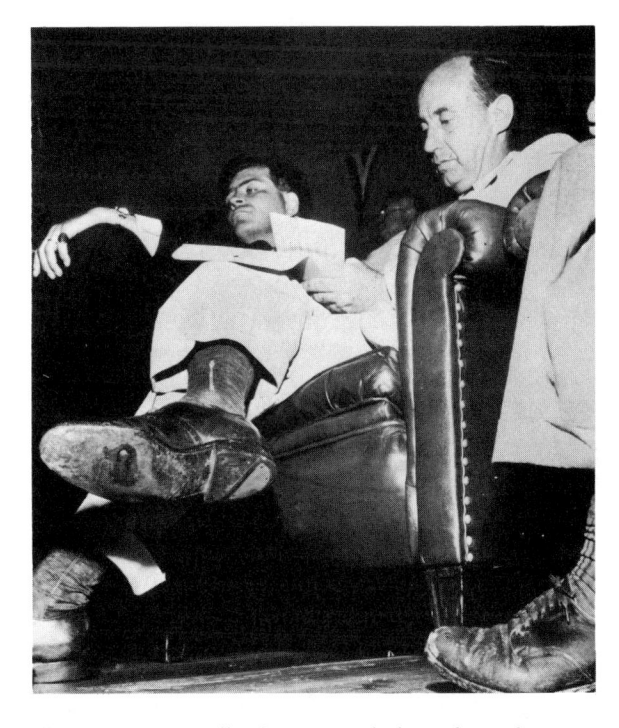

Illustration 5.4 Adlai Stevenson, hole in shoe, photographed in 1952 by William Gallagher of the *Flint Journal*. (Wide World Photos)

Flint Journal in Flint, Michigan, had seen a hole in Stevenson's shoe and gotten a good shot of it. Newspapers across the country ate it up. So notable was the picture that Gallagher won a Pulitzer Prize for it.

Stevenson supporters were delighted. They liked what that hole in the shoe implied about their candidate. For them it "said" a mixture of things, including these messages: "Stevenson is so involved in his campaign that he doesn't have time to get a new pair of shoes"; "Stevenson is a man of the people, who, like the rest of us, has problems with holes in his shoes." And most of all, they thought the hole said: "Here is an intelligent man, a wealthy man, an aristocrat, who has links with the common people of the country." That was particularly important because Stevenson was accused by his critics of being too intellectual, too out of touch with the ordinary citizen.

Shortly after the photograph appeared, some enterprising person manufactured little sterling silver shoe soles with holes in them and began to sell them as a campaign symbol for Stevenson. These little shoe soles could be worn as campaign buttons. Backers of Stevenson, like me, bought batches of these shoe soles, sold them at more than their cost, and gave the profit to help finance Stevenson's campaign expenses.

Then a surprising thing happened.

One day an elevator operator at my college asked me what the silver shoe sole in my lapel was all about. I told her it was a campaign pin for Stevenson, and she was amazed.

"I'm for Stevenson, but I think that's a terrible way to get him elected," she said.

"Why?" I asked, surprised by her comment.

"What that shoe says is that if Stevenson gets elected we'll all have holes in our shoes! Why would anybody vote for that?"

The hole in the shoe meant poverty to her, not all those other qualities I attached to it. The way we perceive things depends on our beliefs, assumptions, and expectations, on the mix of personal experiences that we bring to the event and that are difficult to predict.

Offbeat Perceptions

While differences in perception apply to everyone, some people perceive the world in ways that seem more consistently strange or offbeat to others around them.

Artists Artists often have quite special ways of perceiving things, and they may translate their visions into forms that help the rest of us alter our views, at least slightly.

Frequently an artist notices that something is out of joint in the world, that things aren't the way they might be. He or she may find ugly what others of us see as beautiful or have not seen at all. The artist may express with vigor and clarity (for astute observers) what the rest of us feel vaguely. Many artists have seen for a long time, for example, that pollution is destroying nature and that our decaying cities can be rearranged in constructive ways. They may thus heighten our anticipations, sensitize our perceptions, and perhaps even help us remake the images of the world that we forever carry with us. The words *may*, *perhaps*, and *help* in the preceding sentence are intended to say that change in basic outlook is, at best, difficult to achieve.

Without the precious new perceptions of artists we might all go through life seeing no alternatives to our usual ways. Artists are specialists in re-visioning things for us.

Science fiction writers and filmmakers also create new visions—new worlds, frequently—that are examples of disciplined perceptual trips. For example, director George Lucas's motion picture *Star Wars* is based on a familiar adventure plot in which the good guys win. However, he fills it with characters, settings, and equipment that are imaginative personal projections. While the barroom scene is reminiscent of Rick's Place in the movie *Casablanca*, its customers are fascinating fictions about what the occupants of other worlds might be like. *Close Encounters of the Third Kind*, directed by Steven Spielberg, gives us a brief look at his vision of extraterrestrial visitors and some of their powers. He also plays with a musical communication system that loosens our imagination.

In the *Dune* trilogy, Frank Herbert creates a mythical planet, most of which is a bone-dry desert of sand. Since the inhabitants of the planet are physically much like humans, water is of pivotal importance to them. They must have it, and they preserve every drop they find. When outdoors in remote regions of the planet, Dune people wear "stillsuits," outer coverings of plasticlike material fitting so closely that the water normally lost from the body by perspiration is collected in water pockets in the stillsuit, refined, and then drunk by the wearer. When people die, they are mourned, but the water they have in their possession is inherited. Religious rituals center on water.

Herbert's stunning artistic exercise in creating a mythical planet may not be all that far removed from realities that we may face one day on earth, since fresh water is of increasing concern to us.

Scientists Scientists are also among the people who learn to perceive the world in ways not often accessible to most of us. Louis Pasteur, for example, got the idea that many illnesses come from germs. Most people laughed at him. They couldn't *see* germs (not then), after all. But Pasteur proved his hunch, with the result that millions of lives have been saved.

Illustration 5.5 When the new version of *King Kong* came to town, we saw the friendly monster repeatedly on posters atop the World Trade Center. Addams playfully shaped another vision: Kong captive *inside* a skyscraper, nature dominated by technology. It's funny, but it also presents a vital truth—shown by the offbeat perception of an artist. (Drawing by Chas. Addams; © 1977 The New Yorker Magazine, Inc.)

Physicist P. W. Bridgman, who is quoted near the beginning of this chapter, struggled to perceive the world objectively, but finally concluded that total objectivity is impossible: "We never get away from ourselves." That is a two-edged sword. Most scientists would like to see things objectively. They can't completely, as Bridgman says, and that is disappointing to many. But the other side of the matter is that creativity, for scientists as well as artists, flows from flashes of intuition. A strong expression of this position is in the assertion by Gregory Bateson that "Newton did not *discover* the law of gravity, he *invented* it" (1972, p. 39). The implication is that the world "out there" is subject to many interpretations, which are finally creations of the observer. Some day perhaps another observer will "invent" other ways of talking about the phenomenon we now call gravity.

Seeing Matters from Dramatically New Perspectives

There are ways of gaining new perceptions. One is to go through a severe shift in environment or culture. Sensitive travelers in countries far different from the ones they have grown up in often suffer from culture shock. Events are so different that they cannot be understood in familiar terms. Of course some travelers try to insulate themselves by staying in familiar surroundings and with people of their own culture (such as in American hotels in foreign countries), or by closing their senses, so to speak.

An example: experiences of astronauts Superb examples of new perceptions arising from new perspectives come from astronauts, who, without exaggeration, have seen from points of view that most of us can't possibly duplicate. Ed Gibson, one of the men who circled the earth for eighty-four days in Spacelab 4, the first American orbiting scientific laboratory, speaks of seeing his native planet anew:

> *You see, here on earth, we are accustomed to looking at the earth on maps. And maps always have lines drawn on them that divide one part of the earth from another. Even globes have lines drawn on them. But when you get up there you see, even though you knew it intellectually, that there are no lines that divide one part of the earth from any other part. It's all one. You sit up there and you think, "Why should the people on this plot of ground be shooting at the people on that plot of ground?" It's so obvious that there aren't that many differences, that it's all the same earth.* (Quoted in Ivins, 1974, p. 14)

> If the doors of perception were cleansed everything
>   would appear to man as it is, infinite.
> For man has closed himself up, till he sees all things
>   through narrow chinks of his cavern.
>
> William Blake

Gibson's colleague Gerry Carr speaks in the same general way:

> *I would look at the earth's horizon and see the earth's atmosphere. It is very beautiful. It is blue and white and gold and orange. And it is thin and fragile. It's beautiful but so thin. I really started to get ecology-minded. That atmosphere is all that keeps the earth habitable, but it's no thicker than the skin on an orange, or—no, thinner than that—like the skin on an apple. There's no way to explain how clearly you can see* the *fragility of the earth.* (Quoted in Ivins, 1974, p. 14)

An example: the Andes crash There is a remarkable, and gruesome, story about a change in perception that centers on the incredible adventure of a group of forty-five persons who crashed in a plane on October 12, 1972, while flying from Montevideo, Uruguay, to Santiago, Chile. The plane lost its course and fell in the high Andes mountains of South America, which are isolated from any community and subject to below-zero temperatures each night. For seventy days the survivors remained undiscovered until two of them managed the torturous trek out of the high mountains to get help.

When the plane crashed, some crew members and passengers were killed instantly. Others were severely hurt and died later. Further, there was very little food and few medical supplies aboard. At first the survivors sustained their hope that they would be discovered by search planes. Although extensive searches were indeed conducted, the victims were not found, partly because the top surface of their crashed aircraft was painted white, making it invisible to search aircraft against the snow that everywhere surrounded them.

These are the background facts. Let us now turn to the part of the account relating to perception. As the survivors' food ran out, as their strength began to fail, and as it became clear that they were unlikely to be located by outside searchers, they made a desperate decision, certainly the most shocking decision any of them had ever been required to make. They began to realize that the only source of food remaining to them was the dead bodies of their comrades, which had been preserved by the freezing cold. But how can one eat human flesh? That is cannibalism, one of the most repugnant acts imaginable in most cultures, certainly in Uruguay.

Every person on the plane was religious, respecting human life. Most of the passengers were rugby players who were to represent a Catholic school in Montevideo in a forthcoming international match with a school in Chile. The other passengers were family members, friends, and crew members, also devout Roman Catholics. All the survivors agonized over the decision of whether to consume the flesh of their dead companions, even though it was the only way to survive. Finally, one of the men who had emerged as a leader during those frantic days suggested that from a religious point of view that had a "moral duty to stay alive by any means at their disposal" (Read, 1974, p. 83). He continued, drawing upon religious beliefs, which doubtless, he had never expected to use in this way: "The soulds have left their bodies and are in heaven with God. All that is left here are the carcasses, which are no more human beings than the dead flesh of the cattle we eat at home" (1974, p. 83).

So a new perception was born, agonizingly, after searing soul-searching and from the strongly held religious roots the survivors shared. When newspaper accounts of the incredible survival of sixteen passengers were published and when readers learned that they had eaten the flesh of their dead companions to do so, the world was shocked. Catholic priests who later consulted with the survivors were not all so shocked. They felt that the survivors had acted in keeping with proper religious doctrine.

Lest there be too many turned stomachs as the mere thought of eating another human's flesh, please consider two things. First, to fulfill that critical need for context, read the full account of the ordeal as Read has told it. It is an exciting story. Second, you might pause a bit to ask yourself what you might possibly do under similar circumstances. None of us can really know that, of course, becasue we are not in such an extreme condition. Speculation is one thing, action another. Perceptions occur in contexts.

Other Ways of Achieving Alternative Perceptual States

For centuries people have wondered about, worked for, and achieved a variety of alternative perceptual states. Alternative, that is, to what members of their cultures or subcultures would believe to be "normal." Reality is, of course, a very tricky subject, for reasons that we have already seen. Variations in perception are inevitable, and no sensible person these days should proclaim that he or she has *the* truth. Still, within cultural groups there is a certain rough agreement about acceptable behavior. Charles T. Tart puts the relationship between culture and acceptable "states" this way:

> By virtue of being born a human being, having a certain kind of body and nervous system (the hardware), and functioning in the general environment of spaceship Earth, the individual has a very wide variety of behaviors and experiences potentially available. These may include running a four-minute mile [which was thought to be impossible until Roger Bannister did it in 1954], learning sophisticated mathematics, and enjoying various kinds of esthetic experience.
>
> But any individual human being will develop only a small fraction of his total human potentialities because he is born into a particular culture at a particular place and time, has certain parents, relatives, peers, and teachers, and has various "random" events happen to him. A culture can be looked upon as a group of programmers who had (implicitly) agreed that certain human potentialities are beneficial and should be developed. . . . Trance states, for instance, are a fundamental aspect of American Indian culture but are at best highly suspect to Westerners. (1977, p. 170)

Within the permitted "programs" of the culture, however, some individuals do achieve different perceptual states. Without any attempt to include all alternatives available to us, here are some widely used techniques:

1. *The chemical route.* Various persons strive, in various degrees, to change their perceptual states with chemicals: alcohol, caffeine, marijuana, mescaline, opium, LSD, peyote, and dozens of other ancient and recent drugs that result in "highs" or "lows," but that in any event change the perceptual state. A major problem, of course, is the frequent severe side effects that result, or the tendency of people to get hooked on some drugs in an unexpected way.

2. *The meditation route.* Although various forms of meditation have been used for thousands of years in some cultures to achieve new perceptual states, it is a relatively new phenomenon in the United States, and one that is not widespread.

Generally less harsh on the body than the drug-induced means, meditation requires discipline and continued practice, and it apparently works better for some people than others. The results of most successful meditation include a more relaxed state, greater clarity of sensory activity, and among masters, the ability to control the autonomic body functions, such as respiration or heart rate or body temperature.

3. *The religious route.* Profoundly religious people, in practicing the rituals of their religions, sometimes undergo fundamental change or conversion experiences. In many cases, their practice is akin to forms of solitary meditation; in other instances it involves greater measures of overt communication with like believers or with a deity, through prayer or supplication.

4. *The athletic route.* Peoples in some cultures (Bali, for one) dance themselves into a state that transcends the normal, into a trance. A similar activity, perhaps just as ritualized, is the current American interest in jogging, which for some people results at a certain point in a shifting of perceptual gears, so to speak, so that their everyday concerns are left behind and they experience the world differently. Changes in body metabolism and other shifts in chemical balance are the apparent causes. The fact that physical exertions of some kinds alter our "mental condition" offers personal and first-hand knowledge that the head and the body are part of the same system.

5. *The hypnosis route.* Under hypnosis some people experience sensations that are normally inaccessible to them. They frequently perceive with clarity matters otherwise hidden to them, with the result that they sense the roots of their problems and often are able, in time, to reconstruct their guiding images.

6. *The psychotherapy route.* Many persons have been aided in shifting self-perceptions and perceptions of others through psychotherapy, that is, ongoing intense communication with a highly trained person who can gradually help the patient achieve new views of the way things are or might be.

7. *Other routes.* There are other forms of altering perceptual states, including the use of biofeedback procedures, sensory deprivation, asertiveness training, or sensory awareness training, to name a few. Our purpose here has not been to list all procedures in an exhaustive manner, however. These are merely some suggestions of major forms.

A final reminder about his matter: While change is normal in the course of a life, most of us are fiercely resistant to profound or sudden change. Maintaining our perceptions the way we have grown up experiencing them is the norm; drastic change is the exception.

Psi

Psi refers, in the usage of Laura A. Dale and Rhea A. White, to "a person's extrasensorimotor communication with the environment. Psi includes ESP and PK" (1977, p. 931). *ESP* means extrasensory perception, that is, the ability to sense across time and space what someone is doing or thinking or feeling. *PK* means psychokinesis, or the use of the mind to influence objects or processes without the intervention of known devices or physical energies. Thus the phenomenon of a medium causing a table to be lifted during a seance is a case of psychokinesis. Psi, then, is a general term for both of these mysterious qualities.

Although the ability of some people to project their thoughts across time and space, for example, has not been proved to the satisfaction of all scholars (to understate the case), it is today a legitimate, serious field of study. There have been too many instances of apparent success in human history to dismiss the matter out of hand.

Gardner Murphy, a renowned psychologist, offers an optimistic, although guarded, view:

> *Can parapsychology* [para *means "beyond"*] *move from the realm of the bizarre, absurd and occasionally demonic to the realm of verifiable and intelligible expression of latent human nature? What are these hidden forces at work within us? Our seventeenth-century ancestors knew that blankets gave off sparks in cold weather. Today, electricity drives our machines, lights our halls, monitors our studies of man.* (1973, p. xiii)

The implication is clear. We may have powers within us that emerge now and again and that are seen particularly in some persons, but that might be cultivated further than most scholars have thought to be true. If such is the case, human capabilities, particularly in communication, are not being fully utilized. Nor are they even fully understood.

We cannot explore further here the fascinating subject of psi. At the end of this chapter are listed some references and activities that may seem attractive enough to lead many of you to continue in private pursuit of one of the most tantalizing and little-understood aspects of communication.

SELECTIVE MEMORY

The third selective process is generally called *selective memory*, or selective retention. What selective memory means, in essence, is that we consciously or unconsciously remember certain things and forget other things. Obviously, memory—both short term and long term—is an important factor in communication. If we can't build on memory, then we have to start everything anew each time from scratch. Victims of amnesia have to do that, and it is an excruciating process—living among people who remember facts and faces, events and encounters, that are blocked to the victim.

We Remember What Serves and Doesn't Threaten

To simplify vastly, apparently we remember things that serve our psychological and cultural needs in some way, that are helpful to us in the largest sense of that term. We tend to forget things that do not serve us in a particular context or that threaten us in some way. As with almost everything else in communication, we generally have little or no awareness of these actions.

If we are told that there are thirty-two ounces in a quart in the traditional system of measurement used in the United States, the message is obviously quite simple. If in an hour we have forgotten how many ounces there are in a quart, then the message probably had little importance to us. It may not have seemed relevant. We may have been distracted. We may have doubted the credibility of the source. Both selective attention and perception are now intermingled in the problem. (We'll have a real test of all of these matters when the United States switches to the metric and Celsius systems of measurement.)

Permit another personal anecdote. A few years ago I had a heart attack. It was painful, and I was frightened. I spent three weeks in the hospital and several weeks after that recuperating at home. This is something that happens to many people, of course. There are many kinds of heart attacks, however, that being a very general term. The heart can be damaged in a variety of ways and degrees.

After the initial stages of severe pain were over, I asked my doctor, a kind and considerate man, precisely what kind of heart attack I had had. I was curious. Two friends were with me at the time. They understood perfectly what he said, as did I, and the next day they remembered what the doctor had said. The next day, however, I, presumably the most interested person, had only the vaguest memory of his explanation. I was not under sedation when the explanation was made, so I doubt that the problem was one of perception, although the setting doubtless created anxiety. Certainly the credibility of the doctor was not at issue, for I respected him deeply.

Twice more I asked, once several days later and again two weeks later. Only on the third occasion did I remember days later precisely what had been said to me. Then the information was secure in my short-term memory bank. But now, several years later, I can't call it back to memory. It isn't in my long-term memory bank. A psychiatrist would probably say that I had repressed it out of fear—rejected it from my memory—out of a need to forget it. "Need to forget" is the right phrase, too, for one apparently does not forget accidentally. Unless there is an organic problem present, like the effects of a stroke, for example, we forget because remembering is painful or does not serve our needs, psychologically speaking.

Analyzing dreams gives further insight into memory. Studies show that people dream almost every night, and whether you are having a dream or not can be determined by REM—rapid eye movement—which can be detected by a machine. Yet, even if we dream nearly every night, we often fail to remember many of our dreams. Why? Apparently because it serves us, unconsciously, *not* to remember them. They may be frightening or confusing, and we may not "want" to be frightened or confused. They may also seem irrelevant.

Communication is obviously deeply affected by selective memory (as well as by selective attention and selective perception). We remember things that seem meaningful to us. Many educators—who are, most of all, communicators—forget that failure of the student to remember frequently is as much a fault of the teacher and the subject taught as it is a fault of the student. If students see a reason for remembering something, discover salience in it, they may remember it. Otherwise, they may not remember it.

Memory Can Also Distort

Memory can be likened to the photograph in Illustration 5.6. The images reflect in distorted fashion off old windowpanes that were not made or aligned perfectly. We can vaguely make out what is seen there: a building across the way. Some details are seen more clearly than others. None is a perfect image, if there is ever any such thing. The reflecting windows have no experience, no psychic defenses, no emotional needs, as we do. Still, like us, they are structured in ways that determine how the images bounced off are mirrored. We could compare the particular distorting qualities of the mirrors with perception as well, but there the metaphor of a screen or filter that can be seen through is better. Here we see nothing of the inside.

SO WHAT?

The selective processes greatly influence the way we operate in communication situations, whether we are thinking of intrapersonal communication, interpersonal communication, group communication, or mass communication.

Perhaps the most important result of knowledge about the selective processes is that it badly damages, if not destroys, the notion of total objectivity. While we still hear the phrase "total objectivity" now and again, very few, if any, scholars in the field of communication, or in any other field, believe that full objectivity—keeping yourself totally out of the act—is possible. The best you can do is take into account the fact that you *are* a factor in communication, that you are an *active* part of the system, and try to guess what difference that makes. Even if you strive heroically to be neutral, you cannot be completely so.

All experience is subjective. . . . our brains make the images that we think we "perceive."

Gregory Bateson (1979, p. 31)

SO WHAT? 131

Illustration 5.6 Distorting reflecting windows are like memory, which frequently distorts.

THIS CHAPTER IN PERSPECTIVE

Although the culture into which we are born is a profoundly important context for studying the ways our views of the world are nurtured, it is still important to remember that each of us is an individual; no two of us are identical. Through life experience, almost always in interaction with others, we form individual images about ourselves and all things and events around us. These images shape the meanings that we assign to everything. And, have no doubt: we are the source of meaning. While there are differing views about the exact manner in which they operate, each of us uses three selective processes in communication: selective attention or exposure, selective perception, and selective memory or retention. We attend to communication that interests us or meets our needs, tuning out communication that doesn't; we perceive communication in ways congruent with our assumptions and needs; we remember communication that serves our assumptions and needs. We seldom do any of this in isolation, since we are in constant interaction with others.

The belief that one's own view of reality is the only reality is the most dangerous of all delusions.

Paul Watzlawick (1977, p. xiii)

There are certain groups of people in any culture who use these selective processes in ways other than "normal"; artists, scientists, and persons gifted with the little-understood powers of psi, for example. There are also ways in which some individuals achieve altered states of perception that affect their communicative ability, although these techniques must be sanctioned by the culture. Such techniques include meditation, use of chemicals, religion, participating in various athletic endeavors, hypnosis, and psychotherapy. Shifting to dramatically new settings, as astronauts do, can also allow new perceptions.

The communicator's problem . . . is not to get stimuli across, or even to package his stimuli so they can be understood and absorbed. Rather, he must deeply understand the kinds of information and experiences stored in his audience, the patterning of this information, and the interactive resonance process whereby stimuli evoke this stored information.

Tony Schwartz (1974, p. 25)

One of the major implications for communication that one learns in considering individual differences is that because we cannot totally escape our skins, we can never be completely objective. We can only reduce subjectivity to a certain extent. Also, we can never share meanings totally with another person, although we must forever strive to reveal ourselves and reach toward the other person.

EXTENSIONS

Reading You Might Enjoy

1. Boulding, Kenneth E. *The Image*. Ann Arbor: University of Michigan Press, 1956.

Boulding's little book (175 pages) is used centrally in this chapter. You probably have the gist of the idea by now, but if you want to see how Boulding applies it to several fields of inquiry (e.g., biology, economics, politics, history), go to the source.

2. Castaneda, Carlos. *The Teachings of Don Juan: A Yaqui Way of Knowledge*. New York: Pocket Books, 1974.

Castaneda, Carlos. *A Separate Reality: Further Conversations with Don Juan*. New York: A Touchstone Book published by Simon and Schuster, 1971.

Castaneda, Carlos. *Journey to Ixtlan: The Lessons of Don Juan*. New York: Pocket Books, 1974.

Castaneda, Carlos. *The Second Ring of Power*. New York: Simon and Schuster, 1977.

Carlos Castaneda is an anthropologist who asserts that he became acquainted in the early 1960s with a Yaqui Indian *brujo* (sorceror or medicine man) named Juan, who taught Castaneda to experience "states of nonordinary reality" so different from the way most of us perceive reality as to be absorbing and shocking. The books are written with unusual clarity and lack of technical jargon. Beginning in 1977, the authenticity of the books has been challenged, the allegation being that Castaneda invented Don Juan and thus the whole series of books. If the allegation is true, they are novels, but instructive ones.

3. Davison, W. Phillips, James Boylan, and Frederick T. C. Yu. *Mass Media: Systems and Effects*. New York: Praeger, 1976.

This readable and comprehensive book about mass communication has an excellent section on the selective processes and how they operate in both the reinforcement approach and the uses and gratifications approach.

4. Watzlawick, Paul. *How Real Is Real? Confusion, Disinformation, Communication*. New York: Random House, Vintage Books, 1977.

This superb book, which is advertised as "an anecdotal introduction to communications theory," covers a lot of ground, ranging from matters talked about in this chapter to animal communication to extraterrestrial communication. But Watzlawick's central question, "How real is real?" does come to focus on matters of awareness, perception, and memory. The anecdotal approach makes this book both a readable and a memorable book.

5. Zinberg, Norman E., ed. *Alternate States of Consciousness: Multiple Perspectives on the Study of Consciousness.* New York: Free Press, 1977.

This collection of ten scholarly essays, plus a foreword and bibliography, provides an excellent introduction to the question of states of consciousness different from the norm, how many of these states are achieved, and how they are studied. Some essays in the book are very difficult, others less so. In any event, those who seek a scientific document about alternate states, which we barely touched on in this chapter, will find this a useful book.

Ponderings and Projects

1. Read about the Rorschach test, developed by the Swiss psychiatrist Hermann Rorschach. How does the test relate to the concept of individual differences in perception?

2. Read about the Heisenberg principle, put forth by the German atomic physicist Werner Heisenberg. How does it relate to the selective processes?

3. When Igor Stravinsky's great ballet score, *Le Sacre du Printemps* ("The Rite of Spring"), was first performed publicly, in Paris in 1913, it was disastrously received. Pierre Monteux, the conductor, wrote:

> *The audience remained quiet for the first two minutes. Then came boos and catcalls from the gallery, soon after from the lower floors. Neighbors began to hit each other over the head with fists, canes or whatever came to hand. Soon this anger was concentrated against the dancers, and then, more particularly, against the orchestra, the direct perpetrator of the musical crime. Everything available was tossed in our direction, but we continued to play on. The end of the performance was greeted by the arrival of gendarmes. Stravinsky had disappeared through a window backstage, to wander disconsolately along the streets of Paris.* (Monteux, 1957)

Yet a year later when the piece was played in concert version (rather than a ballet version), it was a great success. Today hardly anyone knowledgeable about Western music regards the piece as anything but a brilliant turning point in the history of music.

There could be an interesting study in the reception of *Le Sacre du Printemps*, as well as other new works of art of whatever type. The phenomenon has been repeated over and over again.

4. You have experienced the selective processes countless times and will continue to do so. Report in a speech, a written comment, or any other form acceptable to your instructor on some of the notable instances that you recall. Or perhaps you would like to keep a log of these events as they occur in the future. And have you ever had a paranormal communication experience?

5. Compare your reactions with those of your classmates about any event of interest to you—a concert, film, play, class, and so on—with an eye to seeing how impressions differ. Attempt not to determine who is "right" or "wrong," but rather simply how perceptions differ.

Two Kinds of Intelligence: The Brain Hemispheres

6

Western man has created chaos by denying that part of his self that integrates while enshrining the parts that fragment experience.

Edward T. Hall

In all human and other living communicators, biological bases are fundamental. For full understanding of these bases we would need to explore such diverse matters as the brain, the nervous system, the sense organs, and body structures and musculature. Space does not permit that, however.

The brain is the master biological control agent. Yet it would be particularly foolish to attempt even an overview of how that complex organ—the "last frontier," as it has been called—operates in our communication interactions. We will, then, probe in this chapter one of its most interesting qualities— the fact that in humans (and some other creatures) the brain has two halves, or hemispheres, each of which processes information in a different way.

Brain bilaterality, as the phenomenon is sometimes called, relates in a powerful way to the two preceding chapters and to the one that follows. How? With respect to cultures, there is evidence that various cultures tend to foster brain hemisphere development in different ways. And one of the many contributors to our individuality as unique members of cultures is the fact that no two of us develop and use the hemispheres identically. Knowing something of the brain hemispheres will also help us understand codification, the subject of the following chapter.

THE DANGER OF CONSIDERING THE BRAIN OUTSIDE ITS RELATIONSHIP WITH OTHER BODY ORGANS

We will concentrate on the brain and something of its structure in this chapter. This will result in an artificial splitting of the brain from the rest of the body, and that split is a bit dangerous, for the brain (or any other organ) cannot possibly be separated forever from the rest of the body and make much sense. Ultimately, the whole body is involved in learning, in processing information, in intelligence. As Margaret Atwood put it in her novel *Surfacing*:

> *The trouble is all in the knob at the top of our bodies. I'm not against the body or the head either; only the neck, which creates the illusion that they are separate. The language is wrong, it shouldn't have different words for them. If the head extended directly into the shoulders like a worm's or a frog's . . . they wouldn't be able to look down at their bodies and move them around as if they were robots or puppets; they would have to realize that if the head is detached from the body both of them will die.* (1976, p. 91)

Still, we will perpetuate that myth of separateness here for convenience and consider one characteristic of the brain in a most elementary way. But, as Gregory Bateson put it, "Lord help you if you think the parts are real [removed from the context of the whole]" (Quoted in May, 1977, p. 90). Let us remember that concentrating on "the knob at the top of our bodies" ignores other components of the central nervous system, the sense organs, the skeletal and muscular system, and other parts of the system known as the body.

THE TWO BRAIN HEMISPHERES

For a long time we have known that the brain consists of two hemispheres, a left and a right, approximately equal in size to each other. For well over a century, neurologists, psychologists, anthropologists, and psychiatrists have also known that specific portions of the brain exercise control over our senses and body parts. In the 1860s, to give one example, a French surgeon, Pierre-Paul Broca, discovered the area in the left brain hemisphere (in most persons) that largely controls the production of speech. Damage to this area can seriously impair ability to speak, although the stricken person can understand and write. Like a newfound geographic feature on the moon today, it was named "Broca's area." As other localized areas in the brain that control such senses as touch, smell, and vision and various motor activities were discovered, they too were appropriately named for their discoverers. For instance, a second speech area in the left hemisphere (associated with the ability to understand speech) was named "Wernicke's area," after its discoverer, Karl Wernicke.

It has also been known for some time that in most of us the right brain hemisphere controls the motor activity of the left side of the body—movement of limbs, for example—and the left hemisphere controls the activity of the right side of the body. They are crisscrossed, in other words. So, if the left side of the brain is seriously injured, the motor activity of the right side of the body is impaired. This is often referred to as brain asymmetry.

The two hemispheres of the brain are interconnected, however, by a large bundle of nerves, millions of them, held together like strands of a rope, known as the *corpus callosum*. The right hemisphere needs to know what the left hemisphere is doing and intercommunication between the two is necessary. In walking, for example, the left hemisphere controls the movement of the right leg and arm, but the left leg and arm must also move at the same time, so the right hemisphere gets into the act as well.

Recently, considerable proof has been brought forward that the brain hemispheres not only regulate motor and sensory activity but also control certain kinds of intelligence or ways of processing information.

LEFT-HEMISPHERE INTELLIGENCE OR INFORMATION PROCESSING

Specifically, current evidence suggests that the left hemisphere in the overwhelming majority of people controls language and mathematical abilities, the ability to reason logically, and the ability to think in an orderly, step-by-step process from facts to conclusion. In short, the left brain hemisphere is analytical, our built-in human digital computer.

RIGHT-HEMISPHERE INTELLIGENCE OR INFORMATION PROCESSING

The right brain hemisphere, on the other hand, apparently controls visual artistic abilities, nonverbal aptitudes, musical abilities, intuition, and feeling for the mythic, spatial, and movement facilities, as in sculpture and dance. It is also the more useful hemisphere in perceiving patterns—in putting matters together, in seeing relationships or *gestalts*, as they are sometimes called in psychology.

As Robert E. Ornstein, a psychologist, puts it:

140   TWO KINDS OF INTELLIGENCE: THE BRAIN HEMISPHERES

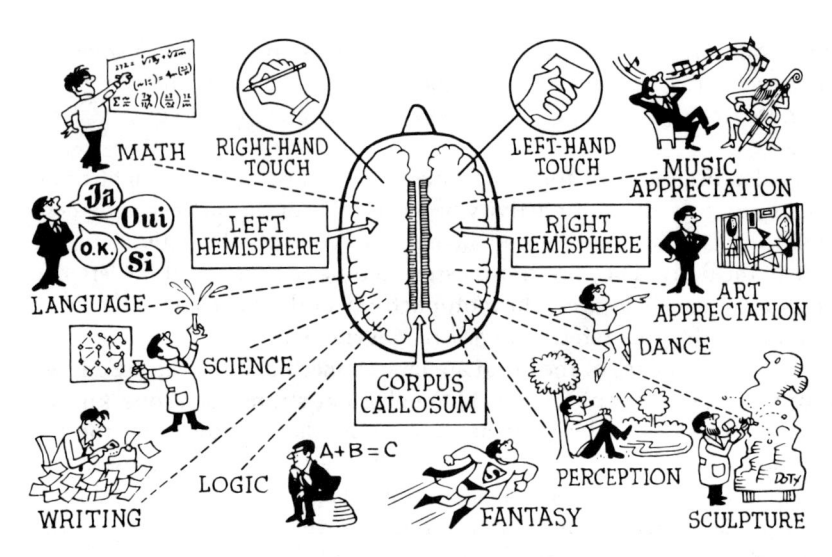

Illustration 6.1 Information processing abilities of the two brain hemispheres. (Illustration by Ray Doty)

Both the structure and the function of these two "half-brains" in some part underlie the two modes of consciousness that coexist within each one of us. Although each hemisphere shares the potential for many functions, and both sides participate in most activities, in the normal person the two hemispheres tend to specialize. The left hemisphere (connected to the right side of the body) is predominantly involved with analytic, logical thinking, especially in verbal and mathematical functions. Its mode of operation is primarily linear. This hemisphere seems to process information sequentially. Since logic depends on sequence and order, this mode of operation must of necessity underlie logical thought. Language and mathematics, both left-hemisphere activities, also depend predominantly on sequence. If, for instance, any set of letters comprising a

---

The brain we know now allows for the experience reported from the spiritual disciplines whereas the brain I was raised on was a computer.

Karl Pribram (Quoted in Paul Byers, 1977, p. 140)

word were ordered in an alternate sequence, the letters would have no meaning.

If the left hemisphere is specialized for analysis, the right hemisphere (again, recall, controlling the left side of the body) seems specialized for synthesis. Its language ability is quite limited. This hemisphere is primarily responsible for orientation in space, artistic endeavor, crafts, body image, recognition of faces. It processes information more diffusely than does the left hemisphere, and its responsibilities demand a ready integration of many inputs at once. If the left hemisphere can be termed predominantly analytic and sequential in its operation, then the right hemisphere is more holistic and relational, and more simultaneous in its mode of operation. (1977, pp. 20-21)

These generalizations are not absolutes, but they are fairly firm. Notice Ornstein's use of qualifying terms such as *primarily, predominantly, more, seems,* and the like, all of which suggest tendencies. This reflects the kind of caution that the mathematician, physicist, and philosopher J. Bronowski insisted on in his statement that "there is no absolute knowledge, and those who claim it, whether they are scientists or dogmatists, open the door to tragedy" (1973, p. 353).

Every night, for the brief duration of a dream, the illogical, emotional, highly visual right brain is almost completely freed from the dominance of the rational left brain, and the result is the torrent of images, sounds and feelings known as a dream.

Laurence Cherry (1977, p. 13)

As pointed out by journalist Warren Brown (1975), one departure from absolute generalization is that among right-handed persons about 5 percent of speech production (which is predominantly a left-hemisphere activity) is controlled in the right hemisphere. Among most left-handers language dominance is still in the left hemisphere, although in about 20 percent of left-handers speech activity is dominant in the right hemisphere or split between the two hemispheres. The whole phenomenon of handedness, and its relationship to hemispheric laterality (as the two-hemisphere phenomenon is sometimes called), is not well understood. It is a tantalizing subject, about which there are some references and suggested activities at the end of the chapter.

PROOF OF LATERALIZATION FROM BRAIN-DAMAGED PERSONS

Much proof of the apparent differences between the two brain halves has come from the study of people who have suffered severe damage to one half of the brain but not to the other half. A famous example is that of French composer Maurice Ravel, who in his later years suffered a severe stroke in his left hemisphere. Since the left hemisphere normally controls language production and other logical functions, Ravel lost the capacity to use language well, and further, he could not continue to write down his compositions on musical staffs. But because his right brain hemisphere was not damaged, his ability to appreciate melodies, harmonies, rhythms, and whole compositions was not hampered in the least, although he could not notate or communicate instructions to others.

Other examples may be found among visual artists. American painter Lovis Corinth suffered right-hemisphere brain damage, after which time his portraits became severe distortions of the subjects. The same is true of German painter Anton Räderscheldt, whose portraits after damage to his right brain hemisphere reflected his inability to depict a subject in his customary realistic style.

CULTURES APPARENTLY REINFORCE HEMISPHERE DEVELOPMENT

The most explosive fact that we need to face, however, is that cultures develop biases through the years favoring one style of thinking or information processing, and this results in recognizing and rewarding one kind of intelligence over the other.

As science journalist Jack Fincher, who rounds up a good deal of the research on questions relating to human intelligence in his book *Human Intelligence*, declares:

> *Our society ... especially in the fields of science and education, is inherently prejudiced against the intellect of the right, or non-language, hemisphere. It is the linguistic, the abstract side of ourselves we test and educate and reward—and by such powerful social strategies catapult to an overarching prominence in the human scheme of things.* (1976, p. 73)

What Fincher is calling attention to (as Hall did in the introductory quotation to this chapter) is the fact that in the United States and in most Western cultures, as contrasted with some Eastern cultures, we clearly spend most of our time and money in our educational systems on reading, writing, and arithmetic, left-hemisphere activities. Parents get depressed when kids bring home negative reports on their progress in the left-hemisphere ventures, although, of course, they don't speak of it that way. We hire tutors and write a hundred books on Why Louis Can't Spell or Why Alicia Can't Read. Those matters pay off in this culture.

We [educators] have subordinated a large area of human experience and neglected the development of one hemisphere of the brain while working very hard to develop the other. . . . At present we are caught between an incomplete theory and the present state of practical pedagogy.

Wilbur Schramm (1977, p. 12)

As a matter of fact, the mere notion that art or music or dancing or design work (to note some of the communicative activities controlled by our right brain hemisphere) are forms of *intelligence* is probably ludicrous in the view of most Americans. Where is the payoff? Given the fact that most Americans see only small pragmatic value in artistic activity, it is seldom at the core of the school curriculum and is generally regarded merely as a hobby or something "nice."

That is not a happy fact, for we may well be in the business of helping to create half-human beings ("half-wits," somebody called it), of stimulating—educating, cultivating—only half of our potential.

No one I know wants to eliminate development of the linguistic-logical-mathematical capabilities that lie inherent in the left hemisphere. Many people do ask, however, that we spend as much of our energy on the right brain hemisphere. As British brain specialist Colin Blakemore puts it:

What we should be striving to achieve for ourselves and our brains is not the pampering of one hemisphere to the neglect of the other (whether right or left), or their independent development, but the marriage and harmony of the two. (1977, pp. 165-167)

AN EXAMPLE OF RIGHT-HEMISPHERE DEVELOPMENT: THE ESKIMOS

As noted, not all cultures emphasize the left hemisphere as sharply as we do. One interesting research project has been conducted among the Eskimo people of Baffin Island in the northeastern part of Canada. Anthropologist Solomon

H. Katz, head of the research project, reports, according to Robert J. Trotter, a science reporter:

> *If variations in cognitive style [the process of acquiring knowledge] emphasizing one kind of thinking over another are possible, says Katz, one of the most likely groups manifesting orientation to right hemisphere functions would be the Inuit Eskimos. They are known for their unusual gestalt (integrated) abilities, such as drawing accurate maps of their territories. They seem to have a sort of symbiotic feeling of oneness with their environment and have traditionally depended on their well-documented ability to find their way out of the most incredible circumstances. Such abilities would probably be highly adaptive in an environment like the Arctic, which demands a high degree of visual spatial ability for survival. In short, says Katz, it would appear that these right hemisphere functions would be more highly developed in Eskimos than in modern urban populations.* (1976, p. 218)

Katz reports, as have other investigators, on the highly developed artistic ability of the Eskimos and the high degree of cooperation between the two brain hemispheres. He finds an

> *almost perfect relationship [in carving] between the right hand doing the detailed, analytical kinds of activities and the left hand doing all of the spatial and touch activities.* (Trotter, 1976, p. 220)

And, Trotter observes:

> *The Inuit environment, language and certain social behaviors (such as their emphasis on teaching by demonstration rather than by verbal instruction) all seemingly combine to foster right hemisphere activity which shows up in the Inuit life style and artwork.* This suggests that modes of thinking (or hemisphere use) can be taught. *It is possible that different cultures channel people into a greater or lesser reliance on one or the other hemisphere.* (1976, pp. 219-220) (emphasis mine)

In a lovely book, *Eskimo*, many Eskimo works of art are reproduced through which one can see the skills referred to in Trotter's observations. The book also presents three outline maps, as shown in Illustration 6.2, with the following commentary by anthropologist Edmund Carpenter:

AN EXAMPLE OF RIGHT-HEMISPHERE DEVELOPMENT   145

The Eskimo are familiar with the most intimate details of this land. In 1929 when George Sutton visited Southampton Island, a land mass of nearly 20,000 square miles, no accurate maps of this island were available, so he obtained from two Aivilik Eskimo, Ookpuktowk and Amaulik Audlanat, the two upper sketches. The amazing accuracy of their combined efforts can be seen by comparing them with a modern map, just below them, prepared years later from aerial photographs. Certain digressions, often shared, are immediately apparent, particularly in the enlargement of

Illustration 6.2 Southampton Island. The upper two sketches were drawn in 1929 by two Eskimos. The bottom sketch is based on an aerial photograph taken years later. Considering that the land mass is nearly 20,000 square miles, the Eskimo renderings, not based on ground surveys or measurements, are remarkable. Their spatial and artistic knowledge are highly developed. (Reprinted from *Eskimo* by Edmund Carpenter, Frederick Varley, and Robert Flaherty, by permission of University of Toronto Press.)

the Bell Peninsula, a favourite hunting ground. But the striking feature is certainly accuracy, especially in the details of the shoreline. (1959)

Carpenter's point is that Eskimos have amazing ability at perceiving spatial relationships, often acoustically rather than visually, because of the snow-blinding conditions and long periods of darkness in which they live. The book *Eskimo* was published before the major work on brain hemispheres had begun, but it adds evidence to Trotter's earlier comment.

JULIAN JAYNES'S HISTORICAL THEORY

Julian Jaynes, a research psychologist at Princeton University, has put forward a daring theory of history drawing heavily on knowledge of the two brain hemispheres. His book bears the mind-corrugating title, *The Origin of Consciousness in the Breakdown of the Bicameral Mind* (1977). The book deals with some highly debatable propositions, a point that Jaynes understands clearly.

Let us consider first what two terms, *consciousness* and *bicameral mind*, mean as Jaynes uses them. *Consciousness* refers to self-awareness—being alert to your feelings, engaging in internal dialogue about your function in life, being worried about money, knowing that death comes to all of us.

Bicameral mind refers to the two brain hemispheres. Today, in most modern industrialized societies, the left hemisphere is regarded by psychologists and neurologists as the dominant hemisphere because it controls language, particularly language production. The right hemisphere is thought of today as the minor hemisphere because of its subordinate role in language. Jaynes believes that at one time the right hemisphere played a major role in a special kind of language activity, namely, hearing "voices of the gods." That is, he suggests, with considerable evidence drawn from a number of disciplines, that through most of history humans quite literally heard voices of the gods, telling them to do this or that, and totally lacked the quality that we now refer to as consciousness. The right hemisphere, he believes, lost this rather special language activity as late as three thousand years ago, due to evolutionary pressures (natural disasters and social requirements) that gradually brought about atrophy of the god-hearing language activity of the right hemisphere, demanding a shift from following those commanding voices to learning uses of logic and other left-hemisphere activities. It was at this time as well—and not before, Jaynes believes—when human self-consciousness began. That is, consciousness was learned, in Jaynes's view.

Jaynes suggests that there exist today carry-overs from our predecessors who heard those commanding voices and followed what they said. These carry-overs are that group of mentally disturbed patients known as schizophrenics. (Schizophrenics hear hallucinatory voices, the source of which they cannot identify, but which are very real indeed to them.) In other words, Jaynes believes that no more than three thousand years ago, all humans heard and obeyed what we now think of as hallucinatory voices. These voices have been replaced by "self-talk," which we think of as a characteristic of consciousness.

Debates about Jaynes's theory abound; scholars meet on the academic battlefield. One of the most provocative aspects of Jaynes's thesis is that it assumes that evolutionary pressure shifted an important human quality, and in the very short time of three thousand years or so. This implies the possibility that evolutionary pressure can again shift the balance between the two hemispheres.

DOUBTS ABOUT THE TWO-INTELLIGENCE THEORY

The material presented so far implies considerable agreement among researchers about the role of the two hemispheres. There is. Still, not all scholars see the case so clearly for two kinds of intelligence, two means of processing information, rooted in a bilateral brain. Caution is urged, for example, by a noted American psychiatrist, Silvano Arieti, who says, "The hypotheses are intriguing, but in my opinion the neurological evidence is by no means conclusive" (1976, p. 395).

While Arieti is clearly in the minority, we may assume that this, like all other discoveries and theories, will gradually undergo modification. So, take a questioning position, and take pleasure in watching new evidence emerge, whichever way it takes us.

THE SO WHAT FOR COMMUNICATION

There are some implications for students of communication in the information being uncovered about brain laterality. Consider these possibilities:

1. *Intercultural complications.* We have seen in earlier portions of this book that people from different cultures, raised on different assumptions and holding different values, are likely to have greater difficulty in communicating with each other than are members of the same culture. This would be true even if they learned to speak the same language and use the same body signals, for subtle differences in background would always inhibit to some degree the possibility of shared meanings. The apparent fact that cultures also tend to reinforce brain hemispheres, and thus styles of knowledge processing, simply magnifies the problem.

2. *Individual hemisphere differences in the same culture.* But even within the same culture there appear to be considerable differences among individuals with respect to brain hemisphere emphasis, as well as among characteristics of their experiential backgrounds. It isn't a question of, for example, Americans being all left-hemisphere oriented and Inuit Eskimos being all right-hemisphere oriented. Individuals within a culture apparently have *degrees* of difference in their reliance on one or the other brain hemisphere. Jack Fincher reports that Roger Sperry, one of the most distinguished researchers in this field, feels that

> *differential balance and loading between these right and left hemisphere faculties . . . could make for quite a spectrum of individual variation in the structure of human intellect—from the mechanical or artistic geniuses on the one hand who can hardly express themselves in writing or speech, to the highly articulate individuals at the other extreme who think almost entirely in verbal terms.* (1976, p. 191)

A key phrase above is "spectrum of individual variation in the structure of human intellect." It suggests that, while nobody is 100 percent left-hemisphere oriented and 0 percent right-hemisphere oriented, or vice versa, that the percentage of reliance on one or the other hemispheres varies considerably within a group of people from the same culture. Thus, in addition to the individual variations that come from our inevitably different background experiences, our variations in brain processing procedures are infinite. These differences undoubtedly are reflected in the way we express ourselves or present ourselves. Communicative style doubtless follows thought style in a close fashion.

3. *A thought about schools.* One of the great agencies of communication in our society is the educational system—schools and colleges. In commenting on Western education and its emphasis on left-hemisphere activity, neurosurgeon Joseph E. Bogen, one of the pioneers in this field, has remarked:

> *Although a school may enjoy an art or music department [right-hemisphere activities], its primary purpose [is thought to be] to encourage intellectuality, i.e., left-hemisphere potential. Which suggests that many students consider their instruction "irrelevant," not just because they find their courses difficult . . . but because they view "life success" differently. . . . They are concerned not only with rationality but with sensitivity. They are concerned not so much with making a living as making a life. They see a world of warring elders, busily Becoming at the expense of Being, who want them [the students] to be unhappy in the same half-brained way. The fight*

with nature for survival is won, they feel; and it is time we learn to live within nature as bilaterally educated, whole persons. (1975, p. 30)

Mere purposive rationality unaided by such phenomena as art, religion, dream, and the like, is necessarily pathogenic and destructive of life.

Gregory Bateson (1972, p. 146)

When Bogen speaks of many students finding their left-hemisphere education irrelevant, he does not mean, of course, that they are able to express themselves in those terms. Indeed, they probably cannot express their rather vague feelings particularly well. For that reason they may feel the great pain of an inability to communicate their deepest feelings. (And is there a greater psychic pain than that?) Such students are involved in a devastating form of communication censorship. Many educators feel that we need to find ways, in school and out, to lift the curtain of silence imposed on those who yearn for acceptance of the many modes of communication that are implied in bilateral brain functioning.

More of that in the next chapter on codification.

The image of mental health that I favor is one in which both capacities, the rational and the metaphoric, are legitimate. It is an image of equal access to the functions of both cerebral hemispheres and to the mind functions celebrated by both.

Bob Samples (1976, p. 190)

THIS CHAPTER IN PERSPECTIVE

Although the existence of two brain hemispheres in human beings and other creatures has been known for some time, the knowledge that each hemisphere processes information in a different way—normally, the left hemisphere in a logical, sequential, step-by-step way; the right hemisphere in an intuitive, holistic, artistic way—is rather new and exciting. We have seen in this chapter some of the implications of recent discoveries about the brain hemispheres, including the fact that various cultures apparently tend to reinforce the role of one hemisphere over the other, another example of the manner in which culture helps shape the individual at a very profound level. In addition to accumulation of different experiences and assumptions, hemisphere preference may be a factor in both intercultural and interpersonal communication.

There is danger, however, in thinking about the two brain hemispheres to the exclusion of other important functions that the brain plays in communication. It is also illusory to think of the brain as the only biological component worthy of consideration. No single part of a system is the key to the system. It is preferable, then, to regard our artificial isolation of the brain hemispheres in this chapter as only a sample of biological underpinnings to communication, not as the whole story.

EXTENSIONS

Reading You Might Enjoy

1. Blakemore, Colin. *Mechanics of the Mind.* Cambridge: At the University Press, 1977.

This is a beautifully clear, beautifully illustrated book about the brain. Historical in orientation, the book moves from early concepts of the brain to current ones. The book is based on a series of lectures given by Blakemore on radio for the British Broadcasting System, so they were designed to be understood by laypersons. They are. You should enjoy this work.

2. Fincher, Jack. *Sinister People: The Looking Glass World of the Left-Hander.* New York: G.P. Putnam's Sons, 1977.

Sinister means "left" in Latin. Sinister people are left-handers, then. (*Dexter* is "right" in Latin, so dexter people are right-handers.) There probably is a relationship between brain hemisphere dominance and handedness, one of the many possibilities Fincher writes about with lucidity and humor. He presents major theories of human handedness, notes left and right dominance in other creatures, in plants, in molecules, indeed, in all of nature. You'll never learn from this book precisely *why* some of us are "lefties" and many more are "righties" or even whether the phenomenon is more than circumstantially related to brain hemisphere dominance. What you will learn, however, is that it is a complex, engrossing subject.

3. Samples, Bob. *The Metaphoric Mind: A Celebration of Creative Consciousness.* Reading, Mass.: Addison-Wesley, 1976.

Samples's book is lovely to read and its graphics are delightful. Based a great deal on bilateral brain theory, Samples nudges us to think of *Homo sapiens* as a species with unlimited potential for development, particularly if we encourage our (Western) maverick mentalities (right hemisphere) as well as our (Western) well-bred, highly organized mentalities (left hemisphere). With stylish verve, he urges us to see and accept our whole selves.

Ponderings and Projects

1. Read, or ask among members of your psychology staff, to discover the kinds of tests available to assess the intelligence normally associated with the right brain hemisphere.

2. There are a number of quick checks, the accuracy of which may be dubious at the moment, that can help determine whether the right or left hemisphere is dominant for a given individual. One of them is a simple experiment designed by Julian Jaynes (1977), which he finds to be about 80 percent accurate. It appears in the form of two faces that are mirror images of each other.

In Jaynes's experiment, you ask a person to look at the two images shown in Illustration 6.3. They are mirror opposites of each other. The stare is to be directed at the nose, briefly. Then ask the viewer which face is the happier one. Right-handed people (generally left-hemisphere dominant) tend to see the left face as the happy one; left-handers (generally right-hemisphere dominant), the right. See the book for further details. Please note that Jaynes regards this little test as an experiment, not a bit of conclusive evidence.

3. The noted French philosopher and mathematician René Descartes (1596-1650) uttered a world-famous dictum, *Cogito, ergo sum* ("I think, therefore I am"). The slogan obviously puts great weight on our logical powers, and thus on what we now presume to be a function of the left hemisphere. Robert Witkin, in the dedication of his book, *The Intelligence of Feeling*, writes:

> *At sixteen I came across Descartes' dictum "Cogito ergo sum." I took it at once to old Les who used to help us examine such things.*

Illustration 6.3 Julian Jaynes's mirrored face experiment. (© Julian Jaynes)

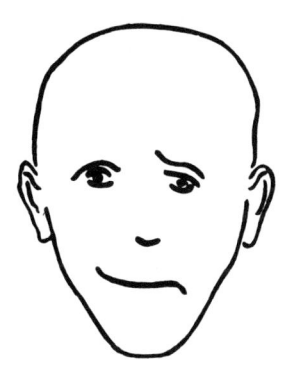

152   TWO KINDS OF INTELLIGENCE: THE BRAIN HEMISPHERES

"I think therefore I am," I announced. There was a pause.
"I feel therefore I am," he replied quietly.
I knew then that there was a beginning to the matter. (1974)

Read and talk about the differences between the notions of thinking and feeling. Are they mutually exclusive? Is one associated more with the left hemisphere than with the right?

"I'll be damned. It says, 'Cogito, ergo sum.'"

Illustration 6.4 (Drawing by Richter; © 1958 The New Yorker Magazine, Inc.)

Our Many Codes

7

People speak in many languages and God understands them all.

Duke Ellington

As we have noted throughout this text, all communication depends on signal systems of various kinds. These systems are frequently called *codes*. Codes take many forms, including spoken language, writing, mathematics, music, painting, architecture, pictures, odors, and touch. No one has ever made an exhaustive list of codes used by human beings and other creatures, so numerous and varied are they.

Underlying all codes are systems, or logics, which must be understood, consciously or unconsciously, by users of the code. The process of putting ideas and feelings into codes is technically known as *codification*.

We will divide the universe of codification into two great groups: the digital and the analogic. Much of this chapter will be devoted to learning the distinction between the two.

Codification is learned in cultures, and for that reason this chapter will bring back echoes of Chapter 4, on the cultural context of communication. It will also resonate with Chapter 5, because codification has individual differences. Further, we will soon see that codification can be analyzed in terms of brain hemisphere specialization, thus recalling Chapter 6.

WE COMMUNICATE WITH MANY SIGNALING SYSTEMS

What Duke Ellington, that superb American composer and performer, refers to in the quotation that heads this chapter is not merely the many verbal languages that peoples around the world use, important though they are. He means as well all the other signaling systems we have devised to communicate facts, to steer our way cooperatively through life, to share our joys, our fears, our anguishes, our accomplishments, our discoveries.

As we know, all communication is based on systems of signals of one kind or another. They are the basic building blocks. Frequently in communication studies these systems are called codes, and students of the field think of *encoding* (putting ideas, emotions, or information into recognizable form) and *decoding* ("translating" back from the code to something approximating the original ideas, emotions, or information).

As Jurgen Ruesch and Weldon Kees, pioneer scholars in nonverbal communication, put it:

For the communication specialist . . . when a person observes a series of events and then wishes to make a statement about them, such a statement has to be represented by signs that are comprehensible to others. The technical aspects of this process are known as codification. (1956, p. 7)

Every code is a system with an underlying logic or set of rules that all parties in the communication process must understand, either out-of-awareness or in-awareness. A major component of the logic of language, for example, is its grammar—the ways words are put together in a given language.

BIOLOGICAL AND CULTURAL CODES

For convenience we can think first of two general kinds of codes: biological ones and cultural ones. For our purposes, the cultural codes are the most important to consider, although we will give a passing glance to biological codes, using the genetic code as an example.

THE GENETIC CODE

It is no news that physical characteristics are inherited. Baby chimpanzees will grow up to be adult chimpanzees, not geraniums. Baby human beings will grow up to be adult human beings, not snails. Beyond that, particular offspring have physical qualities like those of their parents. My children look in some ways like me, in some ways like their mother. I bear resemblances to my parents, as you do to yours.

Genetics—the study of heredity transmission—has been studied for a long time, and most of us know at least a bit about the work of Gregor Mendel (1822-1884), an Austrian monk, who sought out the laws governing heredity and founded the science of genetics (although he did not use the term "genetics").

Only in the last three decades or so, however, have scientists understood by what means characteristics are carried from generation to generation. It has come to be regarded as a problem in communication, in which the signaling system is chemical. The *messages* (and geneticists use that term) are carried by a substance called DNA (deoxyribonucleic acid), which has four subunits making up its "alphabet." As journalist Robert C. Cowen puts it:

> *Just as the dots and dashes of Morse code encode information that can be read by a telegrapher, so [these chemical combinations] encode information that can be read by the chemical machinery of living cells. This is the genetic information that, according to current genetic theory, underlies the development, form, and function of all organisms, from bacteria to humans, and is passed on from generation to generation. . . . The blueprint of a simple bacterium may have a thousand genes, while the gene content of human DNA runs into the millions.* (1977, p. 13)

The greatest single achievement of nature to date was surely the invention of the molecule of DNA.

Lewis Thomas (1979, p. 27)

Further, the exact sequencing—the order of the dots and dashes, to continue Cowen's metaphor—that makes up the information for living substances has been precisely discovered for some very simple forms of life— certain viruses, for example. But science moves rapidly and more complex codes may soon be deciphered.

Meanwhile, debates have begun in scientific and legislative circles about whether we should allow ourselves to tinker with life, for learning the code has led, and will continue to lead, many scientists to a desire to manipulate it. On the one hand, understanding genetic codes permits us to create in the laboratory medically valuable organic substances that might be difficult to come by through natural means. On the other hand, looking over the horizon a bit, there is the natural concern for what ground rules to follow in an age that may not be far away when human beings themselves—or other complex forms of life—can be redesigned to meet somebody's specifications by intervening in the structure of the genetic code. Do we have that right? Can we trust ourselves? By the time you read these words, legislation prescribing guidelines for such genetic intervention may already have been enacted.

But let us turn our attention to a different order of codes, the cultural ones, which we understand at least a bit better, which we use daily.

CULTURAL CODES

There are numberless codes that humans use in communication every day: spoken language, written language, numbers, chemical notation systems, gestures, diagrams, pictures, drumbeats. The word *code* is close to the word *language*, except that *code*, as used here, is broader, intended to include all signaling systems.

The selection of a particular type of codification depends upon the communicative versatility of an individual and his ability to vary statements [verbal and nonverbal] in keeping with the nature of a situation.

Jurgen Ruesch and Weldon Kees (1956, p. 190)

Some codes are consciously invented to serve specific purposes. The Morse telegraphic code is a good example. Other codes, like natural languages (English, French, Urdu, Japanese), emerge over long periods of time. Some, like chemical symbols (H_2O), remain quite stable by agreement over time and space. Some, like natural languages, gradually shift through usage.

In addition to the distinction between invented and natural cultural codes, there is another distinction among cultural codes that helps us further in understanding them. This distinction is between two major classes of codes: digital and analogic.

DIGITAL AND ANALOGIC CODES

Digital codes are the ones we are most aware of. We probably spend more time and money in schools dealing with digital codes than with any other subject. Digital codes are made up of separate and discrete components that are combined according to rules. Among the major examples of digital codes are language and mathematics. They are, by and large, manipulated in the left hemisphere of the brain.

Analogic codes bear some relationship in form to the things for which they stand. Pictures, maps, and most body movements are analogic, for example. They are more flowing and less step-by-step in their operation than digital codes. Their meanings cannot be found in dictionaries. They are controlled generally by the right hemisphere of the brain.

Both digital and analogic codes are *learned* in a culture.

Digital Codes

Digital codes have the following two major qualities:

1. *The individual units in digital codes can be defined rather precisely*, so that the person who doesn't know their meanings can discover them by examining dictionaries or glossaries.

2. *The system that must be used to combine the individual digital units—the grammar—can also be described*, so that someone who hasn't had experience with it can learn the method.

Language Language is, as noted, a digital system. Take the following English sentence:

The man shot the bear.

Now, if you did not speak English, but rather some other language, like Hausa (an African language), those individual words would obviously be nonsense to you. Still, you could get an English dictionary and within reason learn what they mean. You could learn, without getting too precise for present purposes, that:

man = male human being
shot = hit with a bullet fired from a gun (or with an arrow fired from a bow)
bear = a four-legged furry mammal
the = a "function word," as linguists sometimes call them, which precedes certain other words or phrases in English. (This tiny word is the most difficult to define.)

While we are all aware that each of these terms can mean many different things in different contexts (many words in English, as in all languages, have dozens of quite distinct meanings), still you will agree that if you spoke only Hausa you could discover the meanings of those English words in a dictionary.

In English, although not in all languages, it is also true, however, that the words

> bear
> the
> the
> shot
> man

have to be put together in a certain *order* to make sense. Obviously, you get a quite different meaning from the following two orderings of the same words:

The bear shot the man.

or

The man shot the bear.

The ordering "The the shot bear man" makes no sense.

English is a word-order language. That is, the order in which the words are arranged makes a difference in the meaning, a fact not true of all languages. A frequently appearing English sentence structure is that of *actor* ➤ *action* ➤ *goal*. Thus, an actor (man) acted upon (shot) something, a goal (bear).

Chemical notation Another example of a digital code, this time from an invented "language," is chemical notation. Consider the chemical statement immediately below.

$$H_2O$$

Again, the two qualities prevail:

1. The individual units can be defined. You can look H up in a chemistry manual and find it to be "hydrogen." In the subposition it occupies here 2 means "two parts of hydrogen." O means "oxygen." H_2O stands, of course, for water: its components are two parts of hydrogen and one part of oxygen.

2. The order must follow understood rules to keep the same meaning. O_2H is something quite different, so different that it describes no existing substance. O^2H is something else again and is simply nonsense in the system agreed upon by chemists.

Digital systems exist for hundreds of areas of discourse. Following are additional examples.

Morse code The Morse code, with such notations as

• • •   — — —   • • •

is a digital system. This is the written form of three letters in Morse code standing for "S.O.S.," an international distress signal. When heard as sounds, they remain digital, and are still representations of letters of the alphabet, another digital system.

Musical notation Illustration 7.1 is a statement of the first theme of the first movement of Beethoven's Fifth Symphony. It is filled with digital elements, including (1) the words ("Allegro con brio"), (2) the tempo at which the music

FIRST MOVEMENT

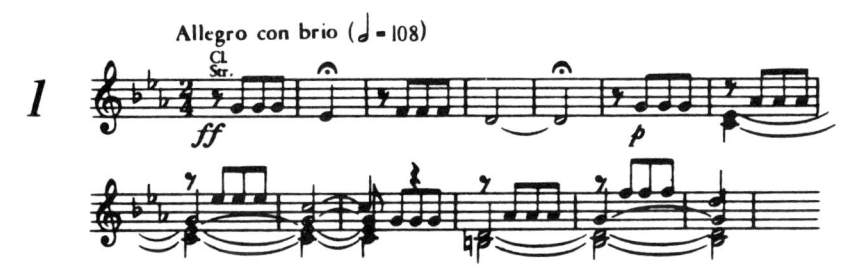

Illustration 7.1 The opening of Beethoven's Fifth Symphony.

is to be played ($\textit{d}$ = 108), (3) the musical staff , (4) the $\frac{2}{4}$ notation, which indicates the rhythm, and (5) the *ff*, which indicates the degree of loudness, plus the many other notations, all of which can be found in musical dictionaries and which are studied and understood by musicians. But be careful to make the following distinction in your thinking: When the score is played—that is, when the music is heard—it is no longer digital. It then shifts to the analogic mode, which will become clear later in this chapter in the section on art as analogical codification.

The manual alphabet of the deaf of North America The individual units (letters) of the manual alphabet of the deaf of North America can all be defined quite precisely, as you can see in Illustration 7.2, and they are combined in the same manner as spelling of the words. (There is another American manual language for the deaf, also digital. It is called Ameslan, and it permits creation of words and phrases rather than single letters.)

The punched computer card The familiar punched computer card is digital because the computer is sensitive to the presence or absence of punched holes at precise positions in the card. The human operator, who creates the punches on a typewriterlike device known as a keypunch, must be meticulously accurate; the computer is unforgiving of error. If a punch is in the wrong place in the card it totally alters the meaning of the message. Since a computer program can consist of anywhere from, say, a dozen cards in length to ten thousand, when an operator makes a mistake it can be a most frustrating experience to find it. A punched card is only one way of feeding information into a computer. Other ways include punched tape and magnetic tape.

160   OUR MANY CODES

MANUAL ALPHABET

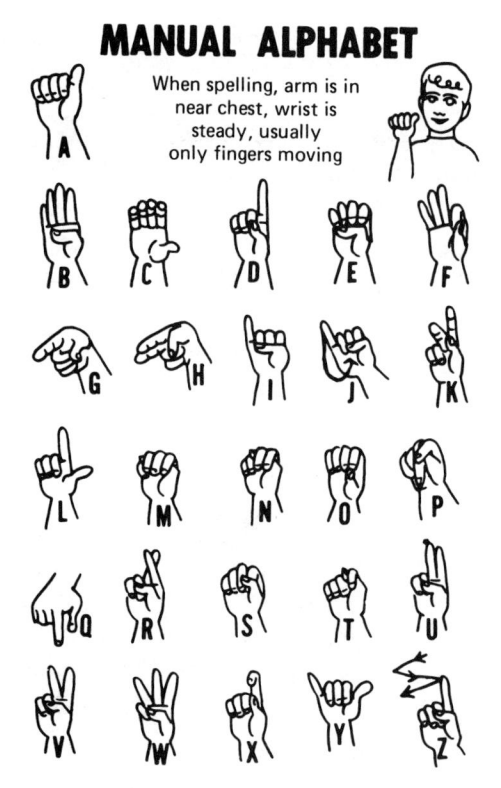

When spelling, arm is in near chest, wrist is steady, usually only fingers moving

Illustration 7.2 The manual alphabet of the deaf. (Printed with permission of Alinda Press, P.O. Box 553, Eureka, Ca., 95501)

Digital read-out instruments Illustration 7.3 shows one of many current forms of digital instruments, in this case a frequency indicator of a radio.

In the past decade instrument dials or readout panels have become increasingly digital, meaning that they present information in an alphanumeric (alphabet plus numbers) way. Thus, the radio receiver in Illustration 7.3 reads 107.1 on the FM frequency range. There is no approximation in the readout, as there is with the older style radio dial, which might leave doubt about whether it is tuned precisely to 107.1. Other instruments for which recent digital versions are available include clocks and watches, thermometers, wind-speed indicators, tachometers, and blood pressure indicators. All of us can think of a dozen more; measuring instruments are rapidly going digital.

Analogic Codes

Analogic codes are quite different from digital codes. *Analogic* means, roughly, "an agreement or likeness or correspondence between things." Unlike the

DIGITAL AND ANALOGIC CODES 161

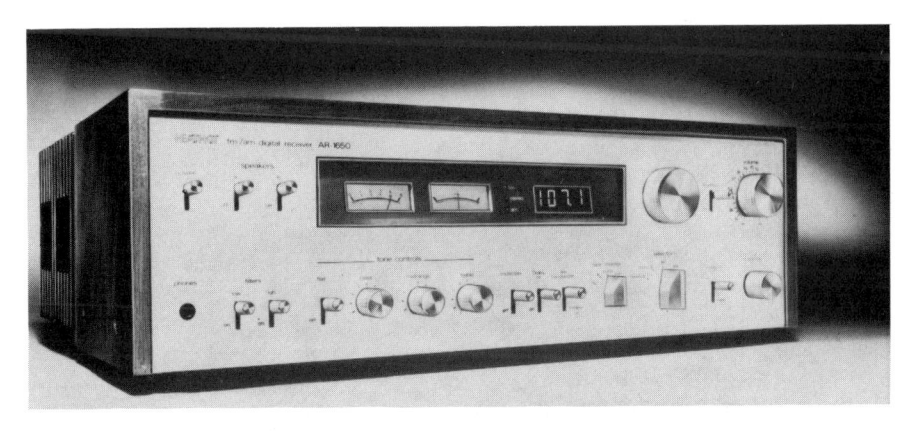

Illustration 7.3 A modern radio receiver with a digital indicator for the frequency (station). The receiver is now tuned to an FM station that operates at the frequency 107.1 (Photo courtesy of Heath Company)

digital modes, one cannot generally define the individual meanings of each unit in an analogic system by looking them up in a dictionary. Nor can one be nearly so precise about how they must be combined to make sense. Here are some examples of analogic coding.

Photographs A photograph is analogic in form. The image in Illustration 7.4 of a woman and child is obviously a photo, not the real thing. It is two dimensional, flat, less than the real size of the woman and child, black and white, not the exact flesh tone of the woman and child. For those of us who have long since learned to recognize photographs easily, there is no question that what appears here represents a woman and child. Still, it is not literally them. It is a representation, and of a passing split-second at that. It is far removed from reality. Many analogic presentations do not have quite the sharp look-alike appearance of this photograph, although they come close.

Maps Illustration 7.5 shows three maps, all forms of analogic communication, and among the most interesting in our time. In May 1976 the United States launched a small (sixty centimeters in diameter) sphere into orbit around the earth. Estimates are that the satellite will be in orbit for eight million years! Its function, by bouncing back laser beams directed at it, is to permit making maps of the earth accurate to within a few millimeters. Engraved on the plaque shown in Illustration 7.5 are three maps of the earth. The one at the top is the earth as scientists think it looked 225 million years ago. In the center is a map of how it looks now, after continents have drifted apart. At the bottom is a

162 OUR MANY CODES

Illustration 7.4 Mother and child. (Photo: Lynn Forsdale)

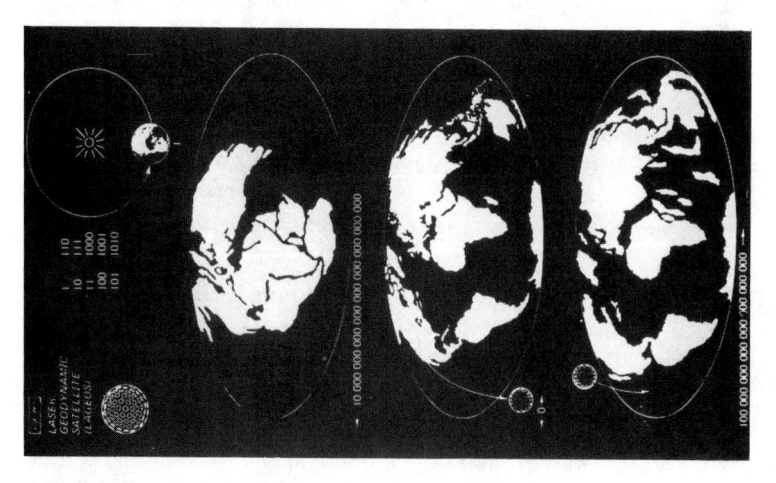

Illustration 7.5 Plaque from Laegost satellite. (NASA photograph)

map of the way scientists think the earth will look in eight million years, the continents having drifted still further apart. Carl Sagan, space scientist and maker of the maps, thinking about some wanderer from outer space finding the globe in orbit one day, writes, "To somebody who may some day come across the satellite it will be like finding a postcard from the past" (1976, p. 41).

This Laegost satellite (Laser Geographic Satellite) plaque also obviously has some digital material on it: the numbers and words.

Dance Illustration 7.6 depicts Judith Jamison of the Alvin Ailey American Dance Theater. As with most Western classical ballet, or its offshoots, Jamison's communication is analogic. Analogic to what? To human *feelings* of power, joy, melancholy, love, and so forth. Some forms of dance—as in India and China—use digital systems, too, in which hands, for example, are held in precise gestures that have exactly defined meanings: the rising moon, a freezing winter, or a rejected lover.

Actually, there are two layers of analogic codification in the photo of Jamison. One layer is the photograph itself, which is representative of the dancer. The second layer is implied. It is the dancer herself performing live on stage.

The analogic clock A simple, old-fashioned clock, with its two hands, one indicating the hour, the other the minutes, is also analogic. What is it analogic to? Perhaps most clearly the cyclical nature of our days—the coming and going of day and night. You can sense the revolutions of earth, sun, and moon in the movement here, something that is not communicated with the same clarity at all in the uncompromising arbitrariness of the digital clock. There are also digital elements in this basically analogical instrument; the numbers and the name that appears on the clock.

DIGITAL/ANALOGIC "ILLITERACY"

There can be "illiteracy" with respect to both digital and analogic systems. The word *illiteracy* is in quotation marks because it is used here in a special sense. Literacy traditionally refers to the ability to read and write. Here its meaning is stretched to include the ability to deal with pictures, movement, music, and other codes not based on words. Nobody doubts that there are people who cannot read words. If you think about it a moment, you probably will not doubt either that very many people cannot read blueprints or maps or electrical wiring diagrams, all analogic.

But it is also true that there are people who cannot make sense—not of the most elementary kind—even of straightforward photographs or motion pic-

Illustration 7.6 Judith Jamison. (Photo by Jack Mitchell. Courtesy Alvin Ailey American Dance Theater.)

tures. How is it that an uncontrived photograph of a human being or an object in the environment cannot automatically be comprehended by anyone on first seeing it? Because it requires *learning* certain conventions, what to look for and how—something like learning the alphabet.

You and I who grow up in cultures where pictures are everywhere from the moment our infant eyes are able to focus may find it difficult to understand that pictures (either still pictures or motion pictures) are based upon *learned* conventions. A couple of anecdotes may help clarify the matter.

John Wilson, a British filmmaker, made educational motion pictures a quarter-century ago in a culture that did not then have films as part of their normal educational or entertainment fare. (Such cultures are getting harder and harder to find!) One of his films was about malaria control, and it simply showed viewers ways to eliminate places where stagnant water might accumulate and become a breeding place for mosquitoes. Among other stagnant-water holders is the upright empty tin can, which catches rain water. So the film taught viewers how to deal with them. Wilson describes that part of the film:

There was a very slow movement of a sanitary laborer coming along and seeing a tin with water in it . . . picking the tin up and very carefully pouring the water out and then rubbing it into the ground . . . and very carefully putting this tin in a basket on the back of a donkey. . . . This film was about five minutes long. . . . We showed this film to an audience and asked them what they had seen. . . . They said they had seen a chicken! (Quoted in Forsdale and Forsdale, 1966, p. 611)

A chicken yet! Wilson could not recall seeing a chicken in the film at all. After searching the film thoroughly, he finally found a chicken in the corner of a shot, appearing for only a second or two. Yet the audience—no comment on their intelligence, mind you, only on their experience with film and the objects shown in the film—could not comprehend the other images on the screen; they didn't sink in.

Now this may partly be attributed to selective perception, but it is also partly a comment about "film literacy." Apparently the viewers did not know the technique of looking at the whole image, so they concentrated on the meaningful details, things that made sense to them. Chickens were important in their lives!

Another anecdote relating to pictorial "illiteracy" as a form of analogic disability is told by John Humphrey, another filmmaker, who many years ago made a film about control of disease, also for people in cultures not accustomed to the motion picture medium. He showed close-ups in the film of, among other things, flies bolding filling the entire screen. In the process he learned something from his audience, a group that was not savvy to the film convention of the close-up:

> *If we showed a close-up of an animal, fly, or an eye, the movement from long shot to close-up had to be step by step to allow [viewers] the feeling that they were actually walking up to see the object close up. If you showed a fly . . . in close-up, and it filled the screen . . . [the audience's comment was] . . . "We don't have flies that big."* (Quoted in Forsdale and Forsdale, 1966, p. 612)

Although these anecdotes relate to people from cultures where the analogic media involved, pictures in this case, were not common, there is evidence as well that there are differences (or preferences) among people in cultures where both digital and analogic systems are widely used. In a developed technological society such as the United States, we probably could not find many examples of pictorial "illiteracy" as striking as those just cited, but we can easily find a considerable range of abilities to take in and use pictorial (and other) analogic representations. This may also relate to the functioning of the two brain hemispheres. In any event, it is not a characteristic limited only to technologically less-developed countries.

ART AS ANALOGIC COMMUNICATION

Art is a special case of analogic communication, although many artists and theoreticians would argue that art has nothing to do with communication, that it is entirely a form of self-expression, with no concern for an audience. As with so many matters, the problem here is primarily one of definition. Also, if the artists assume that communication refers only to digital signaling, which can be translated into language or mathematics, then most people would agree that art is not communication. But if we accept a definition of communication that includes feelings as well as facts, we will be uncomfortable *not* including art in the realm of communication. Beethoven or the Beatles or the Bee Gees share feelings with us, not only in their words but in their music; so do painters like Rembrandt or M. C. Escher or Andrew Wyeth; so do dancers like Judith Jamison or Mikhail Baryshnikov or Fred Astaire.

Still, there are those who cannot accept the idea of communication that cannot be translated into language. The American philosopher Susanne Langer puts the point well, using music as an example:

ART AS ANALOGIC COMMUNICATION

Music has not the characteristic properties of language [or other discursive* systems]—separable terms with fixed connotations, and syntactical rules. . . . But it seems hard for our literal minds to grasp the idea that anything can be known which cannot be named. (1948, pp. 188-189)

What is art analogous to? What is it similar to in form? Using music as the example, Langer says:

Because the forms of human feeling are much more congruent with musical forms than with the forms of language, music can reveal the nature of feelings with a detail and truth. (1948, p. 191)

So, as noted a bit earlier, art is analogous to states of feeling that we experience in our lives. There are other views of what art communicates, but this is one accepted by many.

To take another art form, consider this comment by the American architect Charles Moore:

I keep claiming that buildings speak to people. . . . They speak to people in a great many ways. . . .

It seems to me that buildings should have the license to say things that are trivial or silly or eccentric or winsome or weird—in other words, the license to be representative of the range of emotion and value and decision and responsiveness of everyday life. (1978, p. 24)

Who can say precisely in words what the beautiful Islamic room in Illustration 7.7 says to each of us? Some might weep in its presence, so deeply does it "speak." But if asked, "Why are you crying?" they could only sputter something like "It's so beautiful."

We will return to some of these questions in Chapter 8, on nonverbal communication.

There are four final related matters that deserve our attention in this chapter. They are related to each other only in the sense that they all deal with aspects of codification.

---

* *Discursive*, as Langer uses it, is roughly equivalent to *digital*.

Illustration 7.7 An Islamic room.

CODIFICATION: THE MEANS OF THOUGHT AS WELL AS COMMUNICATION

Apparently we *think* in the codes with which we communicate. Apparently the boundaries of our thought processes are determined by the codes that we learn. Make the word *apparently* a big one in those sentences, because nobody knows precisely how thought works. We are dealing, then, with hypotheses.

The Sapir-Whorf Hypothesis

Let us begin with the Sapir-Whorf hypothesis, which is a proposition about language. It is also a proposition deeply tied to thought about culture, thus being a footnote to Chapter 4 of this book.

Edward Sapir, an American anthropologist, and Benjamin Lee Whorf, a linguist, felt that the language one learns early, which one speaks as a result of being a member of a culture or subculture, is not simply a neutral way of expressing reality, but is in fact a profound means of shaping the manner in which its speakers perceive reality. Sapir writes:

> *Human beings do not live in the objective world alone . . . but are very much at the mercy of the particular language which has become the medium of expression for their society. It is quite an illusion to imagine that one adjusts to reality essentially without the use of language and that language is merely an incidental means of solving specific problems of communication or reflection. The fact of the matter is that the "real world" is to a large extent unconsciously built up on the language habits of the group. No two languages are ever sufficiently similar to be considered as representing the same social reality. The worlds in which different societies live are distinct worlds, not merely the same world with different labels attached.* (1929, p. 209)

Sapir's comment (with which Whorf concurs in his work) says, in essence, that the language you are born into, because of its very form, contributes profoundly to the way you sense the world about you. Thus, if you are born into a culture that speaks Mandarin Chinese you will not—will never be able to—perceive the world exactly in the way a speaker of, say, American English does.

Both Sapir and Whorf, and many others, have suggested, then, although by no means to the satisfaction of every scholar, that various languages of the world are organized with such vocabulary and structural differences that they instill in their users totally different ways of looking at the world.

We saw earlier, for example, that one of the repeated sentence structures in English is that of *actor* ➤ *action* ➤ *goal*, which we use a thousand times a day, as shown in Table 7.1.

The examples in Table 7.1 need not be prolonged: the implications are clear. It is deeply built into the form of the English language that someone takes action toward something or someone. We control things. We grasp the initiative. We build cities. We move rivers. We go to the moon. We believe, this pattern in our language suggests, that we take action against people or things and that people or things take action against us. The cause-to-effect kind of thinking, which was explored in Chapter 2 (on models), is more or less natural to English speakers, then.

Isn't that "natural," isn't that the way all people view the world in which they live, and therefore the way they codify it in communication?

No, as we learned in Chapter 4, on culture, there is no universal, natural set of beliefs or ways of looking at the world. For example, a subculture in the

Table 7.1
The actor → action → goal pattern that occurs repeatedly in the English language.

	Actor	Action	Goal
You, in a routine conversation:	"I	am going	home."
A pilot to the passengers:	"I	will bypass	the clouds ahead."
A baseball manager to the pitcher:	"I	want you to win	this game."
A teacher to a student:	"I	will pass	students with 70 percent scores."
A hunter:	"He	killed	the doe."
A lawyer:	"We	will win	this case."
An engineer:	"We	will divert	the river."

United States culture, one Native American group, the Navajo* Indians, views its relationship with nature quite differently than do most American whites.

Clyde Kluckhohn and Dorothea Leighton, American anthropologists, speak of these two different views:

> *Navahos accept nature and adapt themselves to her demands as best they can, but they are not utterly passive, not completely the pawns of nature. They do a great many things that are designed to control nature physically and to repair damage caused by the elements. But they do not ever hope to master nature. For the most part The People [as the Navajos refer to themsevles] try to influence her with songs and rituals, but they feel that the forces of nature, rather than anything that man does, determine success or failure. . . .*
>
> *Many white people have the opposite view; namely, that nature is a malignant force with useful aspects that must be harnessed, and useless, harmful ones that must be shorn of their power. . . . Their premise is that nature will destroy them unless they prevent it; the Navahos' view is that nature will take care of them if they behave as they should and do as she directs.* (1946, pp. 227-228)

---

* This word is not spelled consistently in English. While I have used in this book the spelling "Navajo," which is probably used more frequently in the United States today, "Navaho" is an alternate spelling.

The Navajo view (and that of many other cultures in the world) is less self-centered than that of white Americans. We speakers of English tend to think of things as revolving around each of us. Like the sun in the Copernican view of the solar system, we tend to view ourselves at the heart of matters, the most active ingredient in the mix. Our language reflects and preserves that view. The Navajo language reflects their quite different view.

Speakers of the Hausa language in Africa express in their language a relationship with the rest of the world that comes much closer to the view of the Navajo than to that of American whites. Although the translation is awkward, let us look at some sentences that represent *tendencies* in Hausa speech.

In English, we might say: "I got sick."
The Hausa speaker might say: "Ciwo ya kama ni." ("Disease it caught me.")

In English, we might say: "He went mad."
The Hausa speaker might say: "Hauka ta kana shi." ("Madness it caught him.")

In English, we might say: "I was born at Kano."
The Hausa speaker might say: "An haihe ni a Kano." ("One bore me at Kano.")

The point to observe is the Hausa speaker's tendency to be less self-centered than the English speaker. The Sapir-Whorf hypothesis suggests, then, that this tendency in the language carries over to the Hausa speaker's view of everything.

Matters that are important in a culture generally appear in the vocabulary of the language spoken by the people of the culture. Snow is important in the Arctic, and many more words for snow appear in Eskimo languages than in English.

In Thailand the national language reflects a need to distinguish among several kinds of carrying. There are at least the following words that are used when speaking of different kinds of carrying. These are not structural (grammatical) differences, but exclusively vocabulary differences, which are important too. It is nearly impossible to simulate these Thai words using our alphabet. For that reason, no attempt will be made to suggest the sound of the words here. Accept the fact, however, that there are at least ten words, unrelated in sound and spelling, that represent different forms of carrying. The meanings of these ten words are indicated below.*

---

* While the meanings of these are not taken verbatim from the dictionary, Mary R. Haas's *Thai-English Student's Dictionary* (Stanford, Calif.: Stanford University Press, 1964) was used as the source of confirmation.

1. To carry or transfer something from one place to another. This word is used by porters, for example.
2. To carry things by use of a pole balanced over the shoulders, behind the neck. This would be used by street vendors, for example.
3. To carry an armful, to have one's arms loaded.
4. To hold or carry something by its handle so that it hangs down from the hand. This is used when referring to carrying buckets or handbags with handles, for example.
5. To hold or carry in the hands, as in the case of a handbag held in the hand. This is different from 3 above.
6. To carry on the shoulder or support on the shoulder or back.
7. To carry on a pole balanced on the shoulders of two people, one walking in back of the other.
8. To carry or hold, embracing with both arms, as in the case of a child or an animal.
9. To carry against the hip at the waist, as in the case of a baby or a younger sibling.
10. To carry by hanging over a shoulder, as in the case of a purse with a long shoulder strap.

We Apparently Think in Nonlinguistic Ways, Too

The immediately preceding examples have dealt with the preposition that we think with language and that different languages organize thought processes in different ways. The idea that we think with words, and only with words, is a very old one. There has always been a minority of people, however, who believe that, while words are doubtless important in our thought processes, we also use other systems of codification—both digital and analogic—when thinking.

[A] definition of thinking as covert verbal behavior [talking to oneself] can reasonably be extended to include not only . . . words and sentences, but also the many other forms of communication used by human beings, such as signs, gestures, mathematical symbols, and the whole nexus of nonverbal communication.

Donald R. Griffin (1976, p. 65)

One contemporary communication theorist, Wilbur Schramm, has put the case of thinking in all codes this way:

[Whenever] one acquires skill in a new coding system, one becomes able to think in a new way, handle more kinds of information, use new mental tools to analyze experience—in other words, to increase one's mental capacity. (1977, p. 14)

Another contemporary spokesperson for multiple modes of thinking is the psychologist Rudolph Arnheim. Arnheim argues that all intelligence, all thinking, begins with sensory data. The sensory data that organisms are able to respond to vary widely from creature to creature. For example, Arnheim observes that humans can't think very well with information gained through the senses of smell and taste:

Although the senses of smell and taste, for example, are rich in nuances, all this wealth produces—for the human mind—only a very primitive order. Therefore, one can indulge in smells and tastes, but one can hardly think in them. (1969, p. 18)

On the other hand, sight and hearing are a different matter, Arnheim believes:

These two senses are therefore the media par excellence *for the exercise of intelligence [in people]. Vision is helped by the sense of touch and the muscle sense. . . . Music . . . is one of the most potent outlets for human intelligence. . . . The great virtue of vision is that it is not only a highly articulate medium, but that its universe offers inexhaustibly rich information about the objects and events of the outer world. Therefore, vision is the primary medium of thought.* (1969, p. 18)

The words or the language as they are written or spoken do not seem to play any role in my mechanism of thought. The physical entities which seem to serve as elements of thought are certain signs and more or less clear images.

Albert Einstein (quoted in Rudolph Arnheim, 1965, p. 12)

RHYTHM AND SYNCHRONY IN CODIFICATION

Rhythm is of great importance to all organisms. Human beings, other animals—indeed, all organisms—operate in the context of large cycles. These large cycles can include the diurnal (day and night) cycle, menstrual cycles, the tidal cycles, the seasonal cycles, the great cycle of birth and death, and so forth. Our bodies, and those of other animals, operate in shorter rhythms, too: those of the heartbeat, breathing, brain waves, and so forth. Further, each individual has certain cycles of rhythms that are appropriate to him or her; a dramatic departure from these cycles is more or less upsetting. An obvious cycle is that of sleep and wakefulness. We all know approximately how much sleep we "require" in order to be at our best, and that amount varies from person to person. Reflecting on the role of rhythm in communication, one researcher, Eliot D. Chapple, writes that

> *all communication is endowed with rhythmic properties. . . . The beat is built up from the length of each action and the interval of silence or inaction in between. . . . It is further elaborated by the rise and fall of amplitude managed by modulation of voice intensity, gesture, and the total postural repertoire of the individual, and by the pitch, timbre, and their nonvocal equivalents. . . . the total rhythmic structure . . . has effects on individuals . . . making all such performances equivalent to a musical form.* (1970, p. 39)

Notice that the codes of interaction are not relevant in Chapple's argument, although doubtless there are individual preferences for forms of codification.

Rhythms of two organisms can be in or out of synchrony, and this is a matter of more than passing interest to students of communication. For example, if you are walking down the street with someone, your steps and other forms of body movement are sometimes precisely synchronized with those of the other person. At other times they are out of sync. In other forms of human interaction—conversation, for example—you can be in or out of sync in eye contact, touch, speech, body movement, and so forth.

Being in sync is itself a form of communication. When signals are in sync, matters are perceived by the communicating parties as going well. We experience the satisfaction of synchrony and the dissatisfaction of lack of synchrony in many contexts: while talking, while viewing or participating in team sports, at musical concerts, even while sitting silently with someone. Best friends probably sync well; being in love may be overwhelmingly a matter of synchrony. Sometimes the syncrony is so effective that we are tempted to say that we are reading each other's minds. More probably, what is actually happening is that we are simultaneously exchanging the tiniest signals with the other person, often of such a subtle nature that neither we nor even trained onlookers can spot them without the presence of recording equipment, such as a motion picture camera, which permits slowing down a sequence.

> [William] Condon speculates that catching another person's rhythm may have roughly the same effect as sharing his posture: it promotes a feeling of closeness, of rapport. People are enormously sensitive to the way other people move. Edward Hall has a collection of photographs taken in art galleries of people unthinkingly sharing the postures of sculptured figures.
>
> Flora Davis (1975, p. 106)

Many researchers have studied this problem, although not as many as have probed questions of the assumed meanings of words, gestures, and other of the more obvious forms of codification. It may well be, however, that the "good vibes" and "bad vibes" that we all know about intuitively are much more basic to our feeling of oneness, our search for being in touch, than are the modes that we normally think of. That is, the signals of synchrony, which are not on the obvious message level as we normally think about communication, may in the long run be much more important to our well-being than we now know.

Although not talking precisely about synchrony, Gregory Bateson makes the same basic point about the importance of the kind of communication that we might think of as "contentless":

> *When A communicates with B, the mere act of communicating can carry the implicit statement "we are communicating." In fact, this may be the most important message that is sent and received. The wisecracks of American adolescents and the smoother but no less stylized conversations of adults are only occasionally concerned with the giving and receiving of objective information; mostly, the conversations of leisurely hours exist because people need to know that they are in touch with one another. They may ask questions which superficially seem to be about matters of impersonal fact—* "Will it rain?" "What is in today's war news?"—*but the speaker's interest is focused on the fact of communication with another human being.* (1968, p. 213) (emphasis mine)

MULTIPLE MESSAGES

A second idea of great importance is that of multiple messages. It is a phenomenon that probably occurs in almost all acts of communication. It means simply that we often signal and receive two or more different messages at the same time. The messages may be contradictory or complementary. They may be subtle or gross. For example, you may be talking with somebody about a political matter, and at the same time, possibly through eye contact, express pleasure in being with that person. An example of contradictory messages might be sitting tensely in a chair during a job interview, saying all the while how nice it is to be there, how good you feel about the opportunity of getting the job. Your fists clench the arms of the chair, so uncomfortable do you feel, while you struggle to say the pleasant words. Some participants and observers pick this behavior up readily; others never see it. Sensitivity to communication signals varies.

METACOMMUNICATION

A third idea of enormous significance is that of *metacommunication*, which simply means communication about communication. It is related to the concept of multiple messages but has a quite specific implication. The idea is that we indicate in a variety of ways how the communication in which we are engaged is to be taken. By tone of voice or by gesture, for example, we give information that says, in effect, "this is serious," "this is a joke," "this is a simple fact," "I'm angry," and so forth.

In this culture, for example, an elementary form of metacommunication is to wink while making a nasty remark to someone. The wink serves as a signal that the statement is not to be taken at face value, that it is not meant seriously. Most metacommunication is much more subtle—being signaled by a slight shift in tone, by a variation in posture, by shifts in duration and rhythm of eye contact. That is, most metacommunication is analogic.

Paralanguage is similar to metacommunication but somewhat more restricted. Paralanguage refers to the vocal signals accompanying normal language (emphasis made by tone of voice, auditory "underlining" of a phrase, shift in rate of speech) that cause the listener to understand that something special, that something beyond the usual meaning of the statement is meant.

We have all been in situations in which the metacommunication signals were inadequate or were not understood. We may have made fun of somebody, as a joke, only to discover that the joke was not taken as such, that the other person felt hurt. We probably reassured the other person with an explicit statement, "Oh, I meant that as a joke." There is also the possibility that what we thought to be a joke was really an expression of antagonism that we did not recognize consciously, in which case the metacommunication signal may have been interpreted accurately.

No communication ever occurs without accompanying metacommunication statements. If that comment seems too sweeping, it is because we are not sensitive to this second layer of codification. An extreme case of inability to recognize metacommunicative signals, and hence how a message is to be taken, is found in those who are classified by society as mentally ill. As Gregory Bateson puts it:

> *He [the ill person] would not share with normal people those signals which accompany messages to indicate what a person means. His metacommunicative system—the communications about communication—would have broken down and he would not know what kind of message a message was. If a person said to him, "What would you like to do today?" he would be unable to judge accurately by the context or by the tone of voice whether he was being condemned for what he did yesterday, or being offered a sexual invitation, or just what was meant. (1972, pp. 210-211)*

We all find ourselves in situations in which we are not certain how to interpret the metacommunicative codes. Bringing the fact of their existence consciously to mind is often helpful as a first step in understanding them. The metacommunicative signals become more difficult to understand as we cross cultural boundaries, as do the basic message signals themselves. In any event, misunderstanding at the metacommunicative level is as profound a communication problem as any of us is likely ever to encounter.

THIS CHAPTER IN PERSPECTIVE

We have seen in this chapter that all communication depends on codes—systems of signals with underlying logic that are shared by members of a culture. Without sharing codes they cannot attain the first step of sharing meanings. The process of putting ideas and feelings into coded form is known as codification.

The universe of codes can be broken into two parts, for purposes of convenience. One is the digital codes, in which the individual elements of the code are arbitrary, can be defined, and the process of putting the elements together can be described in a grammar. Digital codes include everyday language, mathematics, chemical notation systems, and musical notation. The other general class of codes is analogic. These are roughly like something in the world or in one's feelings. Unlike digital codes, the individual units cannot be put easily into dictionaries, nor can a grammar for organizing them be described. Among forms of analogic codification are photographs, motion pictures, and forms of art such as dance, music, or architecture. Illiteracy can exist with respect to both digital and analogic codes.

We also apparently think in the codes that we use for communication, in both digital and analogic ways.

Finally, we have seen that rhythm and synchrony are important aspects of communication, that multiple messages in different codes may be exchanged, and that the phenomenon of metacommunication (communicating about communication) is continuous.

EXTENSIONS

Reading You Might Enjoy

1. Arnheim, Rudolph. *Visual Thinking*. Berkeley and Los Angeles: University of California Press, 1969.

Arnheim, a renowned psychologist of art, argues in this book that people think in a variety of ways, not merely with words. As the title would suggest, he explores the importance of thinking with data gained through vision, but he also treats the uses of auditory and other stimuli in thinking. This is not a simple work, but selective skimming will help you reach sections of the book that are most useful to you.

2. Samuels, Mike, and Nancy Samuels. *Seeing with the Mind's Eye: The History, Techniques and Uses of Visualization*. Copublished by Random House, New York, and the Bookworks, Berkeley, Calif., 1975. Distributed by Random House.

This history of visualization is a lively, richly illustrated account of the course of visualization in human history. The authors also argue, with countless examples and quotations, that visualization is integral to thought and human progress.

3. Shopen, Timothy, ed. *Languages and Their Speakers*. Cambridge, Mass.: Winthrop, 1979.

This is a collection of essays about the structure and cultural context of five languages: Jacaltec (Guatemala), Maninka (portions of West Africa), Malagasy (Madagascar), Guugu Yimidhirr (an Australian language), and Japanese. Why should you be interested in a book that deals with such little-known languages (except for Japanese)? Principally because it is illuminating to see how different languages codify reality for their speakers. The first chapter of the book also provides an elegantly specific example of how a nonspeaker of a language learns the structure of the language. This book is difficult reading; skim it and get a general impression.

Ponderings and Projects

1. Compile a list of as many digital codes as you can think of. Remember that there are some quite specialized ones, such as ships' flags, drum signals, symbols for electrical components in a radio wiring diagram, and proofreading marks. Almost every craft, profession, or hobby has such codes; there are thousands of them.

2. There are alternative contemporary methods to the one we know best for music notation systems. Search out other systems used today.

3. Do some research on dance forms that combine digital and analogic codes in the dance itself, as contrasted with notation systems. For example, much of the classical dance of India requires holding the body in quite precise positions or forming exact gestures with the hands, each gesture having a specific meaning, like "life," "death," "sun," "moon," "love," "hate," or "birth."

4. Attempt to spot metacommunicative signals in a videotape of a conversation between two people. You may have to watch the tape dozens of times to spot those signals that are meant to advise the other person how the communication should be taken.

5. In this chapter we observed that the national language of Thailand has many different words or phrases for describing the way people carry things, because that is an important fact of Thai life. Consider important values for American culture. If they are truly important, we should reflect that importance in our language. For example, we are interested in the size of things, ranging from the very small (miniature radios, say) to the large (buildings, say). One amusing way to get insight into our stock of terms for *large* is to list the number of words that manufacturers use to describe the size of canned or bottled olives.

6. Read about the controvery concerning manipulation of hereditary characteristics as we come to know more about the genetic code. Look also for films, television programs, and novels that will probably begin to use this as the central plot premise.

Nonverbal Communication

8

He that has eyes to see and ears to hear may convince himself that no mortal can keep a secret.

Sigmund Freud

Nonverbal modes of codification have been noted briefly both in the preceding chapter and elsewhere in this book. Because of the widespread recent study of nonverbal communication (there have been scores of scholarly and popular works on the subject in the past ten years), however, it is useful to discuss this form of communication in greater detail in a separate chapter. Nonverbal modes are used both by human beings and other organisms. Our attention in this chapter will concentrate on humans.

WHAT IS NONVERBAL COMMUNICATION?

Nonverbal communication consists of all signaling systems that do not use words. Included are: (1) body modes of nonverbal communication (body movement, posture, body orientation, eye contact, changes in pupil size, odor, touch, body heat, shifts in skin color, spacing, uses of clothing and body decoration); (2) communication of genetic characteristics, which are considered by some scholars as nonverbal communication; (3) various art forms and media such as painting, architecture, music, film, ballet, and mime; (4) the wide range of nonverbal signals used by other creatures, some of which are not used by humans.

THE IMPORTANCE OF NONVERBAL COMMUNICATION IN HUMAN INTERACTION

Ray Birdwhistell of the University of Pennsylvania, one of the pioneer prime movers in contemporary American studies of nonverbal communication, has estimated that perhaps 30 to 35 percent of human communication occurs through words, the rest through nonverbal modes (1970, p. 9). This is a rough guess, of course, but it does suggest, in a gross way at least, the relative importance in frequency of the two systems. Among creatures other than humans, nonverbal communication probably constitutes an even greater percentage of the communication repertory, particularly since their audible utterances are not normally considered by most communication specialists as fully developed languages.

Illustration 8.1 Abundant nonverbal communication at work: gesture, posture, eyes, clothing, distancing.

TOUCH (HAPTICS, TACESICS)

Touch, the study of which is technically referred to as *haptics* or *tacesics*, is among the first forms of communication that any of us experiences, and it continues to be important throughout our lives, although it has seldom been given the position it deserves in the writing about human communication.

Being touched and caressed,
being massaged,
is food for the infant.
Food as necessary
as minerals, vitamins, and proteins.
Deprived of this food,
the name of which is love,
babies would rather die.
And they often do.

Frederick LeBoyer (1976, p. 17)

As Ashley Montagu, an anthropologist and social biologist, says in his book *Touching:*

As a sensory system the skin is much the most important organ system of the body. A human being can spend his life blind and deaf and completely lacking the senses of smell and taste, but he cannot survive at all without the functions performed by the skin. (1971, p. 8)

The incidence of touching varies widely in different cultures and subcultures. Sidney M. Jourard (1971), an American psychologist, observed frequency of touch—a hand, an arm, a shoulder—in cafes over a period of one hour in four places in the world. The results: San Juan, Puerto Rico—180; Paris, France—110; Gainesville, Florida—2; London, England—0.

Jourard's observations in Florida are not necessarily typical of all groups in this country, as his Puerto Rican figures show. Americans of Hispanic background (Puerto Ricans and Chicanos, for example) touch more than do most whites. American blacks also touch more than do most whites.

While we should be cautious in making judgments about the effects of different cultural ways of communicating, we in this culture who are wary of touching may suffer the important consequences of missing that urgently needed message, "You are not alone." Touch may "say" that better than any other mode of communication.

The cultural taboo about touching in the United States that virtually prohibits male companions holding hands while walking down the street does not apply, for example, in many African, Middle Eastern, or Asian nations. There male hand holding does not evoke homosexual overtones, as it does in this country. Male touching male, however, is acceptable in some circumstances in this country, even among wary whites. Athletes, for example, may swarm over each other in the passion of victory, and death is a sufficiently emotional time to permit a separate set of rules, as Illustration 8.2 suggests.

Some animals touch extensively; others do not. Edward T. Hall observes that "contact creatures include the walrus, the hippopotamus, the brown bat, the parakeet, and the hedgehog. . . . The horse, the dog, the cat, the rat, the muskrat, the hawk, and the blackheaded gull are non-contact species" (1966, p. 12).

ODOR (OLFACTION, SMELL)

Apparently all animals, and many other forms of life, use odor as a communication system. Some organisms are much more sensitive to odors (or chemical communication, as some specialists refer to it and taste) than others. A dog, for example, can smell far better than humans can; birds are less well equipped than humans. Fish signal extensively with odors.

Students of communication have not given nearly as much attention to olfaction as its apparent role deserves. Why? Harry H. Shorey, an expert in animal communication, observes:

> *Modern man makes minimal use of chemical communication with others of his own species. Thus, he has little intuitive feel for the great reliance placed on this communication mode by much of the remainder of the animal kingdom.* (1977, p. 137)

Journalist Ruth Winter suggests that "we do not boast about our ability to smell . . . [because it] reminds us that we are animals" (1976, pp. 13-14).

A cultural component conditions human acceptance or rejection of odors, particularly those produced by our own bodies. Arabs and Eskimos, for example, take pleasure in smelling the natural body odors of other people. Most Americans, on the other hand, carefully remove their natural body odors by bathing, using deodorants, and applying artificial odors, such as cologne or perfume.

One current scientific debate turns on the question of whether you or I create *pheromones* as part of our natural life processes. Pheromones are chemicals, produced primarily by the glands of a creature, that are disbursed by a medium (air or water) and when picked up by another member of the

Illustration 8.2 During the Korean war, a male soldier embraces a grief-stricken infantryman whose buddy has been killed in action. In the background a medical corpsman fills out casualty tags. At times of strong emotion, nothing replaces touch. Even if a deep embrace among American men is generally a cultural taboo, it is permitted in certain circumstances. (U.S. Army Photograph by Al Chang)

Illustration 8.3 Two men in Asia walk hand-in-hand, a common mark of male companionship in many of the world's cultures.

species serve one or more robotlike functions, including identification of other members of the species, stimulation of social creatures to come together, triggering sexual arousal, and stimulating aggression. Researchers are not sure at this moment whether humans produce and react to pheromones of their own manufacture, although recent research suggests strongly that we do.

BODY MOVEMENT (KINESICS)

Every body movement has meaning, even though we may be aware of neither making the movement nor its meanings. *Kinesics* means the study of communication through body movement.

Even abstract ballets tell a story, the story of the body, for the body must speak.

Rudolph Nureyev (quoted in Walter Terry, 1977, p. 31)

Some gestures come to mind most quickly when we think of body movement as communicative. We have all probably played the game of comparing our knowledge of gestures from different cultures. For example,

Americans wave goodbye with the plam down. Some Italians wave goodbye with the palm *up*, moving the fingers in the American "come hither" manner. In some Islamic countries one doesn't wave to an acquaintance or try to hitch a ride with the left hand, which is reserved for such "dirty" actions as going to the toilet. Such left-handed signaling, then, is an insulting gesture. In the United States the oath in court to tell the truth is taken with the right hand elevated.

We can all call to mind dozens, perhaps hundreds, of specific gestures that are appropriate to our cultural backgrounds for occasions like greetings, departures, recognizing a friend, gaining the floor in a discussion (as in a class), saluting in the armed forces, indicating decisions while refereeing athletic events, indicating "O.K.," indicating "no good," directing traffic, signaling disapproval, and showing doubt, to name but a few. If you examine Illustration 8.4, you will find clear cases of in-awareness gestures.

In Illustration 8.4 the major gesture is the hand placement of the salesman. Another clear cue of his sincerity (real or feigned) is found in his eyes — directed straightforwardly into those of the customer. The set of his mouth and the drape of his shoulders are somewhat more subtle signals.

Such in-awareness gestures are only the tip of the large iceberg known as kinesics. There are culturally learned body movements, more subtle than these routine gestures, which we use systematiclly and continuously and which are understood by other members of the same culture, but which most of us could not define if asked. This is where most of the contemporary study of kinesics is directed, for it is widely assumed in the field of nonverbal communication that most if not all body movement by members of a culture is systematic and has significance for its users.

Illustration 8.4 "Trust me," the salesman seems to say. Bear in mind some cautions when interpreting this photo: it shows a mere fraction of a second of the action, it shows little context, it was not taken in the United States, and we have no information about the words being exchanged.

Ray Birdwhistell has said frequently that human beings are display boards, forever signaling silently as well as verbally, from head to toe. Birdwhistell (1970, p. 99) has suggested that in North American movement there are probably between fifty and sixty *kinemes* (specific movements with meaning). Of all the visual display areas of the body, the head is probably the most eloquent; Birdwhistell has isolated thirty-two kinemes of the head alone. Consider what can be "said" with the forehead, wrinkled or unwrinkled; the eyebrows, lifted, held steady, turned down; the eyes, shifting or not, nearly closed to slits or staring bug-eyed, fluttering, turned down; the nose, wrinkled, wiggling, twitching, unmoving; the mouth, smiling, laughing, frowning, grim-set, tight, loose; the cheeks, pulled in, loose and puffed out; the chin, firm-set and hanging loose; and so forth.

SHIFTS IN BODY COLOR

Shifts in body color (blushing, "draining color") that occur at moments of excitement, particularly at times of embarrassment or fear, are nonverbal signals, sometimes subtle, sometimes obvious. These changes are particularly visible in the head area, usually confined to the regions immediately around the eyes, cheeks, or ears but sometimes extending to the whole head and neck. While we normally think of shifts in color as signals only among whites, peoples of all pigmentation shift color, and to the person who is alert it is noticeable.

Medical doctors use skin color as an indicator of health. They often speak in general of a person's color being "good." There are also specific body locations—around the fingernails, for example—where color has particular meaning.

EYES (GAZE, OCULISICS)

Use of the eyes is a big enough subject to isolate for special consideration. We look at each other, or don't look at each other, for certain lengths of time, under certain circumstances, always in accordance with the unwritten rules of our culture, tempered by permissible personal idiosyncracies.

Eye contact or avoidance in the United States is a powerful indicator of degree of involvement in a social interaction. Although we scan our environment fairly continuously for quite practical reasons of seeing what we are about to bump into or who is coming our way, eye contact is also a major means of signaling relationships among people.

Generally speaking, in the United States we glance quickly at another person's eyes for two to three seconds to see if we recognize that person, to detect attitude, and to make a general assessment of the other person.

Prolonged eye contact—for ten seconds or more, say—is, as you can prove from a bit of careful observation, something that you do only in exceptional circumstances. Such longer periods of eye contact indicate increasing involvement. If love or friendship is blooming, it normally begins with quick exchanges of glances, followed by more frequent exchanges, followed by longer eyeball locking. Deep involvement of any sort—anger, love, awe— generally escalates to longer periods of eye contact. Lovers, particularly, stare benignly into each other's eyes without fear, as if hoping to see the inner essence of the beloved. Opposing athletes, not so benignly, may attempt to psych each other out with lengthy eye contact.

Erving Goffman, a contemporary sociologist, has called attention to a phenomenon that he has labeled "civil inattention," in which the eyes play a prominent role. It generally occurs in crowded public places, where we meticulously avoid eye contact with strangers. An excellent example is public elevators in the United States. What do you do with your eyes? Unless you know the other people, you avoid even momentary eye contact if possible, directing your eyes almost *any* other place but into theirs in order to avoid unwanted involvement. So you examine your fingernails, check your keys, stare at the ceiling, gaze at the numbers indicating the floors, look at your watch, or inspect your shoes. This unspoken rule can be broken by children in our culture, although at a certain age they must fall into line with adult behavior and accept the rule. Thus you may find children on an elevator staring you straight in the eyes. You, in return, can stare right back. As an adult you are likely to smile or to grimace in friendly fashion.

Another superb example of eyes signaling involvement can be seen in the classroom. Nearly every alert student in this culture knows that he or she should look at the teacher enough to indicate involvement in the class proceedings, whether honest involvement or not. Students also know that too much eye contact with the teacher can result in being called on to speak, and thus may turn away. On the other hand, turning away too abruptly or for too long a time may cause a suspicious teacher to call on the student. It is a very fine line to walk; some learn it better than others.

An interesting subcultural difference in eye contact can be noted right here on home ground, although researchers disagree about it. In the continental United States, among whites at least, there is an old expression, "Look me in the eye when you say that." Our mythology has it that a lie will be detected by "shifty" eyes. How many times have you heard in our Western movies, "Look me in the eyes when you say that, stranger"? How many times have you heard parents say it to their children?

In the Puerto Rican subculture in this country, however, children learn *not* to look into the eyes of those who are, in the opinion of the children, their superiors: teachers, priests, or other persons in positions of authority. For these Puerto Ricans, looking into the eyes of authority figures while speaking is a sign of *dis*respect. No problem occurs so long as the Puerto Rican is with other Puerto Ricans, but cross the border into white-land and the stateside

Illustration 8.5 Civil inattention. There is much more about communication shown here than simply the act of *not* looking at other riders in this subway car. For example, doesn't this photograph confirm the idea raised much earlier in the book that it is impossible not to communicate? These riders are carefully avoiding interaction, and, in so doing, are "saying": "We are keeping each other at a distance; we are maintaining privacy, not intruding." All behavior communicates something. (Photo: Lynn Forsdale)

teacher, for example, is likely to feel that the child who is not looking at him or her is showing disrespect. For the child, of course, it is equally traumatic, since he or she may not understand the source of the "trouble," for trouble it is likely to cause, even with people of good will on both sides.

EYE PUPIL SIZE (PUPILOMETRICS)

A specialized signaling system of the eyes is the size of the pupils, which vary in size not only according to the amount of light but also according to the reaction of the observer to what is seen, a discovery made by the psychologist Eckhard Hess.

The obvious factor that we normally associate with variation in pupil size is the amount of light present while we are viewing something. In bright sunlight, our pupils become smaller (constrict), allowing less light to pass through them. On the other hand, if you walk into a movie theater from the bright sunlight, you need to wait a bit for your pupils to expand (dilate), permitting maximum amounts of the dimmer light to pass through to the optic nerves. If you leave the theater and go again into the sunlight, you will instantly sense the brightness, which can be painful, requiring you to squint or even cover your eyes for a moment. Gradually the pupils of the eyes will become smaller, adjusting to the increased intensity of light.

But if the light level remains constant, pupil size is also an involuntary expression of interest in what we are viewing. For example, if a heterosexual man looks at a woman he finds attractive, the pupils of his eyes will widen or dilate. The woman may not be consciously aware of the increased size of the pupils, yet she may find the man more attractive because of his dilated pupils. Most people don't "read" this signal with any degree of awareness, although it is a skill that can be developed. There was a time when women put a drug—belladonna—in their eyes to dilate the pupils and make themselves more attractive.

One occupational test that uses this principle has been devised. The person who is seeking advice about what job really interests him or her looks through a device that shows slides of people at work in various tasks. An instrument shows variations in pupil size, thus giving clues as to which of the endeavors the subject is most interested in.

INTERPERSONAL SPACE (PROXEMICS)

We distance ourselves rather precisely from each other while speaking, and these distances are culturally determined. In the United States, our conversational distance (or our interpersonal distance) is about arm's length. People in some cultures stand much closer; others further apart. As with most communication traditions, violation of such a cultural habit can cause discomfort, even distress.

It can be amusing to watch two people who were raised in cultures with different impressions of proper distancing do their "spacing dance" in an attempt to arrive at mutually comfortable positions. North Americans and Spaniards provide a good example. A North American speaking to a Spaniard will want more space between them than will the Spaniard. So the Spaniard is likely to step a bit closer, causing the North American to move back a step. Finally, as often happens, the North American will be up against a wall, with no room to retreat further, feeling uncomfortable as the Spaniard "crowds" in. The Spaniard, meanwhile, will feel comfortable. Neither one of them is likely to know what the movement and discomfiture are all about.

Another way of saying this is that humans, like many other creatures, are territorial animals, insisting upon a certain amount of breathing space.

192 NONVERBAL COMMUNICATION

Illustration 8.6 Students cramming for a test. While this scene might be found in the United States (it wasn't), our desire for greater interpersonal space might invite us to arrange ourselves in a totally different way.

ENVIRONMENTAL COMMUNICATION

There has grown up in the last several years a field of study known as environmental psychology or environmental communication, which attempts to assess the interrelationship between people and their environments. This environmental approach considers space, sound, odors, decoration, lighting, color, and other people. Albert Mehrabian, a psychologist and respected scholar in the study of various aspects of nonverbal communication, writes:

> *When environmental psychologists talk of environments, they can mean a cocktail party, your apartment building, a park, the clothes on your back, a retirement community, or a kitchen. Anywhere you are, anything within sensory range, constitutes an environment which can be described accurately and succinctly. Certain guidelines have emerged . . . [that enabled people] to understand why some environments make them feel good or bad, excited or bored, tense or comfortable.* (1976, p. vii)

We cannot deal with all of Mehrabian's categories here. Let us concentrate briefly on certain characteristics of space.

Many of us have experienced in recent years the "open" school. In such schools the traditional classroom walls have been eliminated in favor of movable, low-height space dividers that permit flexibility in the working size of groups. Such schools have been greeted with mixed reactions. Some teachers and students find that they can't function well in an environment without the sight and acoustic barriers of customary cubicle classrooms. They find that they cannot screen out stimuli floating through the larger environment. Others soon learn how to screen out the unwanted sounds and sights and appreciate the ability to change their physical surroundings in a way appropriate to the task at hand. In some ways it is close to the situation faced by many people who cannot function well in a messy office or room. Others can.

We shape our buildings and they shape us.

Winston Churchill (quoted in Edward T. Hall, 1966, p. 100)

Architecture is a form of environmental communication, as noted in Chapter 7. Illustration 8.7, of the new East Building of the National Gallery of Art in Washington, D.C., depicts something of the philosophy behind the widely admired building:

In art museums we should be in the business of practicing what we preach, and we preach very strongly the sensitizing of our fellows to the best in our visual environment. . . . It seemed, that . . . we should have it reflect the best thinking of our time . . . (J. Carter Brown, 1978, p. 5)

Among the "best thinking of our time" is the use of contemporary materials—cement, metal, glass (in huge expanses), and an angularity partly dictated by materials and partly by site. The spacious central area shown in Illustration 8.7 communicates a feeling of openness to the world, spaciousness for crowds, and the incorporation of nature inside in the form of live plants.

A final example of messages associated with environment is related to scale or size. There are many meanings of size, of course: the prestige for some in having a big house rather than a little one; the shift in perception in recent years, because of the energy crisis, of the merits of a large automobile as contrasted with a small one; the preference for coziness at times; and the importance of human-dwarfing size in some places of worship. Illustration 8.8 shows an instance of spatial disorientation, for me at least, resulting from seeing something familiar in a scale so shifted from normal as to be staggering.

Illustration 8.7 This is the East Building of the National Gallery of Art in Washington, D.C., designed by the noted American architect I. M. Pei. Hanging from the ceiling near the center is a free-turning mobile by Alexander Calder, also speaking of our time.

Here is a huge chessboard, made of concrete, with giant chess pieces made of wood. As you see, the players stand to play. When I came upon this scene, I was enchanted at the idea. What an inventive notion! But, as I watched the game, I discovered that I had the greatest difficulty in assessing the desirabilty of the moves the players were making. After a few hours, I imagine one would get the needed new perspective of making sense of the game in its new scale.

BODY ORIENTATION

Another form of nonverbal communication is body orientation, or how bodies of participants are "pointed" or angled toward or away from each other. In so-called high face-to-face cultures (such as in Central Europe) participants in conversation, seated or standing, will in moments of great involvement point their bodies toward each other as much as possible.

You know from your own experience (if your native country is the United States, not a high face-to-face culture in the main) the entrapped feeling at a social gathering when confronted head-on by someone you would prefer not

> Man's feeling about being properly oriented in space runs deep. Such knowledge is ultimately linked to survival and sanity. To be disoriented in space is to be psychotic.
>
> Edward T. Hall (1966, p. 99)

to spend time with. In addition to using body parts, such as arms, to protect yourself (by folding them across your chest, for example), you will probably try your best to turn your body away, off at an angle from the straight-on, high-involvement confrontation. That, hopefully, will lead to full flight, an

Illustration 8.8 Spatial disorientation resulting from seeing something familiar in a radically altered scale. (There is another nonverbal component in this scene, although it cannot be recognized from the photo. The two players did not speak the same language. The young man with his hand on the black king was an Englishman traveling in a foreign country. His opponent spoke no English. They struck up the game through hand gestures, and of course the rules of chess are international.)

eventuality frequently aided by invented tasks elsewhere or manufactured new relationships immediately at hand or across the room.

Dozens of researchers have also investigated whether seating arrangements in a classroom (or library or home or meeting room) make a difference in patterns of interaction. Does sitting in a circle increase cooperative communication? The results are too complex and varied to report here, except to say that such spatial arrangements do indeed make a difference. References that can help you dig into this are listed at the end of the chapter.

POSTURE

Although posture can be subsumed under categories that have already been treated, I mention it separately here. It refers, of course, to the way one stands or sits—to the way one carries oneself. Within cultural norms, you can frequently "read" a good deal about a person through examination of his or her posture, particularly if you have seen the person enough to notice shifts in the hang of his or her body, in the person's dynamics of movement.

Reporter Flora Davis in *Inside Intuition* tells a story about Irmgard Bartenieff, one of the world's experts on body posture and movement:

> *We were behind a one-way screen one day and the sound broke down. We were watching a regular group therapy session and a new young woman came in, very well put together, very vivacious, and she started talking right away. For about fifteen minutes I watched and I got very frustrated. There was something strange in the woman's movement pattern but I couldn't put my finger on it—it seemed as if we didn't have the terms to describe it. And all the time Irmgard was writing away, and after a while she said, half to herself:*
>
> *"Very interesting. I've never seen anything like this before. This woman is very depressed."*
>
> *And I said:*
> *"Depressed? She's a dynamo."*
> *"Oh no. She's suicidal."*
>
> *A few minutes later the sound came on and we listened. And there was the woman talking about poisoning herself. It was really a spooky experience.* (1975, p. 171)

Posture sharing is one of very many interesting phenomena in nonverbal communication. Experts generally regard it as a means, generally unconscious, of getting in sync with another person. Illustration 8.9 shows two women, legs crossed similarly, echoing postures using arms in roughly the same way.

Illustration 8.9 Posture sharing.

Almost all communication, verbal and nonverbal, has *gender signals* embedded in it. Women use one style; men another. One example among many can be seen in a person's posture while seated. Most American women, unlike men, are trained to keep their legs rather close together when seated. (Wearing trousers gives American women greater leeway, of course.)

On the other hand, the woman shown in the full-length portrait in Illustration 8.10 positions her legs in a manner that may seem strange to many American eyes, even though her skirt is quite long. Gender postures vary with cultures.

RATE

Rate is a general term that refers to the speed with which any body signaling is done. Speech can be fast or slow; so can gestures; so can all body movements; so can shifts in posture. Within the culture's rules, the best use one can make of the notion of rate is to see shifts in a person's characteristic rate from time to time. The meaning? Clearly it can be any of several things: interest, lack of interest, tiredness, a burst of energy, anger. The context is all.

CLOTHING AND POSSESSIONS (OBJECTICS)

Our possessions—clothing, jewelry, vehicles, houses or apartments, books— also "say" something. They may speak their messages blatantly (neither a

Illustration 8.10 Gender postures vary with cultures. (Photo: Lynn Forsdale)

CLOTHING AND POSSESSIONS (OBJECTICS) 199

mink coat nor a pair of dirty, thoroughly patched blue jeans is very subtle), or they may whisper much more subtly (the mink coat can be synthetic and the patched blue jeans can be very expensive indeed).

Illustration 8.11 shows side-by-side photos of two women from different cultures. The photos were taken within a month of each other. The woman on the left is dressed in *chador*—the body-hiding garments required of traditional Moslems in some, but not all, Muslim countries. Had this woman known her picture was being taken she would probably have attempted to cover her face more, perhaps by placing the portion of the garment that is seen under her chin in her teeth, thus covering at least her chin. The woman on the right is

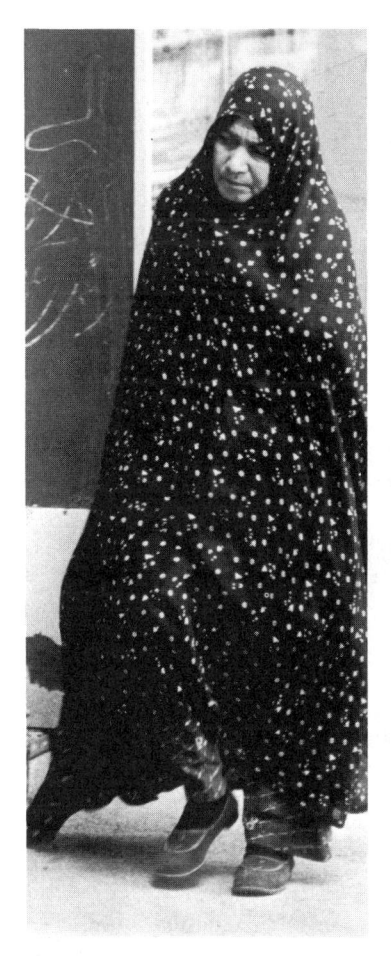

Illustration 8.11 Clothing and other personal artifacts in two cultures.

dressed in rather high style for the culture and the time. In addition to her clothing, notice her glasses, doubtless chosen with a thought to style, and the cigarette in her right hand. The manner in which she carries the cigarette follows cultural rules, as does everything else about her bearing and her display of objectics. There are probably social class differences, as well as cultural differences, between these two women. The photo of the woman at the left was taken in a rather run-down portion of one city; the woman at the right was spotted in a fashionable district of another city.

TIME (CHRONOMETRICS)

All creatures live in time in accordance with rhythms. Further, people, at least, are frequently aware of psychological time. That is, if there is objective time, which can be measured with varying degrees of accuracy by clocks, there is on the other hand our *feeling* about time, which makes it *seem to creep by slowly* or to race by. The latter is psychological time. If you are waiting for someone you want to see, the time can pass very slowly. It can also seem long, of course, if you are waiting for what you anticipate to be a bad scene.

Time is the most overlooked dimension in human nature. Astronomers know more about the timing of pulses [rhythms] from distant radio stars than we know about the pulses of our own bodies.

Gay Baer Luce (1971, p. 4)

Of course, different cultures have different rules about time. Edward T. Hall has called attention to cultural differences in expectations about time and how they can cause feelings of rejection and injustice if not understood, or, alas, even if understood. In his book *The Silent Language* (1959) Hall speaks, for example, of the difference between North American and Latin American expectations about meeting stated time commitments.

In North America we generally set appointments—except for parties, the time for which we often announce by the vague "sixish or so"—and expect participants to be there within minutes. Not being there is a sign of rudeness, regardless of the validity of reasons for missing the moment. A symptom of our deep interest in time is the growing presence in homes and public places in the United States of digital clocks that report time to the *tenth* of a second, as if these split seconds made practical differences in our ordinary lives. In most of Latin America, on the other hand, a meeting time of, say, 4 p.m. means "within an hour or so."

I learned a lesson about time in India a decade ago. I was in the city of Hyderabad, ill, dragging about listlessly, and worried because I was too sick to travel to Madras, where colleagues were expecting me to arrive by plane. Telephone lines were down, and would be for two or three days. I was in despair, worried about not being able to advise the Madras group of the shift in arrival time. Back at the hotel, a group of American colleagues, old hands in the East, took a different view of matters. They reminded me, with annoyance, that I was too sick to travel, so why didn't I just go to bed? And they told me about the flexible Indian sense of time. "Send the Madras people a letter. It'll be there in a week. Meanwhile, they'll notice that you're not on the plane tomorrow. It won't be the first time. They'll go home and wait. Happens all the time."

Most North Americans keep an eye on the clock, propelled by the need to "make good use" of every minute. We often attribute this to the Puritan ethic, which denigrates things that are merely entertaining, leisurely, or self-serving. But other cultures march to different rhythms. It seems, too, that many young people in the United States today—even those from white Puritan roots—are shifting their view of the importance of time. Or are they?

NONVERBAL COMMUNICATION AND WORDS

Quite frequently, perhaps generally, nonverbal signals are used with words. Certainly words are never spoken *without* nonverbal clues accompanying them. If you are in the presence of the speaker, you can learn to spot them. On the other hand, many nonverbal signals, being used more than words, appear alone.

When the two modes appear together, they normally tend to reinforce one another, that is, "say" the same thing. As noted earlier, this is not always the case, however, since mixed messages are frequently given, and when that happens one message is likely to be given verbally, the other nonverbally.

THIS CHAPTER IN PERSPECTIVE

We have seen in this chapter that nonverbal communication is important to all organisms, although various signaling systems are more appropriate to some species than to others. With people, it is damaging to think of nonverbal systems as totally separate from verbal systems, since the two are frequently linked closely together, even though nonverbal communication probably carries much more information between humans than does verbal communication. The nonverbal systems we have touched upon, but by no means exhausted, are touch (haptics or tacesics in technical jargon), odor (olfaction), body movement (kinesics), shifts in body color, use of the eyes (gaze or oculisics), eye pupil size (pupilometrics), interpersonal space and other spatial matters (proxemics), environmental communication, body orientation, posture, rate, clothing and possessions (objectics), and time (chronometrics). While this coverage has not exhausted the nonverbal means of communication, it has examined the major forms. We have also seen, as with all communication matters, that nonverbal signaling systems vary from culture to culture.

Insofar as I have been able to determine ... there are no body motions, facial expressions, or gestures which provoke *identical* responses the world over.

Ray Birdwhistell (1970, p. 34)

EXTENSIONS

Reading You Might Enjoy

1. Birdwhistell, Ray L. *Kinesics and Context: Essays on Body Motion Communication.* Philadelphia: University of Pennsylvania Press, 1970.

Birdwhistell is regarded as one of the half-dozen most important scholars in the field of kinesics in our time. Note that he deals in this book only with kinesics, not with the whole range of nonverbal signaling systems. This book is a collection of essays that were written at various times and drawn together in anthology form. Birdwhistell's work is not easy to read, but it is profoundly important.

2. Davis, Flora. *Inside Intuition: What We Know about Nonverbal Communication.* New York: New American Library (A Signet Book), 1975. (Hardcover edition printed by McGraw-Hill Book Company.)

This is a popular book, designed for the reader who knows nothing of the field and who wants a "friendlier" tone than the scholar is often able to provide. It is an excellent book, accurate in details and with wide coverage. The book is filled with anecdotes and quotations, and you learn the name and work of most of the important researchers in the field through a highly readable document. The book is not illustrated, a single drawback to an otherwise thoroughly engaging volume.

3. Ekman, Paul, and Wallace V. Friesen. *Unmasking the Face: A Guide to Recognizing Emotions from Facial Expressions.* Englewood Cliffs, N.J.: Prentice-Hall, 1975.

Ekman and Friesen deal here with the major display area of the body, the face. The face is dissected systematically to see how the various components, as well as the configuration of those components, contribute to facial kinesics. Although written by respected scholars, the work is designed for the nonspecialist. It is filled with photographs and useful exercises that enable you to try out your skill in "reading" faces. An interesting feature is a section on how to know what your own face is "saying."

4. Knapp, Mark L. *Nonverbal Communication in Human Interaction.* 2nd ed. New York: Holt, Rinehart and Winston, 1978.

This is perhaps the most widely used textbook on nonverbal communication in the United States today. It is a compact, highly systematic overview of the basic scholarship of the field. Knapp also places the study of nonverbal communication in its proper context as part of the larger scheme of human interaction. After completing this book you will know something of the work of major scholars in the field and of major positions and disputes.

5. Luce, Gay Baer. *Body Time: Physiological Rhythms and Social Stress.* New York: Pantheon Books, 1971.

This is a beautifully researched and written book for the reader who is not a scientist. Luce considers the various time (rhythm) problems that influence people, ranging from the day-by-day rhythms to those of a lifetime. In reporting the role of time in our lives, Luce pulls together hundreds of research studies in as painless a way as one can imagine.

6. Morris, Desmond. *Manwatching: A Field Guide to Human Behavior.* New York: Abrams, 1977.

In terms of layout (large format), number of photographs (470, including 290 in color), number of sketches, prints and diagrams (250), this is the most sumptuous of all books on nonverbal communication. Morris deals almost exclusively with visual "body language"—as contrasted, for example, with buildings, icons, and such other sensory modes as smell and taste. His terminology is different from that of many American researchers, but the field is young, so this ultimately is of little importance.

7. Sommer, Robert. *Personal Space: The Behavioral Basis of Design.* Englewood Cliffs, N.J.: Prentice-Hall, 1969.

Sommer is a psychologist who writes in this book about how space and the objects we put in space influence human behavior. He considers such topics as the effect on human behavior of the size and shape of buildings and rooms within buildings, of crowding, and of seating arrangements. In one large section of the book Sommer examines space and associated behavior in four different human-made environments: the mental hospital, the tavern, the college dormitory, and the school.

Ponderings and Projects

1. In comfortable surroundings, violate some of the conventions of eye contact that you know to be true of our culture. For example, in crowded public places such as elevators, buses, or subway cars, look people in the eye

for a longer time than is comfortable for you. Or, if that is difficult for you, "stare down" friends instead of strangers. You will learn a great deal about the duration of eye contact that is permissible.

2. Arrange your classroom, or a small group, so that limited eye contact is possible among students. One technique is simply to turn two rows of chairs back-to-back. Without eye contact, then, conduct a discussion and follow it with a further discussion of how participants felt without the nonverbal visual cues. Another similar technique is to address the class individually from behind a screen, thus blocking visual cues, and note differences in your feelings about the event.

3. Write a short story, perhaps related to espionage, in which something goes astray because one of the characters is not totally at home with the nonverbal ways of a culture.

The Medium Is the Message

9

In operational and practical fact, the medium is the message. This is merely to say that the personal and social consequences of any medium . . . are its meaning or message.

Marshall McLuhan

This is a chapter about the media of communication, but its approach may surprise you. Every reader of this text is aware in some measure of the role of media in the contemporary world, a growing role that was sketched in Chapter 3 when we scanned the history of media. Rather than call attention, then, to the size of audiences that are attracted to mass media or to the ethical, moral, and artistic integrity required in their use (supremely important though those matters are), we will go down another trail. It is a pathway not quite as worn, and it leads to a smashing vista.

All media of communication are extensions of the human body and its sensory apparatus. Radio and stereophonic equipment extend hearing across time and space, film extends sight, as does print. Because media are extensions of the body, they manipulate and change us. These manipulations alter the way we use our senses and therefore the manner in which we perceive ourselves, others, the environment, the culture—our total world. As different languages—calling back to mind the Sapir-Whorf hypothesis—change our world view and the way we think, so do *all* media. This appears to be true *regardless of the content of the media*. A movie-going generation may be as different from a reading generation as an English speaker is from a Hausa speaker.

We will explore that proposition, drawing examples from several forms of communication and from several scholars.

MARSHALL McLUHAN'S INSIGHT

A couple of decades ago a Canadian philosopher of communication, Marshall McLuhan, turned a phrase that focused attention on an aspect of media study that had not been examined with much care prior to that time. His phrase was "the medium is the message." Behind the phrase was a call for students of communication to pay less attention to the *content* of various media—radio, television, newspapers and magazines—and examine more intensely the *form* of the medium and how that form affects us as human beings.

Form, as used here, means how the various materials of the medium are used. Spoken language, for example, uses a system of sounds and a grammatical system. The medium of print uses marks on paper, generally arranged in neat rows to permit easy reading. Movies use pictures, music, sound effects, and language and are viewed in special settings. The telephone uses sound, but sound that is technically inferior to that of face-to-face conversation or a high-fidelity reproduction system, and in industrial societies telephones are everywhere.

The shocking proposition that McLuhan argued was, to paraphrase the statement introducing this chapter, that the nature of the medium—its form—is more influential in shaping our personal lives and social events than is its content. The telephone (to pick a medium arbitrarily) has changed our senses and our living arrangements more by its simple existence, its availability nearly everywhere, than has anything that we say on the telephone. To use an analogy, the invention of the wheel has changed our lives profoundly, a fact that is evident without concentrating on what we carry in the carts, automobiles, and trains made possible by the wheel.

McLuhan (and others) advocated the usefulness of looking at the media, then, without concern for content. It has been a difficult leap for many people, because for so long we have paid such overwhelming attention to the content of the medium that it seems somewhere between ridiculous and insane to change our habits radically and look at something from such a strange new perspective.

McLUHAN'S APPROACH IS LIKE THE APPROACH OF SAPIR AND WHORF

McLuhan's aphorism "the medium is the message" is very close to the Sapir-Whorf hypothesis discussed in Chapter 7. Sapir and Whorf said, basically, that the language you use shapes the way you see the world, and different languages, being different in form, shape people's vision of the world in different ways. McLuhan suggested that all important media in a culture do the same sort of shaping that language does. Like the Sapir-Whorf hypothesis, McLuhan's proposition is by no means universally accepted. Still, we cannot understand contemporary ways of thinking about communication without considering this influential idea.

One of the prime examples McLuhan uses to talk about this "contentless" approach to considering media is the light bulb. He writes:

This instance of the electric light may prove illuminating [McLuhan loves puns]. . . . *It is a medium without a message, as it were, unless it is used to spell out some verbal ad or name. This fact, characteristic of all media, means the "content" of any medium is always another medium. . . . Whether the light bulb is being used for brain surgery or night baseball is a matter of indifference in considering its versatility. . . . The electric light escapes attention as a communication medium just because it has no "content." And this makes it an invaluable instance of how people fail to study media. . . . The message of the electric light is like the message of electric power in industry, totally radical, pervasive, and decentralized. For the electric light and power are separate from their uses, yet they eliminate time and space factors in human association.* (1964, p. 8)

McLuhan believes, therefore, that every medium has influence separate from its content. This influence operates in several ways, among them:

☐ By altering social arrangements among people who use the medium or who are in the environment where the medium is used.
☐ By emphasizing certain human senses (sight, hearing, touch, taste, smell), or what he calls the "ratio among the senses."
☐ By causing consequent shifts in images of ourselves and of our roles in society.

The light bulb, to continue that image for a moment, turns night into day, and thus radically alters our behavior: factories can operate twenty-four hours a day, automobiles and airplanes travel around the clock, leisure activity of new kinds develop, warfare is altered, reading has increased to well beyond the time permitted by sun, candles, and oil lamps. In short, we would be hard pressed to name an aspect of modern life in our culture—and therefore of human arrangements and human sensibility—that has not been altered by the electric lamp and the flow of electricity behind it. You need only to reflect on the dramatic effects of power blackouts to make the influence leap out in bold outline.

ORAL AND PRINT CULTURES AGAIN

It is useful in grasping McLuhan's view to remember that with respect to communication there are two general kinds of cultures in the world, as we have seen in Chapter 3: *oral cultures* and *print cultures*. As noted earlier, oral cultures (sometimes called preliterate) are those in which the written or printed word is not yet in use. There are pockets of oral cultures in such areas as Africa, Asia, South America, and Indonesia, all rapidly disappearing. Information is passed along orally, by word of mouth, the older people telling the young ones the facts they need to know, the old legends, the stories. And, from generation to generation, these things are passed along to the young, often with astonishing displays of memory.

When print with movable type was invented (in the West), by Gutenberg and others, over five hundred years ago, very, very few people could read. Included among nonreaders, even in technologically advanced societies, were many nobles, merchants, and other rich people, although the larger reading disability fell to peasants. Only a comparatively few manuscripts were produced by hand, by scribes, and they tended to be religious documents, some collections of sayings, and some works on science. They were also difficult to read, even for the literate, because what the scribes wrote was not easily legible. Manuscripts were generally read aloud, as a matter of fact, the syllables being mouthed for clarity. There were often reading booths, not unlike our telephone booths, available to permit this babble to go on.

Even after print with movable type was perfected, after the scribes began to lose their jobs, it took a good hundred years or more before people at large began to pay much attention to print. The population as a whole hadn't paid much attention before to manuscripts. They didn't pay much attention to the new "mechanized manuscripts" either. But gradually the new medium of print began to have its effects.

SOME EFFECTS OF MECHANIZED PRINT

In considering some of the possible effects of print on society at large and on individuals, please recall that McLuhan and others are speculating. It would be extremely difficult to *prove* the following propositions to the satisfaction of everyone.

McLuhan suggests that print with movable type has had, among others, the following effects.

Increase in the Importance of Privacy and of Individualism

Generally speaking, oral cultures do not have the same feeling about privacy that print cultures do. The extreme sanctity of the individual, certainly a sister to privacy, may also be an idea developed through the relationship of the reader and the page of reading material in which the reader is engrossed.

Part of the thinking behind this idea comes from the proposition that manuscripts (those written individually by scribes) were read aloud, as noted, while the printed page could be skimmed rapidly and silently. This silent form of reading *required* privacy, but a privacy of a different sort from that needed by the manuscript reader in his or her booth, or wandering about the halls of a monastery intoning material aloud. The reader had a new and special relationship with the author. The individual, whose individualism has defiantly grown over the years, was born behind the printed page. With few exceptions, reading is not a group activity.

The time may come when our descendants will look back on the strong feelings of individuality we have today and wonder how people could be so obsessed by themselves.

Emphasis on the Visual

McLuhan also believes that the major media of communication in any given society tend to emphasize certain of the human senses at the expense of others. Print obviously emphasizes the eyes. He extends that observation further by suggesting that if we read enough, from childhood on, day after day, whether we do it well or not, we may learn to perceive the world principally with our eyes, following the habits of reading. (The word *perceive* is used to include possible impressions or inputs through *all* senses.) If you spend thousands of hours of your lifetime looking at printed pages, whether you like to do it or not, and when everybody around you has his or her nose in a paper, magazine, or book, when you raise your head to take in the rest of the world, you are likely to do so primarily with your eyes—not with your ears or your fingertips.

McLuhan and Fiore write:

> *The dominant organ of sensory and social orientation in pre-alphabet societies was the ear—"hearing was believing." The phonetic alphabet forced the magic world of the eye. Man was given an eye for an ear.... The rational man in our Western culture is a visual man.* (1967, p. 44)

Lineal Thought Habits

Further, reading may teach particular habits of thought, namely, the so-called *lineal* habits. In print, of whatever language, of whatever content, words follow each other, like soldiers marching in single file, one after the other.

(Right now, with your eyes only semi-focused, look at the orderly rows of words, line after line, on this page.) Spending enough time attending to those words on pages in their impeccable files may lead us, subtly and without awareness, to believe that the world around us is constructed that way, too. As McLuhan puts it, "the . . . lineal patterns of the printed page strongly disposed people to transfer such approaches to all kinds of problems" (1962, p. 51).

In point of fact, of course, the world is not built like a book, with pieces put together in lineal fashion like sentences. It is not nearly that neat.

So here are three generalizations about possible effects of mechanized print, quite without respect to content: (1) it may increase the importance of privacy and individualism, (2) it may emphasize our belief in the visual, (3) it may develop lineal thought habits.

Now, switch back to oral cultures, those not dominated by print but rather by spoken words. While there are not many cultures left today that have not been touched by print in some sense, there are many that aren't influenced by print as heavily as we are in North America. And there are still *some* people on this planet who never in their lives have seen a word on a piece of paper. In fact, some of those preliterate peoples are now in the process of skipping the whole stage of literacy, moving from purely oral cultures to cultures dominated by radio, television, film, photography. Then they may return someday to emphasize print. That would be a fascinating turn of events to observe. But that is a different story.

Because oral cultures spend little or no time studying print, McLuhan and others suggest that they do not have the intense need to seek privacy and do not feel militantly individualistic, as do people who concentrate on reading. Thus to many such people the extreme degree of privacy that we often seek is foreign. People in oral cultures apparently enjoy group space much more than you and I are able to. Storytellers are defeated by isolation.

Another result of growing up almost solely with the spoken word is the possibility of perceiving the world quite differently from the way we do. If they are more ear-oriented than eye-oriented, then they may perceive the world more by ear than by eye. Or they may tend to use all senses more than we do. Blind individuals learn to perceive the world with more senses than most of us do.

THE "EYE WORLD" AND THE "EAR WORLD"

Consider how the eye and the ear tune in on the world. The eyes tend to see in an angle out front. While looking we may be aware, vaguely, of what is happening off to the side or at our backs, but we generally must turn our heads to prove to ourselves what we believe may be the case. The eyes are bound by biological blinders.

If you are more tuned to your ears because you come from an oral culture, your world may not be quite so severely bound by that restricting cone of vision. In fact, because one hears from all around—in front, above, to the sides, behind—one is tuned hemispherically to the world. We might be tuned *spherically* except that the earth is below us and forms an omnipresent base so that the oral person is in a hemisphere, a dome. The ear-oriented person, tuned hemispherically, may be extraordinarily sensitive, then, to things happening all around. Eskimos, many of whom are preliterate, are said by some anthropologists to be so aurally sensitive that, in their kayaks, unable to see the shoreline because of fog or darkness, they can nevertheless make quite accurate maps of the shoreline, with its indentations, its juttings out, its irregularities, by evidence of their ears. (Their eyes are frequently less useful because of the long dark artic nights and because of their need to wear protective glasses during the long periods of snow. They could suffer severe snow blindness otherwise.) Their world must be quite different from ours. To be aware, equally, of what is happening to one all around, as encased in a dome, must be an incredible experience.

So there are the two extremes—the oral world and the print world. Today, the print world frequently is filled with other media, too: radio, film, telephone, television. Because of that, although we are still essentially print-oriented, we may be recovering, gradually, many of the qualities of the oral world. The argument behind this thought is that the new media speed up the flow of information to more of our senses and reduce the lineal thought patterns hidden so seductively in the form of print.

THE GLOBAL VILLAGE

As electronic media inexorably surround the globe, particularly with more and more communication satellites in orbit, they act increasingly as a kind of external nervous system around the globe (using McLuhan's term), keeping everybody instantly informed of everything happening everywhere. The main results, again not thinking in terms of content, will be the accelerated flow of information—any kind of information. McLuhan refers to this as living in a global village, akin to the village in an oral culture.

Today, after more than a century of electric technology, we have extended our central nervous system itself in a global embrace, abolishing both space and time as far as our planet is concerned.

Marshall McLuhan (1964, p. 3)

Illustration 9.1 The ubiquitous telephone helps create the global village.

McLuhan's provocative invitation to think of the medium itself as a major force in shaping the way we relate to each other and the manner in which our senses are used—entirely without respect to the content of the medium—has already become a significant approach to the study of communication. It will probably become even more important in years to come.

SHIFTING MEDIA CHANGE PEOPLE

Whether or not we are moving back (or forward?) to an oral culture because of accelerated information flow, there is no question that shifting balances of media are profoundly disruptive to any culture into which they are introduced. They turn things upside down, far more than most people yet realize. We should consider that further.

> The major advances in civilization are processes that all but wreck the societies in which they occur.
>
> A. N. Whitehead (quoted in Marshall McLuhan and Quentin Fiore, 1967, pp. 6-7)

HUMAN-MACHINE COMMUNICATION SYSTEMS

Our shifting communication environment heavily involves machines, always as extensions of the human body. The technology is likely to increase, not diminish, for that is the general history of our relationship with gadgets. Restlessly we develop new communication technology as if fulfilling a preordained destiny. If we do not transform ourselves literally into cyborgs (combinations of human and machine: a person with a heart pacemaker embedded permanently in the body, for example), we can nevertheless look forward to an ever more intimate relationship between our communication technology and ourselves.

For example, as I sit in my study, I merely look around to confirm this human-machine relationship. Across from me is a portable cassette tape recorder. Beside it sits a compact television set. Nearby in an aluminum case is my still photo equipment: two camera bodies and a variety of lenses, filters, flash equipment, and associated gadgetry. A digital clock, constructed from a kit, sits on a filing cabinet. A Super 8mm motion picture projector is ten feet away on the floor. Near at hand is a pocket-sized transistor radio. A telephone sits at the ready six steps away. I am typing this manuscript on a portable electric machine, having long since lost the facility to write easily by hand. A hand calculator is ready to help compensate for the arithmetic skills that I never learned well in the first place. Loaded bookcases line the walls. A cork bulletin board is thick with notices in layers, making me resent Gutenberg's ingenuity. Filing cabinets are pregnant with material that can be located about a third of the time, luck prevailing. In adjoining rooms are a good stereo system and an antique manual typewriter. Bookcases line more walls. The kitchen can be converted into a darkroom in ten minutes.

There is something in the structure of the human animal which compels him to produce superfluously.

Norman O. Brown (1959, p. 256)

In addition to photographs and paintings, some of the walls are decorated with the still-inept computer graphics that I've been struggling to produce.

I feel ambivalent about being part of this human-machine system. On the one hand, I enjoy these adult tinker toys, and it can be argued they are necessary for a teacher of communication. On the other hand, I sometimes yearn for a simpler life, for the wilderness area that I spoke of in the Introduction.

And, just as Socrates was afraid of the effects of writing in that first revolution in communication discussed in Chapter 3, we should probably

Illustration 9.2 A contemporary composer, Laurie Spiegel, creating music with electronic equipment.

view with wariness, as well as with great expectation, effects of the exploding human-machine union in the field of communication.

PEOPLE CAN GET LOST IN HUMAN-MACHINE SYSTEMS

A basic problem that some observers find in human-machine systems is that we are likely to forget the respective functions of humans and machines. A good way of making this point sharply is to draw upon a controversial book, *Computer Power and Human Reason*, by computer scientist Joseph Weizenbaum, particularly so since computers represent far and away the most sophisticated machinery that we have yet developed.

Consider first a passage from Weizenbaum telling, amusingly, of the compulsive programmer, sometimes known as the "computer bum."

> Wherever computer centers have become established, that is to say, in countless places in the United States, as well as in virtually all

other industrial regions of the world, bright young men of disheveled appearance, often with sunken glowing eyes, can be seen sitting at computer consoles, their arms tensed and waiting to fire their fingers, already poised, to strike at the buttons and keys on which their attention seems to be as riveted as a gambler's on the rolling dice. When not so transfixed, they often sit at tables strewn with computer printouts over which they pore like possessed students of a cabalistic text. They work until they nearly drop, twenty, thirty hours at a time. Their food, if they arrange it, is brought to them: coffee, Cokes, sandwiches. If possible, they sleep on cots near the computer. But only for a few hours—then back to the console or the printouts. Their rumpled clothes, their unwashed and unshaven faces, and their uncombed hair all testify that they are oblivious to their bodies and to the world in which they move. They exist, at least when so engaged, only through and for the computers. These are computer bums, compulsive programmers. They are an international phenomenon. (1976, p. 116)

Weizenbaum's description also reminds me vaguely of the scene of my study I've just described. It calls forth some other memories and observations: my own youth, hunched down in rhapsody hour after hour in movie theatres, staring red-eyed at variations of the same style of cowboy show; city kids today strutting the streets, lugging radios and tape playback machines so that they won't be separated from that sound "out there"; old and young people hypnotized from dusk to dawn by television's scanning trace of light (hypnotism literally involves extreme concentration of a single sense); old and young gabbing voraciously on the telephone; photo darkroom technicians struggling hopefully in the half-light to bring out the proper shading in a print; eager but exhausted authors drumming at the typewriter keyboard, awaiting the right "inspiration"; young people transported by the sound of records blaring; older people transfixed at the sound of *their* records; people of all sizes, shapes, and ages glued to books, magazines, and newspapers as if their salvation depended on finishing, or scanning, the products before them. (Print, remember, is a product of technology, although many people seldom think of that.)

But back to Weizenbaum and computers, far and away the most complicated communicating machine we have yet made.

Weizenbaum is deeply disturbed about the assumptions some learned people have made about computers. Years ago he developed a computer program called ELIZA, which was akin to a certain style of psychotherapeutic counseling.

The program was made specifically to illustrate how easily one could communicate with a computer in natural English. He also wanted to poke fun at the thought that a computer could replace a human psychological counselor. But he was soon shocked by the unexpected fame that he and his program received. ELIZA was acclaimed by a number of psychiatrists, as well as by his colleagues in computer science. This was a totally unexpected reaction. Weizenbaum did not, to repeat, believe that the computer could replace psychiatrists, yet optimistic predictions were made that it soon would. And when his secretary first asked him to leave the room while she was at the computer terminal with her "psychiatrist," Weizenbaum realized how badly misinterpreted his intentions had become.

The role of the machine in relation to people was not understood in this case. Still, it never has been fully understood and may never be. The message for us is important. We should probably assume, with McLuhan, that all our communication tools inevitably change our lives and that we had better be alert to the kinds of changes coming about. Some of the changes we can resist if we wish; others we may be able to do little about, except when possible to comprehend what is happening to us. And other changes we have no reason to resist. We should glory in many: they offer pleasure, information, new art forms. But, like highly processed and packaged food, they can so alter our communication intake as to alter the nutrient value of more human interchange.

A COUNTERVIEW

If Weizenbaum and others argue that no machine can ever take over all of the functions of which a human being is capable, there are, of course, other views in the controversy. One is stated with sharp clarity by George A. Miller, a noted American psychologist:

> It is quite clear that man is a miserable component in a communication system. He has a narrow band-width, a high noise level, is expensive to maintain, and sleeps eight hours out of every twenty-four. Even though we can't eliminate him completely, it is certainly a wise practice to replace him whenever we can. The kind of routine jobs that men like least are just the kind that machines do best. Our society has already made the first steps toward eliminating human bottlenecks from communication systems, and the years ahead are sure to bring more. (1975, p. 50)

It will not be astonishing, perhaps not even sad, to see parts of our role in the communication process reduced or shifted. Gutenberg, after all, reduced the role of the scribes; the telegraph eliminated the Pony Express. But Miller and others who agree with his position are talking about a bigger game; it is a game that Weizenbaum fears. And we will not resolve the argument here.

Illustration 9.3 New media of communication profoundly alter societies into which they are introduced. The outlook of these two men (and other villagers where they live) is dramatically different from that of their parents, who did not have a radio, the new "ear on the world." The chances are high that these men are illiterate, yet they are increasingly part of McLuhan's global village. In this village radios can receive four or five stations, which program mainly music and news. Everybody in the village wants a radio; a fine radio is a status symbol. People save for long periods of time to buy one. (Photo: Lynn Forsdale)

But on this we can probably agree totally: Media as extensions do change us. They totally change our communication world, and in the process, each of us. They are not neutral.

Of all the changes in what has come to be called the quality of life, none has had a larger direct impact on human consciousness and social behavior than the rise of communication technology.

George Gerbner (1972, p. 153)

FINAL THOUGHTS ON OUR COMMUNICATION EXTENSIONS

We have been pondering the role of communication sources that extend our bodies. To keep matters in perspective, it is important to recall that such extensions are really nothing new. The first stylus gouging marks into a clay surface was a system of extending human communication. The problem, if there is one, is that the devices have multiplied to the point where we may literally confuse their functions with our roles as the creators and users.

Edward T. Hall, the anthropologist whose name has appeared many times in this book, puts the point eloquently. On the one hand:

> [*An*] *important feature of extensions is that they make possible the sharing of human talents that could be accomplished in no other way.... every time a viewer turns on his TV set, he shares the creative talents of hundreds of other minds.* (1976, pp. 37-38)

One of the attributes of a television society is an historically unprecedented sharing of the same experience. The only comparable sharing prior to television are religious and patriotic rites.

George Comstock (1978, p. 19)

On the other hand:

> *Man has dominated the earth because his extensions have evolved so fast that there is nothing to stand in their way. The risk, of course, is that by enormously multiplying his power, man is in the position of being able to destroy his biotope — that part of the environment that*

contains within it the basic elements for satisfying human needs. Unfortunately, because they do have a life of their own, extensions have a way of taking over. The mathematical genius Norbert Weiner in his book God and Golem, Inc. [*much like Weizenbaum's work*] *shortly before he died, saw the danger of his brain child, the computer, and warned against letting it play too prominent a role in human affairs. The automobile is another mechanical system that has so many people and so much of the American economy dependent upon it that it is difficult to see, short of catastrophe, any possibility of reversing the take-over trend. Everything has fallen to the automobile—the livability of cities, the countryside, clean air, healthy bodies, etc.*

Extensions fragment life and dissociate man from his acts. This is serious. Modern warfare is a dreadful example of how mechanical systems can be used to kill at a distance without any involvement in the process. It is so easy for a president to say, "Drop more bombs, and that will bring them in line." (1976, p. 38)

In short, we suffer the danger of losing touch, almost literally, with ourselves and our fellow riders on Spaceship Earth, because of our ingenious, fascinating, informative, beguiling extensions.

Yet, the danger of losing touch with our humanity because of our interest in the machines that extend us is only one view of the message of those extensions. Two more positive observations by that gifted medical doctor and writer, Lewis Thomas, may apply as well.

One message of the extensions with which we try to connect ourselves with all the outposts of the world—yes, even the universe—is that we need to try for the connections, bumble as we may, because, as Thomas puts it:

We are by all odds the most persistently and obsessively social of all species, more dependent on each other than the famous social insects, and really, when you look at us, infinitely more imaginative and deft at social living. (1979, p. 17)

Thomas implies a second reason for connecting as many parts of the earth as we can:

It seems to me a good guess, hazarded by a good many people who have thought about it, that we may be engaged in the formation of something like a mind for the life of this planet. (1979, p. 18)

This latter view, highly speculative and somewhat mystical, follows from Thomas's view that the earth is a living organism, a coherent system, with every component connected to every other component. Human beings may be scurrying about developing the communication network—to use my term, not Thomas's—that is essential to the operation of a mind for that system.

So we are in a quandary. We will doubtless continue to proliferate our communication extensions. They may alienate us from ourselves and others, or they may bring us closer. Being on the alert is the key. We must observe as skillfully as possible what is happening, preserving the best, resisting the worst. Chapter 11 will suggest ways of being on the alert, that is, of being continuous observers of communication in action.

Every technological advance contains within itself a monster, for each one expresses in one form or another man's monstrous narcissism as well as the simple desires of which it appears superficially to be an expression.

Philip Slater (1974, p. 12)

THIS CHAPTER IN PERSPECTIVE

We have observed that all media of communication are extensions of ourselves. Communication instruments extend our senses across time and space, and in so doing they alter us individually and collectively. Although we are particularly fond of pondering the content of media of communication, this is not the only way of looking at them. Marshall McLuhan and others suggest that we should consider how the media, by their very form, change our senses and our arrangements for living with each other, regardless of what content they carry. Thus print makes vision our most important sense, places a high value on isolation, and is congenial to habits of lineal thinking. Film, while it also maximizes the importance of vision, places a greater value on coming together in tribal fashion in the ceremony of viewing and may induct us gradually into a style of thinking that is more congenial to camera movement and editing flexibility. There is danger in our enchantment with communication technology, because we may conceive of the instruments as the highest product of which we are capable, thus losing sight of something more basic in our humanity. On the other hand, pushing the communication technology as far as we can, creating a global village, may be as high a mission as we can fulfill.

EXTENSIONS

Reading You Might Enjoy

1. Kozinski, Jerzy. *Being There*. New York: Harcourt Brace Jovanovich, 1970.

This short novel is a brilliant exploration of the influence of media. In the novel, a man named Chance is orphaned at an early age and grows up in a mansion owned by an eccentric man. Chance never leaves the house and its garden. As he grows older, he becomes gardener for the mansion owner, but still never sees the world behind the high garden walls. He never learns to read or write. His only association with the outside world is television. When the owner of the mansion dies, Chance is forced into the outside world with no knowledge of it except the limited and romanticized knowledge that comes from television. His sensibilities have been shaped by that medium alone. As you can imagine, he has an interesting time "out there," since television is not the world. You may have seen the film based on the book.

2. McLuhan, Marshall. *Understanding Media: The Extensions of Man.* New York: McGraw-Hill, 1964.

This is the book in which McLuhan first developed systematically his ideas about how media influence our sensibilities and our social arrangements. Of the many books McLuhan has written, this is the one that has been most influential in turning attention to "the medium is the message."

3. McLuhan, Marshall, and Quentin Fiore. *The Medium Is the Massage: An Inventory of Effects.* New York: Bantam Books, 1967.

This is a more popularized account of much of the material found in *Understanding Media*. It is highly illustrated and is laid out with great attention to graphics that you should find interesting.

4. Winn, Marie. *The Plug-In Drug: Television, Children, and the Family.* New York: Viking, 1976.

This readable, controversial book is McLuhanesque in the sense that Winn is concerned not with the content of television programs in the United States but rather with the personal and social effects of the medium on children and families. The title suggests Winn's thesis succinctly: Television is like a drug that sedates the young and acts as a pernicious baby-sitter. She is largely speculative in approach.

5. Weizenbaum, Joseph. *Computer Power and Human Reason: From Judgment to Calculation.* San Francisco: W. H. Freeman, 1976.

As you will recall from the chapter, this book is about the uses and misuses of computers. In a sense, Weizenbaum asks the question, "What is the message of computers?" Some of the book is very technical, but it is not necessary to understand those sections to make sense of the rest of the book.

Ponderings and Projects

1. When television first became widespread in the United States in the 1950s, many thoughtful people predicted that it would bring the family closer together. The logic was that everybody in the family would probably watch programs together. In point of fact, however, television probably hasn't done much to bring the American family together. Rather, it may have fragmented the family still further. Do you agree? Why? If you agree, what do you think went wrong with the prediction?

2. The coming of television was also seen by professionals as a profound challenge to both radio and movies. Yet there are more radio stations in this country today than there were when television came. What happened? How was the challenge of television met by radio station owners? (The answer is that the nature of radio programming changed in basic ways. What were those ways?) Filmmakers also responded, principally by using certain technical innovations and introducing new subject matter. What were some of those innovations and shifts in subject matter?

3. Today electronic hand calculators may be in almost every American home, perhaps even in most schools. Is there any evidence yet about how those calculators are shifting personal attitudes and skills toward the study of mathematics? Can you think of any implications as well for social arrangements?

4. One of the most exciting communication developments of our time is interactive cable television. The key word is "interactive." If you aren't familiar with it now, investigate the subject. Your life is likely to be changed dramatically in the next few years by the phenomenon represented in the three words "interactive cable television."

Other Creatures Communicate

10

There is a popular notion . . . that the crucial event which primevally separated humanity from the rest of the animal kingdom, was the discovery of speech. The result being a persistent delusion that somehow all other creatures are, well, dumb. That they are missing something. And that this something gives humans the obvious edge over all other living things.

Christopher Andreae

Most of this book has dealt with communication among humans, although frequent references have reminded us that you and I have no monopoly on that activity. This chapter will make the point that all other species on the planet also communicate, some using quite elaborate communication systems. Some of the attempts at cross-species communication will be described. The chapter will leave unanswered the question of whether we are supreme in the animal kingdom—as is widely assumed—because of our ability to use language better than any other species. Why will the question be unanswered? Because nobody knows the answer. Some of the questions posed here and some of the opinions given, however, are as interesting as the "ultimate" answers that we will one day learn.

ALL SPECIES COMMUNICATE

There may be no more exciting aspect of communication today than the study of communication by creatures other than humans and the possibility of humans communicating with other creatures. We appear to be on the threshold of some important discoveries. Whether they will alter drastically long-held assumptions about differences between people and other creatures remains to be seen. At the very least, however, readjustments in thinking are being made.

During the past thirty years we have been repeatedly surprised by discoveries about animal behavior, especially in the area of orientation [in space] and communication.

Donald R. Griffin (1977, p. 26)

There is no question that creatures other than humans communicate, by almost any definition of that term. Dogs romp and play or engage in angry battle, wolves run in coordinated packs, deer send out scent signals indicating sexual interest, whales transmit elaborate songs over great distances, dolphins use a variety of noises to which other dolphins respond, bees dance, touch, and use odor to show the distance and location of food, and so forth. All of these actions require communication. Further, as biologist Donald R. Griffin points out:

Almost every sensory system is employed by some species of animals for communication. . . . Chemical signals . . . are ordinarily detected by the olfactory system and are especially important in insects, flying phlangers, rodents, cats, and monkeys. . . . Sounds are extensively used by many groups of invertebrates, as well as by all classes of vertebrate animals. . . . Surface waves are used by aquatic insects. . . . Tactile communication includes not only direct contact between animals, but communication via vibrations of the ground or vegetation. Leaf-cutter ants stridulate [create a shrill grating sound] when acidentally buried, and other members of the colony locate them by vibrations transmitted through the soil. . . . In certain spiders, the male begins his courtship by setting the female's webs into a particular pattern of vibrations. Many groups of fishes that use electrical orientation . . . also communicate by electrical signaling. . . . Communication by visual signals is widespread. . . . An especially striking example is the courtship of certain fireflies, which exchange light flashes signaling sexual readiness. . . . But visual signaling has not been studied as extensively as has acoustical communication, primarily because it is technically more difficult to record and play back visual signals. (1976, p. 16)

That is quite an array of signaling techniques and is by no means a full account.

INTRASPECIES COMMUNICATION

These have been examples of intraspecies communication, that is, communication among members of the same species: whales to whales, dogs to dogs, bees to bees, fish to fish. Most of this book so far has been devoted to another form of intraspecies communication, that among *Homo sapiens*—people.

There is a very old and widely held idea in the communication field (and in biology, ethology, philosophy, religion, and many other disciplines) that no other species comes close to humans in the refinement of their communication system. Indeed, as the quotation at the beginning of this chapter suggests, the use of language has been thought to be the single most important quality that sets humans apart from other creatures. This is sometimes referred to as the *discontinuity* theory, meaning that there is not an unbroken flow of communication development (the *continuity* theory) from "lower" creatures to *Homo sapiens*, but that somewhere along the line in evolutionary development, humans made a big leap forward in language development, leaving our nearest biological neighbors far behind, on the other side of a great gap much too wide to bridge. Let's call this the Great Gap theory. The Great Gap theory is now under fire from many quarters, although it still overwhelmingly dominates most scientific thinking. Although the communication methods of dozens of animals, fish, insects, and other organisms have been described, in some detail at least, and always from *our* point of view, very few researchers have suggested that other creatures command communication techniques as powerful as ours, shaky though ours frequently appear to be.

INTERSPECIES COMMUNICATION

Much work is also being done now on the question of whether one species can learn to communicate with another. From our point of view, the big question is whether humans can learn to communicate in a sophisticated way with such animals as chimpanzees, apes, and dolphins. The key word is "sophisticated." We have all experienced communication with dogs and cats, at least at the level of ordering a dog to heel or scolding a cat for clawing at the furniture. Many of us have had pets with whom we have established strong mutual ties through speech, touch, body movement, and other signals. But has anybody ever seriously discussed, in a two-way process, the state of the world with a member of another species? Some researchers feel that we *may* be near the day when that can happen.

> Now that we have seen how similar we are to other animals we must wonder whether communications will soon be established. No human has ever analyzed, or really ever *known*, the thoughts of a cliff swallow, so there is no way of knowing whether the swallow might also feel that it was made in the image of the creative force. But a future communication might well reveal that the cliff swallow feels it is unique, blessed with the image of the creator, and so must take care of the human.
>
> John Janovy, Jr. (1978, p. 208)

The possibility of interspecies communication at a high level is not a new thought to writers of fiction, nor should the intuition of such artists be dismissed. Among modern authors, Robert Merle, in his book *Day of the Dolphin* (1969), later made into a motion picture (1974), told a tale in which dolphin researchers established a highly developed communication system with those intelligent mammals. Both book and film end sadly when the communication is turned to evil uses by a group of human beings.

Pierre Boulle, in his novel *Planet of the Apes* (1964) and in the subsequent motion pictures in that series, used a neat reversal in which humans became subordinate creatures in a world dominated by apes. There was an excellent example of cross-species communication—the English language and non-verbal communication—in operation, but the major point, adventure aside, was the ethical one of what it would be like if you and I were dominated by another species. We've spent a lot of time dominating other species.

But these are both works of science fiction. Even though science fiction frequently points the way long before science and technology catch up with it, let us turn now to what is known in a scientific way both about intraspecies communication among other creatures and about attempts at interspecies communication. The focus will be on two examples—honeybees as the intraspecies case and chimpanzees and humans as the interspecies case, with a passing note about apes and dolphins. These choices are not intended to imply that other important work has not been done. On the contrary, there are hundreds of studies of intraspecies communication and dozens of studies of interspecies communication.

COMMUNICATION AMONG HONEYBEES: AN IMPORTANT DISCOVERY

One of the most influential studies of communication among members of another species is the pioneer work in the 1920s and 1940s of biologist Karl von

Frisch, who studied honeybees. While working with bees, von Frisch observed that a scout bee would find a source of food and come back to the hive, after which time other bees would fly unerringly to the same food found by the original scout. And what's more, the new group of bees was not physically *led* to the food by the original scout bee. So, von Frisch concluded, the scout bee had communicated information to her sister bees (for it is the female honeybees that do all of this) in some fashion. But how? What was the means of communication?

Von Frisch discovered the answer in an ingenious series of experiments described in his book *Dancing Bees* (1953). He first constructed a hive that would permit him to observe the bees' behavior. Then he set up a source of food and placed a spot of color on the bee that had found that source and would soon head back to the hive carrying the good news. The color spot was necessary to permit observation of that crucial bee—the scout—on her return to the swarming mass in the hive.

The Bees' Basic System: Dance

Von Frisch's careful observations finally led him to the astonishing discovery that the scout bee communicated information about the presence of the food and about the distance and direction of the food from the hive partly by means of scent and partly by means of a dance! Scent carried on the scout bee's hairy body indicated the kind of flower the other bees needed to search for, while distance and direction were indicated by the dance, which was detected in the dark hive largely by touch.

The dance takes the form of a figure 8, with the scout bee repeating the movement time and again. If you study Illustration 10.1 you will see that the bee continually returns to the center line of the figure 8 after performing clockwise and counterclockwise "round dances" on either side of the center line. If the scout bee performs the dance on a flat surface, outside the hive, the direction of the center line in the figure 8 points directly toward the food supply. If performed inside the hive, vertically and in darkness or semidarkness, the center line is executed so as to point to the position of the food with respect to the sun at that moment. If, for example, the direction of the food is 20 degrees to the right of the sun (as in the diagram), the scout bee will dance that center line at a 20-degree angle from the vertical. Even on an overcast day, the bees know the position of the sun and can execute the correct angle. (The reason that the center line undulates in the diagram is because the dancing bee waggles the rear portion of her body while traversing the line.)

The distance of the food from the point where the dance occurs is communicated by the duration of the waggly line portion of the dance. Biologist Edward O. Wilson asserts, for example, that among one particular

228 OTHER CREATURES COMMUNICATE

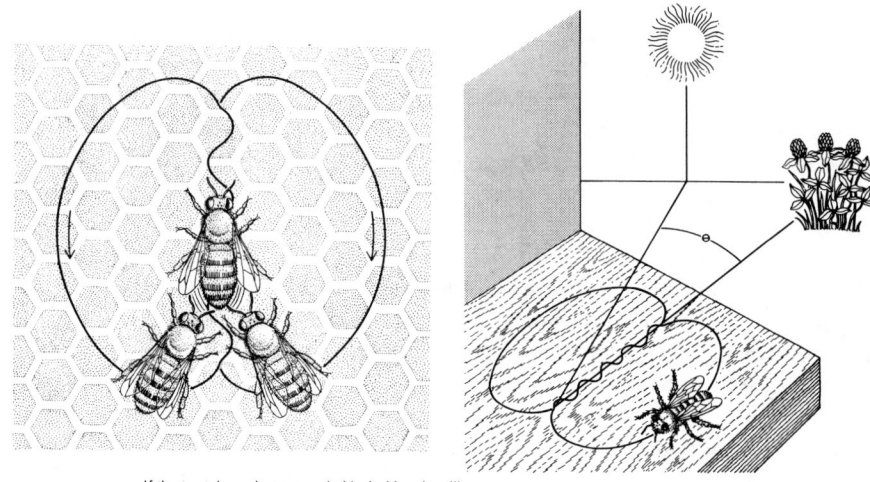

If the scout dances her message inside the hive, she will perform on a vertical surface, as noted in the diagram below.

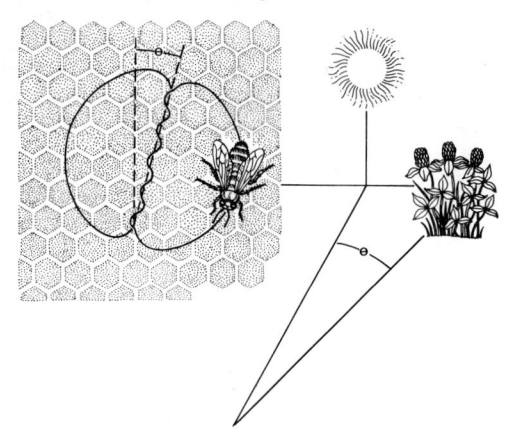

Illustration 10.1 The dance of the honeybee. (From "Animal Communication" by Edward O. Wilson. Copyright © 1972 by Scientific American, Inc. All rights reserved.)

type of honeybee, "a straight run lasting a second indicates a target about 500 meters away, and a run lasting two seconds indicates a target 2 kilometers away" (1975, p. 177).

Further, it has subsequently been learned that the bee's gestural form of communication can be used for other purposes. For example, scout bees can "tell" their comrades in a deteriorating hive the location of a suitable site for a new hive construction project (Griffin, 1976).

A Qualitative or Quantitative Difference from Human Language?

As impressive as the honeybee's feat of communication here may seem at first glance, most scholars in the fields of biology and communication have argued that it is greatly different from the kind of communication of which you and I are capable. While that argument is beginning to be questioned by some scholars, it is still accurate to say that an overwhelming number of students of communication believe that there is a Great Gap between our communication abilities and those of other creatures. They argue that the difference is one of quality, not merely quantity.

The quality/quantity distinction can be illuminated in the following way. Would you say that the aerial activity of the flying fish (which leaps from the water and has no wings) is slightly or greatly different from that of a sea gull? Obviously they are greatly different. The so-called flying fish merely leaps extraordinary distances—for a fish—out of the water. It doesn't fly in the "true" sense. The difference is one of *quality*, not *quantity*. On the other hand, although the bird known as the roadrunner spends a lot of time on the ground, it is quite capable of extended flight, employing the same biological mechanism —wings—as the sea gull. The difference between these two is one of *quantity*, not *quality*.

Wilson puts the idea well, arguing the classic position that you and I are qualitatively superior to other creatures in our communication behavior:

> *The great dividing line in the evolution of communication lies between man and all of the remaining ten million or so species of organisms. The most instructive way to view the less advanced systems is to compare them with human language. With our own unique verbal system as a standard of reference we can define the limits of animal communication in terms of the properties it rarely— or never—displays. Consider the way I address you now. Each word I use has been assigned a specific meaning by a particular culture and transmitted to us down through generations by learning. What is truly unique is the very large number of such words and the potential for creating new ones to denote any number of additional objects and concepts. This potential is quite literally infinite.* (1975, p. 177)

Note and tuck away for future reference the idea that our language, not our nonverbal means of communication, is the key distinguishing us from other species. The Great Gap theory almost always turns on this.

THE DIFFERENCE BETWEEN SIGNS AND SYMBOLS IN COMMUNICATION

Another approach to understanding the Great Gap theory more fully is to know the distinction between two kinds of communication signals—signs and symbols. It is frequently argued that you and I can use both signs and symbols but that other creatures rely much more heavily on signs, using symbols rarely or never.

Signs

A *sign* is logically related to a natural event or is a portion of a natural event or act. For example, among chickens there is a phenomenon known as the pecking order. As occurs frequently among a group of people, a dominant or "boss" chicken emerges from the flock. At first the boss chicken literally pecks the other chickens into submission. Real pecks with real pain are involved. Then gradually the boss chicken stops the actual pecking and simply moves its head in a gesture that is the beginning of the peck, without following through. This head movement is logically related to the natural event. It is also a shorthand reminder—a portion of the event—that is sufficient to keep the other chickens in line. People do that, too. Signs are also logically related to natural events, such that smoke accompanies fire and a wake in the water follows naturally after the passage of a boat or an alligator. Puddles of water are logically related to rain.

Symbols

A *symbol*, by contrast, is something that stands for something else but that has no necessary natural relationship with the object or phenomenon that it stands for. Thus the word *tree* in English is not part of the natural object (a tree growing in nature) and neither looks nor sounds like it. The word is a completely arbitrary sound or set of marks that humans have agreed to use to stand for the natural object.

It is widely thought that animals other than human beings cannot use symbols, or more accurately, cannot use a considerable stock of symbols— arbitrary sounds or gestures or touches or other sensory signals understood to stand for such-and-such.

Going back to the dance of the bees, it can be argued that the straight line portion of the dance on a horizontal surface—the part of the dance showing direction—is merely a mini-version of the flight itself. It actually points the way. And the length of the run in that center line is also merely a model of the distance itself. Some researchers, then, say that this is a sign. Others argue that it is quite as arbitrary and agreed upon as is human language.

THE ARGUMENT THAT HUMAN BEINGS ARE THE ONLY LANGUAGE-USING CREATURES

As noted, sometimes the distinction between human beings and other creatures is not made in terms of the ability or lack of ability to use signs and symbols, but rather in terms of the assumption that other creatures cannot use language in the sense that we do. In order to remove the possibility of simply arguing back and forth—yes, other creatures can use language; no, they can't—a number of scholars have suggested qualities that must be present for a system to qualify as a language.

For example, W. H. Thorpe (1974) listed sixteen features identified by himself and several other researchers as indicative of the existence of language. It is not useful to repeat all sixteen of these criteria here. Still, to give the flavor of that list, let us consider some of them. Included as indicators of existence of language are, for example:

- *Interchangeability*—the ability of the user to act as *both* transmitter and receiver of the signal.
- *Complete feedback*—the ability of the receiver to perceive all necessary aspects of the signal that the originator has generated.
- *Arbitrariness*—that the signal is not merely a sign in the sense of being part of a natural event; rather, it has no relationship with the object, event, or idea symbolized.
- *Discreteness*—the quality, such as found in human language, that small elements (like words) can be separated from the full flow of the utterance.
- *Tradition*—the signals and their meanings are transmitted through instruction, not genetically (by heredity).
- *Openness*—the creation of new messages by making endless new combinations of the discrete elements. The units can be put together in ways that haven't been used before and with meanings that will be understood.
- *Reflectiveness*—the ability to "talk" about the communication system itself. This is identical with the notion of metacommunication described in Chapter 7.
- *Prevarication*—the ability to lie using the signaling system. (Yes, the not-too-admirable quality of ours to lie is considered an indicator of whether a true language is at work or not.)
- *Displacement*—the quality that permits users to refer to things or events not physically present at a given time and in a given place.

Not many scholars believe that the signaling of honeybees—to take one creature that we know a bit about—for example, meets these (and other unlisted) criteria. Donald Griffin (1976), among others, is an exception. He argues, for instance, that the vertical dance of the bees *is* arbitrary, is an agreed-upon system, since it does not merely point the direction, as does the horizontal dance. He argues, to give another example, that the criterion of *displacement* is also present in the dance of the bees, because they can go to the food source even though that source is at a distance and even though time has elapsed since the scout bee that discovered it communicates her information to other members of the hive.

But the work of von Frisch, and others not mentioned, with honeybees is not nearly so startling as recent work with chimpanzees and apes, who are being taught to communicate across species with human beings. It is this recent work more than any other that has led some researchers to see tentative bridges appearing over the Great Gap that has been assumed between our language and the communication systems of other creatures.

COMMUNICATING WITH CHIMPANZEES: IMPORTANT CROSS-SPECIES STUDIES

Humans have for a long time been interested in the communicating ability of chimpanzees, those close primate relatives of ours. But for decades researchers made a major error in their studies: they assumed that chimps, intelligent creatures though they were, were still markedly inferior to us because they could not be taught to talk, although a number of attempts were made in that direction. The blunder was corrected when the simple observation was made that chimpanzees, because of their biological makeup, could not control their vocal mechanisms particularly well. Therefore some researchers decided to try other tactics, such as seeing if chimpanzees could use the gesture sign language used by deaf people or some other nonvocal technique. This was quite a breakthrough. As journalist Eugene Linden puts it:

> *In 1966, R. Allen Gardner's and Beatrice Gardner's infant chimpanzee said "more" in Ameslan, the American Sign Language for the deaf. Since that time, this chimp, named Washoe, has learned 180 other words, and a number of other chimpanzees have learned to communicate in this language as well.*
>
> *Also since that time Washoe and other chimps have taken to using language in different ways. They swear, invent names, learn signs from each other, have demonstrated syntactic capabilities, have translated from spoken to sign language, and have used words to express emotion, to joke, to converse, to lie.* (1975, p. 35)

Although the research with Washoe was the turning point, over a dozen other chimpanzees have been taught to sign, according to reporter Flora Davis

> What sort of culture, what kind of oral tradition would chimpanzees establish after a few hundred years of communal use of a complex gestural language? And if there were such an isolated continuous chimpanzee community, how would they begin to view the origin of language? Would the Gardners and the workers at the Yerkes Primate Center be remembered dimly as legendary folk heroes or gods of another species?
>
> Carl Sagan (1977, p. 123)

(1978). Davis also addresses herself to the question of the difficulty of using Ameslan:

> *Lest the reader think it's a trivial matter to learn sign language, let me describe my own experience. The accomplishments of the signing apes became very real to me in a personal way when I decided to take a few lessons in American Sign Language myself. I had some idea, I think, that if I could zip through a crash course in ASL, I could hold up my end of a conversation with Koko [a gorilla, not a chimpanzee] or one of the signing chimps. Although I was never exactly adept at language, I was sure a gestural language would be different: I expected something simple, with lots of pantomime and body English thrown in. However, I soon discovered that, while there were elements of pantomime, ASL is a language as complex as any other. My teacher's hands, flowing through a signed sentence, were as hard to follow as a comment rattled off in Greek. I found myself desperately rummaging through my memory for vocabulary: surely that gesture was familiar—one of those I had memorized only last week. . . . Though I persevered through half a dozen lessons, when I was introduced to Koko, it took me only a minute or two to learn that she was far, far ahead of me in signing, in fact, completely out of my league.*
>
> *When an ape learns to sign, then, it is no small accomplishment; or is the ability to read [signing] easily achieved.* (1978, p. 14)

Chimpanzees have been taught other means of communication with their human researchers. Sarah, for example, has been taught by Ann James Premack and David Premack to communicate by manipulating on a magnetic bulletin board plastic symbols constructed in different shapes and colors. Sarah learned to interpret, that is, decode or read, the symbols that the

234 OTHER CREATURES COMMUNICATE

Illustration 10.2 Sarah with her plastic symbols. Premack and Premack (1972) comment: "Sarah, after reading the message 'Sarah insert apple pail banana dish' on the magnetic board, performed the appropriate actions. To be able to make the correct interpretation that she should put the apple in the pail and the banana in the dish (not the apple, pail and banana in the dish) the chimpanzee had to understand sentence structure rather than just word order. In actual tests most symbols were colored" (p. 92). (From "Teaching Language to an Ape" by Ann Jones Premack and David Premack. Copyright © 1972 by Scientific American, Inc. All rights reserved.)

Premacks set out for her and to perform the actions called for in the message. In a sense, Sarah learned a "written" language. The researchers say:

> *Compared with a two-year-old child . . . Sarah holds her own in language ability. In fact, language demands were made of Sarah that*

would never be made of a child. . . . It is our hope that our findings will . . . lead to new attempts to teach suitable languages to animals. (1972, p. 99)

Washoe and Sarah are not the only chimps that have been taught to use language. By now there are dozens. Another star among language-using chimps is Lucy, at the Institute for Primate Studies at the University of Oklahoma. Lucy's mentor is Roger Fouts, and Illustration 10.3 shows Lucy and Fouts engaged in a conversation in which the crucial issue of using language syntax (word order) properly is tested. (Washoe, first instructed by the Gardners in Nevada—and named after the county in which Nevada State University is located—is also now at the Institute for Primate Studies.)

A third star is Lana, at the Yerkes Regional Primate Research Center in Atlanta. Lana works with neither Ameslan nor plastic figures but rather with a keyboard connected to a computer. When Lana pushes a key, the word is flashed on a screen. As the other chimps do, Lana learns words and proper syntax and is able to ask for the names of things that she doesn't already know. Duane M. Rumbaugh, director of the project, states:

We've obviously always underestimated the intellectual ability of chimpanzees. It's now clear that we're not pushing Lana at all. She can learn a lot more things if we can only figure out how to teach her. (Quoted in Rensberger, 1974, p. 45)

Let us consider briefly only one other example, that of Cetacea (the order including porpoises, dolphins, and whales).

A GREAT HOPE: UNDERSTANDING THE CETACEA

There is a certain irony in the fact that the breakthrough in cross-species communication with chimpanzees and apes came as a result of abandoning the attempt to teach acoustic (sound) communication techniques to those animals. On the other hand, only limited success has been achieved in learning the means of intraspecies communication or of teaching interspecies communication codes to mammals that have legendary ability in the production of sound —the Cetacea. Still, there is a persistent faith in some scientific quarters that it is with these creatures that we may make our most challenging breakthrough.

John C. Lilly, a neurophysiologist and psychoanalyst, is doubtless the most well-known American scientist in the field of dolphin communication. For twenty years—with brief forays into other areas of inquiry—Lilly has concentrated on dolphin communication. A cornerstone of Lilly's belief is that

236   OTHER CREATURES COMMUNICATE

1 Roger Fouts signs "Roger" in saying, "Lucy tickle Roger."

2 Lucy signs "Roger..."

3 "...tickle..."

4 "...Lucy," confused that her name is not used as the recipient of tickling.

5 Roger signs "no" and repeats: "Lucy tickle Roger."

6 Suddenly comprehending, Lucy leaps to tickle Roger.

Illustration 10.3 Roger Fouts, in a conversation with Lucy, testing word order. (Illustrations by Madelaine Gill reprinted by permission of E.P. Dutton from *Apes, Men and Language* by Eugene Linden. Copyright © 1974 by Eugene Linden. A Saturday Review Press Book.)

"these Cetacea with huge brains are more intelligent than any man or woman" (1978, p. 1) (Lilly's emphasis). Strong words.

The Cetacea realize that man is incredibly dangerous in concert. It is such considerations as these that may give rise to their behavioral ethic that the bodies of men are not to be injured or destroyed, even under extreme provocation. If the whales and dolphins began to injure and kill humans in the water, I am sure that the Cetacea realize that our navies would then wipe them out totally.

John C. Lilly (1978, p. 8)

Cetacean Intelligence

How do you go about determining the intelligence of a whale or a dolphin? Aside from the kind of brightness that all of us perceive as we watch dolphins jump through hoops on command at an aquatic amusement park, there is a more precise means that professionals such as Lilly employ, although it still results in an educated guess. Lilly observes:

> *Paleontological evidence shows that the whales and the dolphins have been here on this planet a lot longer than has man. Dolphins . . . have been here on the order of fifteen million years with brain sizes equal to or greater than that of modern man. Apparently some whale and dolphin brains became the equal of that of present-day man and then passed man's current size about thirty million years ago. . . . human skulls in large numbers with a cranial capacity equal to present man are found only as far back as one hundred fifty thousand years. Thus we see that man is a still evolving latecomer to this planet. He may not survive as long as the Cetacea have survived. (Man may also ensure that the whales will cease surviving within the next generation or two.)* (1978, p. 9)

It is not mere brain size, however, that is at issue. The composition of the brain—what portions of that organ have developed in what creatures—is also significant. We do not have time to go into that matter here, but references at the end of the book, particularly Lilly's *Communication between Man and Dolphin* (1978), will lead you further if you wish.

Cetacean Acoustical Powers

The Cetacea have superb acoustical equipment. Biologist Edward O. Wilson writes of the abilities of the humpback whale:

> *The most elaborate single display [ritual signal] known in any animal species [other than man] may be the song of the humpback whale. . . . the song lasts for intervals of 7 to more than 30 minutes duration. The really extraordinary fact . . . is that each whale sings its own particular variation of the song, consisting of a very long series of notes, and it is able to repeat the performance indefinitely. . . . Few human singers can sustain a solo of this length and intricacy. The songs are very loud, generating enough volume to be heard clearly through the bottom of small boats at close range and by hydrophones over distances of kilometers. The notes are eerie yet beautiful to the human ear. Deep basso groans and almost inaudible high soprano squeaks alternate with repetitive squeals that suddenly rise or fall in pitch. The functions of the humpback whale song are still unknown. . . . The most plausible hypothesis is that it serves to identify individuals and to hold small groups together during the long annual transoceanic migrations. But the truth is not known, and the phenomenon may yet hold some real surprises.* (1975, p. 220)

Even though the Cetacea have enviable acoustic ability, at least one experimenter, William Langbauer, has adopted the Premacks' technique of getting porpoises* to move symbols around on a magnetic bulletin board with their noses under water as a means to establish human-dolphin communication (Linehan, 1979).

But acoustic ability remains the primary lure with respect to establishing interspecies communication between humans and dolphins and other cetaceans. Cetaceans have a remarkable ability to mimic human sounds and in addition can generate and react to sonar signals, which, although beyond the range of human hearing, can be translated into visual form, according to Lilly (1978, p. 158), which might be viewed on a video screen.

Lilly and his colleagues, at the time of this writing, are working on a human-dolphin communication system called JANUS. Journalist Edward J. Linehan, reporting on Lilly's goal, says:

---

* See Lilly (1978) for a discussion of the complexity in terminology with respect to dolphins and porpoises.

> *When completed, the array [or equipment] will enable man and dolphin, each in his own element, to exchange precise sounds adjusted to their comfortable hearing range. Once both sides have learned to use a code of 64 sounds, communication will be rapid.* (1979, p. 538)

Lilly refers to this apparatus as a "vocoder" and explains it at greater length in his book *Communication between Man and Dolphin* (1978).

Let us consider now the question: Why has it taken so long to challenge the Great Gap theory of distinctions in communicative ability between humans and other creatures?

WE MAY BE CAUGHT IN A BIND OF ASSUMPTIONS

For a very long time the notion has existed in the West (less so in certain segments of Asian and African thought) that human beings and other creatures are massively separated by virtue of the communication system that one species can use and the other can't. This is an assumption that may require shifting because of the work that began with Washoe and continues with individuals of other species.

> The melancholy truth is that we are blind to our own blindness and will continue to be so until science forges a postive link between humans and the rest of the animal world.
>
> James L. Gould (1979, p. 75)

If we have been held back or misdirected by an assumption, it would not be the first time that has happened. By no means. For example, people thought for a very long time that the earth was flat. Finally that intellectual apple cart was upset by a shift in assumptions. Shaking loose old assumptions and replacing them with new ones is probably the most impressive intellectual act that anyone ever achieves. That appears to be happening all around us today with respect to our own place in nature's scheme. Worth repeating here is Lewis Thomas's observation used in the Introduction about our tendency to think of ourselves as outside nature:

> *Nor is it a new thing for man to invent an existence that he imagines to be above the rest of life; this has been his most consistent intellectual exertion down the millennia. As illusion, it has never worked*

out to his satisfaction in the past, any more than it does today. Man is embedded in nature. (1974, p. 1)

We may have been trapped in an act of tunnel vision with respect to the communicative ability of various other species of earth. Carl Sagan suggests:

Our difficulties in understanding or effectuating communication with other animals may arise from our reluctance to grasp unfamiliar ways of dealing with the world. For example, dolphins and whales, who sense their surroundings with a quite elaborate sonar echo location technique, also communicate with each other by a rich and elaborate set of clicks, whose interpretation has so far eluded human attempts to understand it. One very clever recent suggestion, which is now being investigated, is that dolphin/dolphin communication involves a re-creation of the sonar reflection characteristics of the objects being described. In this view a dolphin does not "say" a single word for shark, but rather transmits a set of clicks corresponding to the audio reflection spectrum it would obtain on irradiating a shark with sound waves in the dolphin's mode. The basic form of dolphin/dolphin communication in this view would be a sort of aural onomatopoeia, a drawing of audio frequency pictures—in this case, caricatures of a shark. We could well imagine the extension of such a language from concrete to abstract ideas, and by the use of a kind of audio rebus—both analogous to the development in Mesopotamia and Egypt of human written languages. It would also be possible, then, for dolphins to create extraordinary audio images out of their imaginations rather than their experience. (1977, pp. 107-108)

Such statements as these by Thomas and Sagan suggest a rethinking of the human position in nature. Most technological cultures have lost sight of our position in nature, although, interestingly, not all societies have. Perhaps, as Marshall McLuhan has suggested, we truly believe that the world of machines, buildings, highways, bridges, and the like really is the part of our environment that counts most and nature is merely decoration, colorful leaves to be dried in a book, samples to be retained in zoos and museums.

THE EFFECTS OF ENVIRONMENT ON OTHER CREATURES

One aspect of the debate about the superiority of humans over other creatures turns on another simple observation, as productive as the notion that chimpanzees don't have good vocal mechanisms was, *after it was thought of.* So much of our thinking works that way: hindsight excels.

Many observers have suggested that other creatures do not live in environments requiring them to perform the feats of communication they might very well be able to handle, given a shift in environment and thus of expectations. Paul Watzlawick, a psychiatrist and communication theorist, makes the point nicely, adding a little bonus idea about the potential of *Homo sapiens:*

> The natural environment of apes [and other creatures] is such that they are hardly ever called upon to perform the remarkable achievements of which we now know them to be capable. In other words, their mental abilities are potentially far greater than their everyday life in the wild seems to require, but they can be brought out and developed in completely "unnatural" contacts with humans. This raises precisely the same question with regard to ourselves: how much of our own potential are we actually using and what superhuman trainers could help us to develop it further? (1977, p. 157)

Lest this end with the implication that the world of scholars is rapidly dismissing the discontinuity theory of communication—the Great Gap theory, as I have called it—a corrective note should be repeated. A poll of scientists concerned with such matters would doubtless show an overwhelming belief to the contrary, namely, that there *is* a great qualitative difference between the communicative ability of human beings and other creatures. Still, there is no question that the debate has heated up, and we live at the dramatically productive time when the idea is being debated.

In ending his detailed book *Intelligence in Ape and Man*, David Premack states well the dilemma in which he and many other scholars find themselves when they attempt to make precise distinctions between humans and other species:

> [My work] did not lead to the discovery of qualitative differences between man and other species. [That is, he did not find evidence to support the Great Gap theory.] Those who find satisfaction in this failure will insist that this is the simple truth of the matter: there is both mental and anatomical continuity from one species to another; all differences are quantitative. It is also possible, however, that the inability to find more radical differences reveals not the genuine lack of such differences but simple ignorance [on our part]. (1976, p. 355)

EXTRATERRESTRIAL COMMUNICATION

One bonus that may come from exploration of interspecies communication—and we of course are highly speculative here—is that our sweeping searches across deep space by radio antennae for the presence of intelligent life elsewhere should doubtless proceed with the strong suspicion that "they" will not use our communication systems. That highly anthropocentric (based on a human outlook) assumption simply has a very low probability of being true. Perhaps we can gain knowledge for the possible day of encounter with "them" by learning whether we can communicate in a sophisticated way with other species on our own planet.

THIS CHAPTER IN PERSPECTIVE

We have considered in a brief way the fact that all creatures communicate. They do so with a variety of codes, using many senses. From our position as human beings there is an ancient assumption that humans are supreme among earth's organisms because, among other things, of our ability to communicate with greater sophistication than any of our co-inhabitants on the planet. Although this view is still by far the most widely accepted position among scientists who study the problem, rust spots have begun to appear recently in that armor-plated idea. Looking quite selectively, we have seen that honeybees communicate among themselves in a way that some scientists would say is quite sophisticated—with a system of dance augmented by other cues. We have also looked, far too briefly, at the exciting work that has been done to establish cross-species communication between chimpanzees and great apes and human beings, using nonvocal techniques because chimps and apes don't have vocal equipment equivalent to ours. Finally, we have looked hastily at both completed and proposed work in establishing communication between humans and the large-brained Cetacea (whales, dolphins, and porpoises), who have superb acoustical equipment, including the ability to mimic human sounds. On a speculative note, we have observed that understanding other creatures on earth might help us if and when we encounter intelligent life in our increasing looks at outer space, for in both cases we need to reexamine our assumptions about the means of communication employed. We did not settle the issue—because nobody can at this point—about whether we are supreme among earth's creatures because of our language ability.

EXTENSIONS

Reading You Might Enjoy

1. Davis, Flora. *Eloquent Animals: A Study in Animal Communication.* New York: Coward, McCann & Geoghegan, 1978.

Davis is a free-lance writer who has talked directly with researchers in animal communication and writes for the layperson. She discusses work being done with many creatures, including apes, chimpanzees, fish, ants, crickets, birds, and whales. Anecdotal in approach, Davis's book makes difficult information accessible to the nonspecialist. I suspect this is the most useful book in the reading list for students who want a good understanding of where we stand now in animal communication research and who prefer not to keep one eye on the dictionary while doing their reading.

2. Frings, Hubert, and Mable Frings. *Animal Communication.* 2nd ed., rev. and enl. Norman: University of Oklahoma Press, 1977.

These two zoologists, long-time students of animal communication, have written in this book one of the best short (207 pages) and readable accounts about nonhuman communication that I know of. It discusses the sensory systems and communication functions of animals in a humane and clear way. Illustrations enhance the text at many points.

3. Lilly, John C. *Communication between Man and Dolphin: The Possibilities of Talking with Other Species.* New York: Crown, 1978.

Lilly is undoubtedly the best-known American researcher into the possibility of cetacean communication with human beings. This book pulls together much information about the historical interest in the communication systems of cetaceans and in Lilly's attempts at cross-species communication. It also contains information about Lilly's plans for future research, many illustrations, and a large annotated bibliography. Some chapters of the book have been published elsewhere as well.

4. Linden, Eugene. *Apes, Men, and Language.* New York: Penguin Books, 1974. (First published by Saturday Review Press/E. P. Dutton, New York, 1975. Published by Pelican Books, 1976.)

Eugene Linden is a journalist who has done his homework thoroughly in telling the story of work with Washoe, Lucy, and other chimpanzees. The book is beautifully written and illustrated. Although no primer, it is easier going than some of the highly technical works written by scientists.

5. Wilson, Edward O. *Sociobiology: The New Synthesis.* Cambridge, Mass.: Harvard University Press, Belknap Press, 1975.

This is a weighty book that discusses a great deal of biology not of direct interest in the present context, but is has three excellent chapters on communication among creatures other than humans. It is a traditional book in the sense that Wilson subscribes to the Great Gap theory. For that reason, it would go nicely with other books that take the counterposition.

Ponderings and Projects

1. What would a world be like in which all species are regarded as equal? Silly question? Not really, because there do exist cultures of people today who have as much respect for an earthworm as they do for another human being. Interested? One way is to begin the search with the key word *Buddhism*. And here is another useful hint: The attitude is frequently associated with belief in reincarnation, in *any* form.

2. As a follow-up on the last paragraph of the chapter, consider extraterrestrial communication. Now that our interest is turning increasingly to space, the question is being asked: "Shouldn't we be sending out signals and searching for signals sent from elsewhere to see if intelligence exists beyond the earth?" We are doing that, of course, although the project could easily fail because of our assumption that such intelligent forms of life will recognize language and mathematical forms which *we* know and use on earth. For some provocative leads look for articles on the plaque that was attached by NASA to the Pioneer 10 rocket in 1972. Also, check out leads on signals sent from the Arecibo Observatory in Puerto Rico to outer space, first on November 16, 1974, keeping the same question in mind. And if you want to turn to artistic treatments of the same problem, see, among others, the film *Close Encounters of the Third Kind* (1977).

3. Should there be rights for species other than *Homo sapiens*? Although ecological battles have long been fought in the United States and other countries for the preservation of endangered species, there appear to be signs of a growing feeling that other creatures have rights (similar to human rights) that should be extended to them. Illustrative is an incident in which two employees at the Kewala Basin Marine Research Facility of the University of Hawaii released two Atlantic bottle-nosed dolphins, leaving in their place toy rubber dolphins marked "Slave no more" and "Let my people go." In explaining why they had freed the dolphins, one of the employees said:

> *Their freedom is more important than that research. All the research keeps demonstrating how intelligent dolphins are. How much do we have to know before we see they have rights of their own?* (Turner, 1977, p. 23)

The men who freed the dolphins were charged with grand theft, and one was tried and convicted. This is probably not the last instance when the "rights" of other animals will be tested legally or morally. The matter should be worth following. Robert Merle wrote about it in his interesting novel *Day of the Dolphin*, later made into a film.

4. Washoe, the first chimpanzee to learn human sign language, has been pregnant twice and has lost both babies. During her second pregnancy, Roger Fouts was looking forward to seeing whether Washoe would transmit her sign language to the infant, something that many scientists believe is unlikely or impossible. Fouts and his colleagues planned to keep Washoe and the baby away from most humans to avoid the possibility of the baby imitating human signs. At the time of this writing they plan to find an infant chimp for Washoe to raise. More developments will doubtless have occurred when you read this, either with Washoe or another chimpanzee.

Learning to Observe Communication in Action

11

*I can tell that you're a logger,
And not just a common bum
'Cause nobody but a logger
Stirs coffee with his thumb.*

Traditional American

Most of this book has been an invitation to look at interesting aspects of communication as specialists see them. Now let us do an about-face and look at ourselves as students of communication. Most of us probably have grown up believing that the best way to become a good communicator is to learn a set of rules as laid out by experts. While learning rules is indeed a good way to solve some of our communication problems, it is not the high road to the desired goal. There is too little known about communication to trust the route of rules. There are also too many differing communication situations in which we find ourselves to expect any set of rules to cover all of them.

The better way to proceed is to learn to be continuous observers of communication in a variety of contexts. From such continuous observation—which can serve us throughout our lives—we can personally draw our own rules, revising them as required.

Observation of communication can be conducted in many ways, but we will learn in this chapter some of the elementary characteristics of the style known as naturalistic observation, concentrating on examples of some procedures that can be started right now.

OBSERVATION LEADS TO GENERALIZATION

The verse that begins this chapter, humble though it may be, is an example of observation leading to generalization. The narrator has spotted a bit of behavior—not for the first time, clearly—and from it draws a conclusion.

Without question, the most effective way of learning to be a good communicator is to constantly observe communication in action around us. From continuous observations we can draw our own conclusions, our own "rules" about what makes for effective communication. The technique serves us endlessly.

Formally or informally, part of every day of your life will be spent as a communication inquirer.

Gerald R. Miller and Henry E. Nicholson (1976, p. 251)

We all learn the communication systems into which we are born by unconscious observation, and we all continue this unconscious observation, to some extent at least, long after childhood. Others go about the job systematically. Fortunately, we can all learn the basic skills.

YOU HAVE TO BE CURIOUS

The first requirement in learning to observe communication is to be motivated. You have to be curious. It does no good for someone to try to force you into a routine if you neither see the reason for it nor want to do it. Although curiosity killed the cat, it may be the student's best friend.

LEARNING BOOK RULES ALONE WILL NOT DO THE JOB

Most of us have been taught that the way to learn effective communication is to read basic books of rules. We are far past the time, however, when it is even remotely possible to learn enough lists of rules to guide us in every communication situation. The modes of communication available to us (and the contexts in which they are employed) are so many and so complex that nobody really has been able to analyze and state the rules that underlie their operation, except in a very general way. Probably nobody ever will be able to.

This is not to say that printed resources about communication are without value. On the contrary, we should begin with such material when it is available. With respect to language, for example, we would be either arrogant or insane to ignore dictionaries, those great depositories of information about the history of languages and, insofar as they are up-to-date, about the current

> Don't accept things on the say-so of established authority: look at the facts, then judge for yourself.
>
> Bryan Magee (1979, p. 222)

usage of words. Thesauruses are frequently helpful in suggesting choices of synonyms or antonyms. Manuals of style are doubtless the simplest sources we have for learning the conventions of writing term papers and other formal reports. With respect to other modes of communication—nonverbal systems and the various media—there are also hundreds of critical analyses of processes.

The point is to use such books as appropriate guides. Many gifted scholars have spent their lives on them. The point, further, is to understand that such books alone will never relieve us of the need for careful, personal observation.

THE GOAL IS TO INCREASE YOUR ALTERNATIVES

It is vital to recall now a point made much earlier in the book: The systems of communication we learned in our homes, our neighborhoods, and our cultures are complete and effective, *within those systems*. To forget that may make us vulnerable to a dangerous illusion, that the reason for learning about other systems is that they are inherently better than the ones we already know. The more sensible reason for learning other communication systems is that they will give us the option of becoming active participants in alternative ways of life.

Essentially this means that we may be able to cross barriers if we want to. We may be able to enter, for example, into academic enterprises, into other socioeconomic groups, into the pleasures of other cultural or subcultural groups.

A footnote should be added. Even if our general social system is as complete and adequate as that of another cultural group, every system can deteriorate, can become "sick," so to speak, just as a human body (quite adequate in its normal state) can degenerate. That state can be detected—not always easily—by observation, too. The communication of a family can also degenerate, for example, often with disastrous results.

EMPHASIS ON NATURALISTIC OBSERVATION

There are many ways to seek information about communication through your personal efforts. One—using printed resources—has already been mentioned. Professional scholars in communication use a range of additional techniques for getting new information. Essentially there are two general settings within which research of a scientific kind can be conducted. One is the *laboratory*, where various kinds of carefully controlled experiments can be conducted. A psychologist, for example, can bring people into a laboratory, give them tasks to do, and draw conclusions from their performances. The other general setting where scientific research is conducted is the *field*, that is to say, in offices or schools or communities where people go about their normal behavior. Experiments can be performed in the field, as they can in laboratories, but frequently field research consists of careful observation of the way people behave; it is often called naturalistic observation. It is that mode of seeking information that we will emphasize here.

Colette Grinevald Craig writes that fieldwork and naturalistic observation mean

> *to be in direct contact with the source of information. In this context, the word "field" has the general meaning of "natural setting." It designates any type of location ranging from an urban center to a desert, from lush jungle to arid mountains. . . . Going to the field usually implies an expedition of some importance, settling somewhere for a stay of a few weeks to a few years, although one can do field work only a few blocks away in the same city, a few hours at a time.* (1979, p. 4)

For our purpose we should recognize that we are always in the field; for our fieldwork we need not go even a few blocks away. We are forever and always surrounded by communication. Further, studying communication in our omnipresent "field" should be part of a constant agenda, wherever we are, for whatever amount of time we have at that moment. Once we have tucked in the back of our heads the idea that there is always something fascinating around about communication, and once we have learned some of the methods of seeing that fascinating something, then it becomes a happily irresistible habit.

WHAT IS IT TO BE SCIENTIFIC?

I have suggested that we will be talking about scientific ways of obtaining information. What does that mean? What is it to be scientific? The answer is difficult, but to oversimplify, it means proceeding in such a way that a minimum amount of our personal biases get in the way, that we work with an open mind, accumulating facts that can be counted on as being accurate, for that time and place at least. The procedure seeks empirical evidence, that is, evidence based on careful observation of actual situations that can also be observed by other trained observers.

A Crucial Test Is to Try to Disprove Your Theory or Hunch

Sometimes hypotheses are developed by the investigator. A hypothesis is essentially a hunch, carefully stated, that one then tries to *disprove* or falsify. Disprove or falsify? Why not *prove*? The answer is that it is more effective to disprove something than it is to prove something, and the results are the same. The notion of verifying information by trying to disprove it is generally attributed to a German philosopher, Karl R. Popper, who says:

What characterizes the empirical method is its manner of exposing to falsification, in every conceivable way, the system to be tested.
(1968, p. 42)

For example, take the bit of verse that begins this chapter. Obviously, the playful point of the verse is that loggers are tough; we are never really expected to believe that they literally stir coffee with their thumbs. But let's take the verse literally for the purpose of making a point. From that distorting perspective, would you agree with the following? (1) The narrator has seen enough loggers stirring coffee with their thumbs to conclude that many, or most, of them do perform the task that way. (2) By the same token, the narrator has presumably *not* seen persons of other occupations stirring coffee with their thumbs. The hypothesis, stated or unstated, then, is that only loggers stir coffee with their thumbs. How do you knock off that hypothesis? By disproving it, that is to say, by finding persons other than loggers stirring coffee with their thumbs. Thus if you wander from shore to shore, from culture to culture, carefully watching people stirring their coffee, and you find a number of exceptions to the hypothesis—society gentlemen in England stirring coffee with their thumbs, peasants in Argentina doing the same—then you have disproved or falsified your hunch and are obligated to revise it.

How Much Falsification Is Necessary to Disprove a Theory?

Most people who seek empirical evidence—that is, who proceed scientifically—today do not conclude at any point that they have achieved unending truth. While the basic point of scientific activity is to help us predict what will happen in a given situation, many scientists, especially in the social sciences (psychology, anthropology, sociology) state theories in terms of the *probability* of such-and-such happening. The contemporary communication researchers Gerald R. Miller and Henry E. Nicholson state the proposition this way:

Many communication theories . . . specify what probably will happen. . . . a single discomforting observation does not constitute

> *sufficient grounds to label the theory false, since the instance observed may be one of the minority of cases.* (1976, p. 77)

Thus our hypothetical observer searching for exceptions to the rule that only loggers stir coffee with their thumbs will not necessarily abandon the hypothesis if he or she sees a *single* instance of someone else engaged in the practice. The observer will feel a little shaken in confidence about the theory, of course, and presumably will keep a sharper eye out for other exceptions. Meanwhile, our researcher will change the verse to read something like:

> *I can tell that you're probably a logger,*
> *And not just a common bum,*
> *'Cause, generally speaking, nobody but a logger*
> *Stirs coffee with his thumb.*

How many instances of disproof or falsification can your hypothesis tolerate? There is no fixed number. Common sense is involved in seeking empirical evidence. If you see a thousand cases of one way of behaving and find a single exception, then you've probably got a good hypothesis. If in a thousand cases you find a dozen exceptions, however, your hypothesis has begun to tremble, if not quake.

HOW TO GO ABOUT OBSERVING

Observing anything, including communication, is not easy. John Collier, Jr., an anthropologist, feels that

> *we moderns are not good observers.... We moderns have drifted out of an embracing relationship with our surroundings.... In contrast, the perception of the aborigine is related to his interaction with his total environment. The native with limited technology necessarily has to live in harmony with surrounding nature. He has to be an astute observer of all his world or perish!* (1967, p. 1)

Aside from Collier's generalization, there are at least two other reasons why communication, in particular, is hard to observe.

1. In the United States, at least, we have seldom been invited in school to observe communication. Rather, we have been taught that the truth lies in a set of rules to be learned. Problems arise immediately with that, as we have seen, but the idea is hard to banish.

2. Whatever we live in the midst of is hard to perceive. And, without question, there is little in our lives that is closer to us than communication.

That is why it is easier to see instantly new communication (or other) behavior in a foreign culture, or in a different family, than one's own. We are more removed from it.

Four Tips from Anthropology

Naturalistic observation of communication is the kind of task that anthropologists are good at. Let us borrow some clues, then, from social anthropology, a discipline concerned with gaining information about the structure, values, beliefs, and rules that peoples of different cultures follow.

Alfred G. Smith suggests that anthropologists look for four things, as follows (1979, pp. 62-68). They:

1. *Look for nothing.* By this, Smith means that anthropologists, like all good scientists, try to clear their minds of preconceptions and therefore perceive with relatively unencumbered senses. This is a monumentally difficult task, since each of us is a mass of preconceptions, and we are unaware of most of them. But we should try to clear out our assumptions. The best way is to bring them to consciousness. Being aware of our assumptions is an aid to our intellectual activity in the same way that knowledge of our bodily strengths and weaknesses is an aid to physical activity.

Scientists . . . try to examine the universe without prejudice. This is an ideal that they do not always attain, but they at least try. It is an expressed ideal, maintained by constant vigil and criticism.

Marston Bates (1950, p. 260)

---

2. *Look for differences and distinctions.* This is a technique that we will be emphasizing a great deal. Looking for differences in communication means being *surprised* by something that we perceive. It is probable that we never perceive anything except that it differs in some way from that which we expected (consciously or unconsciously) to perceive.

3. *Look for contexts.* If an observer's attention is drawn to something—generally because it is different—the next step is to study the physical and social surroundings (context) in which the surprise is found. The purpose of seeking context is to see if meanings for a particular form of communicative behavior can be found. Studying the context of a communicative behavior also permits us to see whether that behavior is found in other contexts or only in that one setting.

4. *Look for freedom and order.* The words *freedom* and *order* are used in a special way here. On spotting a bit of communicative behavior, the anthropologist then tries to discover by continued observation in many contexts whether that behavior appears to be required in such-and-such a situation or whether there is a choice given to the individual about whether or not to employ that behavior. If two friends in a culture on meeting each other *always* greet each other with a hug, then it is a highly ordered—that is to say, *required*—form of behavior. It is a rule for that culture. If observation shows, on the other hand, that friends do not always hug each other on meeting, although they sometimes do, then freedom of choice is possible. Further observation might reveal, of course, that hugging always occurs in certain contexts, but not in others.

THE USE OF INFORMANTS

In the process of observation it is also possible to use *informants*. An informant is someone who has grown up with that communication system and therefore knows it more or less automatically.

There are certain warnings that we should understand about using informants. Colette Grinevald Craig writes about the qualities of a good informant in the quotation below. Because Craig was studying the nature of Jacaltec, a language spoken in Guatemala, the following quotation includes many references to *language* and *linguistics*. In your thinking, expand these words to include other coding techniques as well.

> *The basic prerequisite is that the informant be an intelligent person with a good linguistic intuition. This means someone who is sensitive to the workings of language and can convey to the linguist what nuances of meaning are, someone who likes his/her language and is proud of it, and someone who enjoys discovering together with the field worker its mechanisms, laws, and exceptions. In all cultures and societies, some people are good with language while other people have little curiosity about it or feel for it.* (1979, p. 10)

Obviously, if you are studying something in a culture or subculture quite foreign to you, it would be desirable to have an informant who speaks your language as well.

Further, it is very important to understand that the manner in which the informant is asked for help will partly determine the results obtained. Consider the regional use of words in this country, for example. Many people in the United States enjoy a piece of sweet pastry as part of their breakfast. In some regions this tasty bit is called a "sweet roll." In other places it is called a "Danish." If you were to ask an informant in a particular part of the country, holding the morsel in your hands (or pointing to it), "Do you call this a 'sweet roll' or a 'Danish'?" you might actually confuse the informant. It is often best to seek an answer without giving the alternatives you know, since they might be limiting. The best of all possible methods is to set up a situation in which the informant is required to use the term without any nudging on your part. Thus you might wait until the informant is eating breakfast with you in a public restaurant, point to the object, and say, "I want one of those; what shall I ask for?" This should bring back a spontaneous response.

Even setting up a spontaneous response does not ensure accuracy. Other informants might be asked, or you could accept the response of the first informant, tuck it in the back of your head as a possibility, and see if experience over time brought forth any alternatives.

All this skepticism in approach, all this protection against error, may seem excessive. It is necessary, however, because so much of our communicative behavior is unconscious and is therefore difficult to call to mind and use simply by desiring to do so.

THE USE OF RECORDING INSTRUMENTS

Observation is often enhanced by the use of instruments permitting you to obtain a record for later study. If you study spoken language, an audio tape recorder is very useful. If you study nonverbal communication or various visible codes (writing, pictures, advertisements), then still photographs, motion pictures, or videotapes are often extraordinarily helpful. Obviously, the still photograph has distinct disadvantages where motion is recorded. The still photograph, however, should not be ignored. When taking stills, most researchers today use 35mm cameras; for some purposes the smaller and less expensive 110mm size cameras serve admirably. Telephoto lenses help bring distant subjects into better view. For recording motion, with and without sound, 16mm and Super 8mm motion picture cameras or portable video cameras are all used.

In recording either sound or images, researchers must face an ethical question: Should the subject know he or she is being recorded? Certainly if extended amounts of material are recorded, the people being recorded should know. Further, the material should not be used without their knowledge and consent. Obviously, one does not record and present to a class material that would in any way be embarrassing. Privacy should not be invaded. Caution and decency are the key words.

In addition to the ethical and legal questions, researchers should be aware of the fact that the presence of an audio tape recorder or a camera will, in subtle or gross ways, influence those being recorded. Most researchers feel that the effects of the presence of technology wear off after a time, particularly if the researcher has managed to fade into the distance as much as possible — not moving around much, not ordering subjects to do this or that, and so forth.

Comparing [motion picture] footage of a subject who is unaware of a camera, then aware of it — fully aware of it as an instrument for self-viewing, self-examination — is comparing different behavior, different persons.

Edmund Carpenter (1975, p. 456)

A final observation in this brief account of how recording instruments can be used is that, in the case of visual recording, the greatest error that most beginners make is the failure to provide adequate context. It is a good idea to be certain of having one or more still photographs or moving image shots that show as wide a visual context as possible. Further, the camera operator should avoid the temptation to move the camera around constantly or to use too many tight close-ups. Communication is an interactional process, and thus it is desirable to show all participants in addition to considerable chunks of the environment. (In my own visual records I generally shoot a lot of pictures: some to provide context, others to show specific pieces of action. I tend to use the still photograph more than either motion picture or video images, even though the still has obvious disadvantages. I like the relative inexpensiveness of the still camera and am prepared to compensate for its disadvantages with my own vision. Still, one must recall that I do not do the kind of detailed research studies that many scholars do.)

FOUR MINI–CASE STUDIES IN OBSERVING

Let us examine four photographs, keeping in mind Smith's four suggestions for naturalistic observation: (1) clear your mind of preconceptions as much as possible, (2) look for differences, for unexpected things, (3) study the context, and (4) ask whether the thing spotted is part of something required in that society or whether it is something where a good deal of freedom is permitted.

A Street Sign

Look at Illustration 11.3. It is, quite clearly, a street sign. The words are not difficult: "Bus Stop, No Standing." Still, wait a minute! There is a paradox in the statement. "Bus Stop" is clear enough: that's where you wait for a bus, and waiting a bit easily confirms that. But how can you wait for a bus if "No

Illustration 11.1 A medium context photo. This still photo provides a lot of interesting context to play with in analysis. It could easily be supplemented by closer shots. Notice the wealth of verbal material that one could profitably ponder. It is also rich nonverbally. Notice the posture sharing (of arms) by the two men to the left of the door. Notice the walk of the man about to enter the door. Does it seem somehow different from American walking? A series of cross-cultural stills would be needed to study that matter more. Or, better yet, some Super 8mm film footage would help. And there's more in the photo. (Photo: Lynn Forsdale)

Standing" is permitted? Let me confess that I did not consider this sign unusual because I've seen it dozens of times a day for years. One of my students from out of town spotted it, however, and told me about the embarrassment it caused her. Assuming that she couldn't stand right there, she backed up against a building, a sidewalk's width away from the sign. The bus driver stopped to let other passengers off and then chided the student when she ran from her place of refuge against the building to get on the bus. "I wouldn't have stopped for you," he said, "if somebody hadn't rung the bell to get off. You gotta stand closer or you won't catch the bus."

The paradoxical statement on the sign is easily explained if you hold a New York City driver's license, in which case you know that "No Standing"

258 LEARNING TO OBSERVE COMMUNICATION IN ACTION

Illustration 11.2 A fib told by a still camera. All lenses distort in some way. In this photo I was interested in a shot of the sunbathing man. The women in the background, who seem so unconcerned about his presence, are actually a good deal further away from him than the photograph would suggest. They were actually about one hundred fifty feet from the man. They appear to be closer because a telephoto lens was used, and telephoto lenses foreshorten distance. Using this picture for analytical purposes, then, has a built-in drawback.

means that *automobiles* cannot stop in that area. In all probability most pedestrians in New York City don't know that meaning of "No Standing" at all. They have simply learned, by watching, that passengers waiting for buses wait by those signs.

The hypothesis about this minor observation, then, is that "No Standing" refers to automobiles. Can that hypothesis be disproved? Not easily. The driver's manual spells out the meaning of those words when used on street signs.

It is quite another question whether this sign is *effective* or not. But studying effectiveness is a step beyond what we are now attempting to do — namely, learning how to observe the existence of something.

A Numbering System

Illustration 11.4 shows something "different" that will probably catch your eye as it did mine. This is the number of an apartment in a building located well outside the United States. (Remember, explanatory notes about the context of photographs appear at the end of the book.) I lived in Apartment 12 opposite this one. The apartment number 12 was written exactly as it appears in this sentence. I developed a hypothesis on the spot: This culture is super-

Illustration 11.3 Bus Stop, No Standing.

stitious about the number 13, just as we tend to be. My hypothesis continued with the thought that they have solved the problem in the interesting way shown in Illustration 11.4.

I began to check in my wanderings if the number 13 appeared in other places as 12 + 1. It did. Repeatedly. At the same time, I asked an informant, who spoke good English in addition to his native tongue, "What's that?" pointing to the number on the apartment.

He was confused by my question. "It's the apartment number."

Although I was aching to get at the basic question ("Are people in this culture superstitious about the number thirteen?"), I held off, not wanting to signal a possible answer.

"Why is it written that way?" I asked.

"What way?"

"Twelve plus one," I replied.

He was still confused, so I asked, "Is that apartment number thirteen?"

"Sure," he said. Then, eyes brightening, he knew what I was after. "We are superstitious about the number thirteen."

"So are we," I replied, hoping to remove any sting of oddness from his musings. "But I have never seen anywhere in the United States the use of 'twelve plus one' as a solution to avoid writing 'thirteen.' "

"Really?" He was a bit surprised. "We do it a lot."

My hypothesis was given further validity by his testimony. But I continued to watch and ask, hunting for those crucial exceptions that might disprove my hypothesis. In six weeks, I did not find any exceptions in which the number 13

Illustration 11.4 12 + 1.

was used alone, as in an address, an apartment number, or a floor number in a building. But I still don't feel secure in saying that all people of that culture are superstitious about the number 13. I'd like more evidence from various regions, from various age groups, and from various social class groups. Are you prepared to say that Americans are universally superstitious about the number 13?

Another Sign

Illustration 11.5 shows another sign that caught my eye because it leaped out at me as a surprise, as something different. To my eye, this verbal statement is a rather amusing philosophical observation, the kind of thing that would make a gloriously pessimistic slogan on a wall poster. I've purposely not provided much spatial context in the photograph. The words appear on a subway turnstile, however, as you may have guessed. I looked around the subway station for the flip side of this statement, and, sure enough, I soon spotted a sign reading "Way Out." Again, the contemporary American usage of that phrase struck me, and I laughed aloud, doubtless to the bewilderment of many passersby. Context quickly suggested the obvious meaning of both phrases. "No Way Out" was the equivalent of the American expression, "No Exit." "Way Out" was the equivalent of our "Exit." Were there exceptions? I didn't find any in the subway system, but there were plenty of alternative usages in public buildings. Tentative conclusion: This usage has been adopted by the people who run the subways, but it is not the only possible usage in the culture.

FOUR MINI-CASE STUDIES IN OBSERVING   261

Illustration 11.5 No Way Out.

A Backward Limousine

Illustration 11.6 depicts what might be called a "backward limousine." The photograph is not printed in reverse; the lettering on the front is as it appeared on the vehicle. There is internal evidence of that fact in the illustration. That is, if you look closely at the photograph you will find at least several bits of evidence that back up that assertion without taking anybody's word for it. Those bits of internal evidence include:

☐ The lettering on the side of the limousine is straightforward. The name of the corporation is clear here, as is its telephone number.
☐ The license plate is clearly not backward: "Virginia" can be read.
☐ The manufacturer's name of the vehicle—Plymouth—appears to be as straightforward as the day it left the manufacturer.

Certain other bits of information give added proof that the picture is not printed backward. Knowing that the vehicle is being driven in the United

Illustration 11.6 Backward limousine.

States, we can assume that it should be in a right-hand lane (not a left-hand lane, as for example in Great Britain), and it is. Also, the driver's position is on the left side of the vehicle (again, not on the right, as in Great Britain). Doubtless there are additional bits of evidence, some less convincing than others.

The name, carefully and professionally printed backward under the windshield, is "airport limo, inc." It is a clear "difference" from the norm. But why?

I've seen this technique used on ambulances in various places. Some commonsense deduction, reinforced by conversation with informants (ambulance drivers) led to the conclusion that backward printing on the front of ambulances is done to permit drivers who see the vehicle through their rearview mirrors to recognize what it is and immediately pull out of the way to permit the ambulance to proceed as quickly as possible. (Hold the photograph of the airport limousine to a mirror to prove that it will read in a perfectly straightforward fashion.)

But why print this information backward on a limousine? Why would it be helpful if you were driving a car to see these words printed backward? Obviously there is no message of crisis involved as there is with an ambulance —or is there? So, to hypothesize: There is advertising value in what the corporation has done. Seeing the name from the rearview mirror of a car might fix the name in mind. Seeing it with the naked eye, backward, probably piques the curiosity. It's an attention grabber, which people will try to decipher, and they thus will become actively involved, at least for a moment, with the visual problem.

I sought out an informant about this offbeat practice, turning to a manager in the corporation. He confirmed the advertising hypothesis—it was an attention grabber—but added another dimension that hadn't occurred to me. On thruways between Washington, D.C., and its airports, one lane is kept open for buses and also for limousines, which are defined as buses. In that open lane, buses can bypass traffic jams in the other lanes and move a good deal more quickly to their destinations. The advertising agency for Airport Limo, Inc., felt that if drivers of automobiles were stalled in their lanes and watched buses and limousines going by them to their destinations, some drivers, at least, would see the name of the limousine company in their rearview mirrors as they went by in the reserved lane and might conclude, if they were headed to or from one of the airports, that next time it might be better to leave the car at home and go by limousine.

How common is the practice of backward printing on vehicles? My observation suggests that it is rare in the United States, except for ambulances and other emergency vehicles. Does the advertising work? That's another problem, one that we can't dig into here. As we have noted at other points in this book, thinking about effects—or *probing* effects of communication—is an agonizingly difficult task.

OBSERVATIONS ARE SELDOM EARTHSHAKING

We have just looked at four miniobservations of minicommunication events. The earth has not trembled as a result. Which is to say that the observations have been of little matters. By and large, however, this is what observation of the kind you and I do is all about: getting into the habit of studying little things, endlessly.

IMPROVE YOUR WRITING BY OBSERVING

One of the big problems we all go through as students is learning to write papers that meet the standards of our teachers. Again, part of the answer lies with observing carefully as we read. In our natural concern for getting meaning from texts and other written material, we often fail to notice form— the way writers package their material.

Consider this book, for example, not as an instance of something special, but because it is handy. What can we learn by focusing attention beyond the content to style and technique? Of the thousands of possible answers to that question, let us consider six specific qualities, not offered as *the* six most important matters to look at, but as six varied items.

1. *Chapter-opening quotations.* Each chapter in this book starts with a brief quotation designed to encapsulate a theme central to the chapter. They are generally comments by writers who are important in one of the many fields upon which communication research draws. There is no rule stating that you should start chapters—or papers—that way. Having observed that small technique, however, having called it to the forefront of your thinking, you may want to tuck it in the back of your head, see in what other books you find it, and decide whether or not you like it. If so, you may want to use it; if not, put it aside. Again, we've made no major breakthrough in seeing this device. But learning skills in communication consists of thousands of small gains.

2. *Use of "I," "you," and "we."* Sometimes in this book I use the word "I" when referring to myself and "you" when referring to you, the reader. Often I use "we" to include both of us. Some writers of textbooks use neither "I" nor "we," choosing to avoid both in their manner of address. If you were to pick six textbooks at random and glance through them, you would see quickly what decision the authors have made. For example, some writers refer to themselves as "the writer," or more likely these days, simply bypass any reference to themselves at all. (You had better find out, by the way, if you are writing college papers, whether your instructors like the "I" mode of identification or not. Chances are there will be differences of opinion among your teachers.)

Examination of randomly selected texts also will reveal a variety of methods of referring to the reader, including making no direct references at all.

3. *Anecdotes.* Anecdotes are used frequently in this book; less so in other books. Again, this is the sort of thing you can observe by looking behind the content to the form in skimming several texts. I personally use anecdotes for the same reason that I use the "I/we/you" mode of address: for informality and to try to make points memorable.

4. *Quotations.* Quotations from other writers are used often in this book, partly to vary the style, but mostly to acquaint you with important writers and their ideas. Check this in other books, too, but also notice the way the quotations are handled physically on the page. If they are long quotations they probably are printed in a manner slightly different from the rest of the text—indented, for example, or in another style of type—to make it clear that they are indeed quotations. You may be required to use quotations in papers. In addition to consulting style manuals about how to handle them, you can get clues from examining the printed material you see every day.

5. *Citations and references.* Close examination of the citation and reference technique used in this book will reveal what items about each book or article are included and the order in which those items are introduced. These forms will vary somewhat from document to document, so do not assume that you have all the answers from this one examination. Check several style manuals, too.

6. *Sexist references.* Sexism is built into the English language; no reader of this book needs to be advised that our language favors males. Thus in English it is common to use the words *man* or *mankind* to refer to women and men collectively. If we want to talk about a hypothetical student, having neither sex in mind, we tend to say or write *he*. Those of us who want to give women an equal break are likely to use a variety of neutral words. Thus, I don't think I ever use the word *mankind* in this book, substituting such words as *people*, *human beings*, or *Homo sapiens*. Problems of sexism arise on nearly every page. You may not agree with my solutions, but they are there to be noticed and therefore accepted or rejected. Notice also how writers who are quoted in this text handle the problem.

The generic use of "man" simply cripples our minds. . . . So, I invite you to remove the words "man" and "mankind" from your vocabulary and to struggle with using the alternatives. Maybe someday we can use "man" and it won't matter, but not in this century.

Elise Boulding (1977, p. 63)

The point of the preceding list is merely that some matters that at first seem mysterious become less mysterious if you merely allow yourself to notice how other people deal with them.

We could continue almost endlessly this listing of qualities about form that you could discover from looking "behind the scenes," so to speak, of any book, including this one. There are so many: how chapter titles are stated, what appears on the title page (the source of bibliographic information when you need it in writing papers), the author's preference in sentence length, the use of pictures, the typestyles used, the page layout, the handling of student exercises or questions, the nature of the index, the color of the book cover.

SPOTTING LONG-RANGE TRENDS

It is difficult to see long-range trends, as we noted earlier. It is still possible, however, particularly if you are interested. We all know people, not necessarily specialists, who can speak with considerable accuracy about how rock music has changed in the last decade, or how men's and women's clothing fashions have shifted in recent years, or how automobile design shifts year by year. The major key, as always, is in spotting *differences*, small and large. Another key is knowing what is likely to change and therefore where to focus attention.

In the years immediately ahead we will undoubtedly undergo some of the most dramatic changes in the uses of communication media in human history. Some observations about the site of those changes have been made earlier, but they bear repeating. The biggest generalization that we can make with a fair assumption of accuracy is that electronic media will continue to change rapidly.

Below is a list of probable media developments, by no means exhaustive, that will be interesting to watch. The questions raised by each item on the list are many, but perhaps the following queries will help focus our observations. (1) How will the development of one medium affect other media? It is almost impossible for a major change to occur in one medium without causing changes in all others. A medium seldom simply dies, but it may shift its role quite sharply. (2) How will the development change our sensibilities, how we think, how we perceive the world? (3) How will the development change our habits of relating to other people, our social arrangements?

Added Access to Television Signals

We will undoubtedly continue to have access to more and more television channels in our homes. The developments that will make this possible include improvements in satellites (and more of them), substitution of glass fiber for copper wire in transmission, and perhaps shifts in government regulations (in the United States, at least) in the direction of encouraging new initiators of televised material. Some engineers who study this question feel that we may soon have access to over a thousand signals that can feed various kinds of material to television sets.

Video Discs or Tapes

Both video discs and home videotape recorders and reproducers have been available for some time. Videotape, in cassette form, came first, but video discs are swiftly entering the market. The discs can only be used to play back material, but they will make possible home libraries of motion pictures or other visual material. The motion picture entertainment industry keeps a sharp eye on the implications of home videotapes and discs, both of which could profoundly influence the distribution of films.

Automated and/or Electronic Postal Systems

It is possible and, in time, probable, that the postal system in the United States and in other highly industrialized countries will need to increase automated handling of mail and perhaps move beyond that to the distribution of mail by electronic means. Such systems could be tied in with computer systems and/or increased television access. The U.S. postal system is technologically ready for it now. Great Britain and France are already using "electronic mail" in limited experiments. Several American corporations are developing privately owned systems.

Holography

Holography, that fantastic three-dimensional image-making procedure, is still in its infancy. We can see holographic exhibits here and there, now and again, but its future, whatever that may be, lies in systematic development of the medium. We will doubtless all have a chance to witness that development in the years ahead.

Physical Transport Systems

Some students of communication like to consider physical transportation of the body and of materials as a form of communication. Others do not. Whichever you personally feel, it is almost impossible to imagine a future in which the role of automobiles, airplanes, trains, and other vehicles will dramatically change in our society, primarily because of the necessity to conserve energy. One viable possibility is the gradual reduction in movement of bodies from here to there and increased use of electronic media (two-way television, video telephones, computers) to keep us in touch with places of work, study, and play.

Cross-species Communication

What *will* happen with respect to cross-species communication? Will we be able one day to hold sophisticated conversations with chimps, apes, dolphins, and perhaps other creatures? Research will doubtless continue and expand. Where will it take us?

The Crisis in Knowledge

Underlying much speculation about the future of communication media is the encouraging but frightening fact that we are generating new information at a rate that is unequalled in human history. The problems of storing that information (how long can libraries in their present form exist?) are enormous. Perhaps even more important is the problem of *finding* what we want to in the stored information. It is an old cliché by now that we are drowning in a sea of information. How will we learn to swim in those crowded waters? Many scholars and businesspeople feel that the most likely answer is the continued development of linkages between powerful centralized computers and cable television, which will permit subscribers to the system to call up desired information to be displayed on television screens.

Information . . . can now be moved at the rate of 1.5 million words per minute. *Gone With the Wind* can be transmitted in about twenty seconds. The Bible would take a little longer—about half a minute.

W. M. Ellinghaus (quoted in Ralph Lee Smith, 1972, p. 9)

THE PASSING PARADE OF LANGUAGE

Language is forever changing, and it is fun to watch the passing parade. If we keep our senses open we will see, hear, and produce wondrous concoctions. I would like to use as an example of a language observer William Safire, a former presidential speech writer who has a Sunday column in the *New York Times Magazine* called "On Language," in which he records with infectious wit his observations on the Great Language Parade. For example, Safire notes:

- The rise of the word "gorilla" in the music industry to mean a resounding hit (1979a, p. 107). It apparently follows the earlier usage of "a monster" to refer to an entertainment hit. Where has usage taken "gorilla" (in this sense) by now? Is it part of everyday usage? Has it disappeared?

  The "on-line" syndrome, which apparently is restricted to New York, where people stand "on line" (not "in line") to get tickets to a movie (1979b, p. 9). In the rest of the country people stand "in line." True, according to your observations?

- The relatively new American phenomenon of people saying "Have a nice day," at the end of a conversation. Referring to it as the "H.A.N.D." phenomenon, Safire notes that telephone operators have been instructed to say it, that indeed the phrase pops up everywhere. Safire notes that "when H.A.N.D. is spoken with sincerity and eye contact, it is a social asset and a note of civility in a hurried world; but when it is spoken automatically, in the same tone as 'Get lost,' it comes across with a resounding clank of falsity" (1979c, pp. 9-10). A favorite instance of usage is reported about a courtroom episode in Cortland, New York, where the judge had just committed a man to prison for seven to ten years and ended his statement of sentencing with the phrase: "You are hereby remanded to the custody of the sheriff's department for delivery to the custody of state officials. Have a nice day."

☐ The offbeat use in baseball of "He flied out," as in occasions when the batter hits a fly ball. We would all get an ugly red mark in the margin if we used "flied out" in a paper for school, but Safire points out that, in baseball, the only time " 'flew out' would be correct is if the batter dropped his bat, flapped his arms and soared out the stadium" (1979d, p. 8).

THIS HAS BEEN ONLY A BEGINNING

This brief introduction to naturalistic observation of communication gives us only a glance at how researchers work at communication. We have seen only some hints about naturalistic field observation, and this is but one means of investigating communication. There are hundreds of survey techniques, questionnaires, and reaction scales, not to mention controlled experiments, statistical approaches, and elegant experiments that require years of background and practice to perform.

But we have seen a beginning.

THIS CHAPTER IN PERSPECTIVE

The major point of this chapter has been that we should all become lifelong observers of communication in action. The major reason for this, aside from pleasure, is that it is impossible to rely on rules for gaining the kind of skill that we all hope for in communication. Books of rules, while useful, are simply not adequate for the task of preparing us to behave sensibly in the endless communication contexts in which we will find ourselves day in, day out. There are many ways of observing communication in action, but we have centered here on the technique known as naturalistic observation, as contrasted with accumulating information through experimental procedures. We frequently borrowed guidelines of what to look for from anthropologists, a professional group that contributes much to the study of communication. We settled on Karl Popper's way of determining whether we have hit upon a truth—no matter how temporary: not being able to disprove a hypothesis. Finally, we saw some examples of observation leading to hypotheses and to temporary truths, since the notion of permanent truths is generally foreign to the scientific outlook.

EXTENSIONS

Reading You Might Enjoy

1. Hocking, Paul, ed. *Principles of Visual Anthropology*. The Hague: Mouton Publishers, 1975.

This large collection of essays centers on the simple thesis that motion pictures, still pictures, and video images serve profoundly well a variety of functions in which anthropologists are interested. If you have any interest in how culture—and therefore communication—can be studied by visual means, you will find more information here about a variety of approaches than in any other single document I know. The essays range from technical matters (what camera, what film, what technique) to philosophical matters (why record with cameras at all, how do people unaccustomed to cameras react to their own images?).

2. McLuhan, Marshall, Kathryn Hutchon, and Eric McLuhan. *City as Classroom: Understanding Language as Media*. Agincourt, Ontario, Canada: Book Society of Canada, 1977.

The authors of this book take the position that school is a point of departure for learning the nature of the larger world. They suggest hundreds of experiments, activities, and observations specifically intended to help you learn about the properties of media and their effects, to detect changes in the communication environment, and to sharpen your capacity for continuing observation. The book is straightforward and clear.

3. Miller, Gerald R., and Henry E. Nicholson. *Communication Inquiry: A Perspective on a Process*. Reading, Mass.: Addison-Wesley, 1976.

This is a careful, readable explanation of the procedures that professionals use in studying communication. It is necessarily general—it doesn't describe in detail *all* of the techniques that researchers employ. It does, however, provide a basic outline of steps to be taken from asking the right question, defining terms, developing a theory, engaging in unbiased observation, and evaluating the results. Although the authors are sophisticated researchers, going well beyond the techniques suggested in this chapter, their frequent down-to-earth examples make the book attractive to beginners.

4. Webb, Eugene J., Donald T. Campbell, Richard D. Schwartz, and Lee Sechrest. *Unobtrusive Measures: Nonreactive Research in the Social Sciences*. Chicago: Rand McNally, 1966.

Perhaps the best way to describe this fascinating book is to say what *reactive research* means and thus understand what *nonreactive research* is. Reactive research, to oversimplify, refers to the use of such tools as questionnaires and interviews with people, items to which people must necessarily react. The authors here suggest many means of supplementing questionnaires and interviews by looking for other kinds of physical evidence without relating directly to the people involved. It's frequently similar to, as the authors point out, using the kind of evidence that Sherlock Holmes so often used: seeing a deposit of ashes, noticing wear in a carpet, noticing a pair of eyeglasses. The book is fun to read, as well as being quite scientifically respectable.

Ponderings and Projects

1. Study the same newspaper across fifty years of time. Look at copies of *The New York Times*, for example, from half a century ago and from today. Study, for instance, the average number of words in sentences fifty years ago and today. Do you have any hypotheses before beginning about whether the average number of words per sentence in newspaper stories and advertisements has increased or decreased over time?

2. Look at two recent novels, one published in the United States, the other in Great Britain. Hunt specifically for dialogue in which quotation marks are used. Find dozens of instances of dialogue in each novel. Then search for four patterns of punctuation in sentences in which quotation marks are used, as follows:

a) "_____ _____ _____ _____ _____."
b) "_____ _____ _____ __ __ _____ __".
c) "_____ _____ _____ _____ _____," __ _____.
d) "_____ __ _____ __ _____", _____ __ __.

If there are differences in British and American practice, note it and draw a generalization about the rules that seem to operate.

3. Make observation studies of sexism in American writing and speech. Read papers and magazines closely to see if writers and editors avoid use of the terms *he, him, man, mankind*, and so forth, when they refer to all people. Listen as well to television newscasters, your teachers, your friends, and yourself.

4. Look at Erving Goffman's book *Gender Advertisements* (1976) (see the references near the end of this book), both to become familiar with his techniques of analyzing advertisments and to point the direction for a similar study of your own. You may wish to shift the subject of your inquiry from how men and women are depicted to, say, how children or older people are shown. Your study could be even more revealing if you conducted it across cultures, getting advertisements from, say, American and British magazines, unless you read another language.

5. With permission, make an audio tape recording of a conversation with a friend. Make a written transcript of *exactly* what each of you said for about ten minutes. Include in the written version all the pauses, *hmms, ahs*, false starts, and stops of the conversation. This should reveal how different speech is from writing.

6. Where you live do young people—normally teenagers—carry radios and tape recorders with them on the street? If so, do you detect prestige value of large radios, as contrasted with the pocket-sized transistors everywhere available today? What symbolic value is found in the large portable radios? After developing a hypothesis, use informants (carefully) to see why they chose large over small.

7. If you are fortunate enough to attend a school that has students from other cultures or subcultures, make friends with someone who will serve as a good informant about the communicative ways of that culture and offer in return your own services as an informant about the communicative ways of your culture. Remember, whatever you find out, the cultural ways of one culture are neither better nor worse than those of another culture, only different.

Postcript

At the beginning of this book I welcomed you to the forest, the wilderness area of communication, where so little is really known, although specialists labor daily to accumulate new knowledge and interpret it with wisdom.

We've traveled together down many trails in the forest, getting perspectives. There are, however, many trails on which we didn't set foot, many perspectives we didn't see. But you have a lifetime to explore, and I hope you will be interested in doing that. It's fun.

Do you know where the most fun lies in wandering through this forest of communication? Precisely in pursuing the study yourself, in big ways and little ways. There's nothing more abundant in our lives than communication: we live forever and always in a spacious communication laboratory. We cannot exhaust it. Search away.

What communication is all about is crossing barriers, so that two can cooperate, three can dance, three hundred can hold a class reunion, a nation can pull together. Even the passing thought of being totally alone is frightening enough to put most of us into instant freeze frame.

May I repeat something that I wrote in Chapter 4? I mentioned the truth of John Donne's famous sermon ("No man is an island . . .") but said that there was another side to the story, too:

> *Every person is an island, isolated from all others in his or her self, forever physically separated after the umbilical cord is cut. The anxiety, the loneliness of the isolation moves us to create bridges*

between our islands. We extend our hands, fingers touching; we span the distance with our eyes. We speak; we smile. Through such strivings we construct transitory bridges, pathways of signals, that carry delicate freight of meaning. In fair weather the bridges hold; in foul weather they collapse. We work a lifetime keeping the bridges open between our personal islands. The tolling bell signals the death of an island, the collapse of a bridge, punctuating the eternal state of isolation that we endure, seeking always to alleviate.

Building those bridges of communication is an eternal task. Sometimes it's tough, because it's always a guessing game. Our hardest job as communicators is making sensible guesses about how the other person is receiving the conscious and unconscious signals that we continuosly spark off. Husbands and wives who have crowned a happy life together with a fiftieth wedding anniversary still make guesses about what the other is thinking. New friends, shyly or boldly, struggle to get in sync. Writers for big and varied audiences—

Illustration P.1 Now rest.

writers of textbooks like this one, for example—make the scariest guesses of all. There are so many of you. You are similar in some ways, quite different in others. (I hope I've made some good guesses about your backgrounds and interests. To say it more directly, I hope you've learned and enjoyed.)

Have a healthy skepticism about what you've read in this book. The minute ideas go on paper they begin to be obsolete. Knowledge moves fast these days. Major new insights grow slowly, although they often fuse into consciousness in an unexpected instant. The function of skepticism is personal growth. Skepticism permits you to say, "Well, I'm not so sure about . . ." What follows then is thought, self-dialogue, conversation with friends, perhaps leading one day to insights, exploding like sunburst rockets on the Fourth of July.

In any event, we are at the end of this journey. We've tramped some trails and glanced from time to time in the direction of other trails or uncharted territory. Keep trekking.

But now, it's customary to rest.

Notes about the Illustrations in This Book

As promised in the Introduction, I would like to provide you with information about the location of the photographs used in this book, where that information is not fully given in the caption or otherwise explained in the text.

I will not provide technical information about the photographs (the cameras, films, lenses, printing paper, etc.) because this is a specialized bit of lore that would probably be of interest to only a small percentage of readers.

Frontispiece São Paolo, Brazil. A park in the center of the city, Sunday morning, during a fiesta.

I.1 Kenya, Africa, several kilometers outside the capital city of Nairobi, in coffee-growing country.

3.1 Self-explanatory.

3.2 (*Top*) Directly outside the main post office in Lahore, Pakistan. The scribe, with white hat, serves a client under the shade of a tree in 125°F weather. (*Bottom*) One of several color television studios in the modern facilities of the Pakistani Broadcasting Corporation, Lahore, Pakistan.

3.3 A portion of the Frankfurt, Germany, international airport.

3.4 Self-explanatory.

3.5 Self-explanatory.

3.6 Self-explanatory.

3.7 Self-explanatory.

4.1 A family in Kensington Park, London, England, on a lovely spring day.

278 NOTES ABOUT THE ILLUSTRATIONS IN THIS BOOK

4.2 London, England, near St. James' Park in the city center, summer.

4.3 Self-explanatory.

4.4 Self-explanatory.

4.5 Self-explanatory.

5.1 New York State. A girl with a silk or nylon stocking over her head.

5.2 Window of a drugstore, New York City.

5.3 Schoolchildren on a guided tour of the great art museum, the Hermitage, in Leningrad, Russia.

5.4 Self-explanatory.

5.5 Self-explanatory.

5.6 Windows of St. James' Church in London, England, consecrated in 1684.

6.1 Self-explanatory.

6.2 Self-explanatory.

6.3 Self-explanatory.

6.4 Self-explanatory.

7.1 Self-explanatory.

7.2 Self-explanatory.

7.3 Self-explanatory.

7.4 In a village in Kenya, near the capital city of Nairobi.

7.5 Self-explanatory.

7.6 Self-explanatory.

7.7 A room adjoining the Friday mosque in the Maidan (square) in Isfahan, Iran.

8.1 Inside the Hermitage, Leningrad's great art museum.

8.2 Korea, Harcong-Ni area, 1950.

8.3 In the renowned Shalimar Gardens, Lahore, Pakistan.

8.4 A salesman in the covered bazaar in Istanbul, Turkey, bargaining with an American tourist.

8.5 Subway, New York City.

8.6 A park in Istanbul, Turkey, end of the school year.

8.7 Self-explanatory.

8.8 A park near Finlandia Hall, Helsinki, Finland.

8.9 Two Brazilian women in an auditorium, São Paolo, Brazil.

8.10 Bamako, Republic of Mali, West Africa.

8.11 On the left, a woman in Tehran, Iran. On the right, a woman in London, England. Both photographs were taken in 1977.

9.1 Heathrow Airport, London, England.

9.2 In the composer's loft working area, New York City.

9.3 The village of Kirango, about 230 kilometers from Bamako, the capital city of the Republic of Mali, West Africa.

10.1 Self-explanatory.

10.2 Self-explanatory.

10.3 Self-explanatory.

11.1 A street in Machakos, Kenya, East Africa.

11.2 Hyde Park, central London, England, on a good spring day for sunbathing.

11.3 New York City.

11.4 Apartment number, Tehran, Iran. The apartment is in a cosmopolitan section of the city, hence numbering is not done in the Persian system.

11.5 In a subway—or "underground," to use their term—station in London, England.

11.6 A few hundred feet from the terminal building, National Airport, Washington, D.C.

P.1 Outside the Hermitage, Leningrad's major art museum.

References

Arden, H. (1975). The pious ones. *National Geographic* 148:276-298.

Arieti, S. (1976). *Creativity: The Magic Synthesis*. New York: Basic Books.

Arnheim, R. (1965). Visual thinking. In Gyorgy Kepes (ed.), *Education of Vision*, pp. 1-26. New York: George Braziller.

——— (1969). *Visual Thinking*. Berkeley and Los Angeles: University of California Press.

Atwood, M. (1976). *Surfacing*. New York: Popular Library.

Barna, L. M. (1976). Intercultural communication stumbling blocks. In L. A. Samovar and R. E. Porter (eds.), *Intercultural Communication: A Reader*. Belmont, Calif.: Wadsworth.

Barnlund, D. (1968). *Interpersonal Communication: Survey and Studies*. Boston: Houghton Mifflin.

——— (1970). A transactional model of communication. In K. K. Sereno and C. D. Mortenson (eds.), *Foundations of Communication Theory*. New York: Harper & Row.

Bataille, G. (1955). *Prehistoric Painting: Lascaux or the Birth of Art*. New York: Skira.

Bates, M. (1950). *The Nature of Natural Science*. New York: Charles Scribner's Sons.

Bateson, G. (1968). Conventions of communication: where validity depends upon belief. In J. Ruesch and G. Bateson, *Communication: The Social Matrix of Psychiatry*. New York: Norton.

——— (1972). *Steps to an Ecology of Mind*. New York: Ballantine Books.

——— (1979). *Mind and Nature: A Necessary Unity*. New York: E. P. Dutton.

Baugh, J. (1978). The politics of black power handshakes. *Natural History* 87(2):32-40.

Benedict, R. (1946). *Patterns of Culture*. New York: Penguin Books.

Bertalanffy, L. (1967). *Robots, Men and Minds: Psychology in the Modern World*. New York: George Braziller.

Birdwhistell, R. (1970). *Kinesics and Context: Essays on Body Motion Communication*. Philadelphia: University of Pennsylvania Press.

Blakemore, C. (1977). *Mechanics of the Mind*. Cambridge: At the University Press.

Bogen, J. E. (1975). Some educational aspects of hemispheric specialization. *UCLA Educator* 17(2):24-32.

Boulding, E. (1977). Women in community. In M. Katz, W. Marsh, and G. Thompson (eds.), *Earth's Answer: Explorations of Planetary Culture at the Lindesfarne Conference*, pp. 59-70. New York: Harper & Row, Lindesfarne Books.

Boulding, K. E. (1956). *The Image*. Ann Arbor: University of Michigan Press.

Boulle, P. (1963). *Planet of the Apes*. New York: Vanguard.

Bridgman, P. W. (1959). *The Way Things Are*. Cambridge, Mass.: Harvard University Press.

Brockman, J. (1977). Introduction to *About Bateson*, edited by J. Brockman. New York: E. P. Dutton.

Bronowski, J. (1953). *The Common Sense of Science*. Cambridge, Mass.: Harvard University Press.

——— (1973). *The Ascent of Man*. Boston: Little, Brown.

Brooks, J. (1976). *Telephone: The First Hundred Years*. New York: Harper & Row.

Brown, J. C. (1978). Introduction to *United States, National Gallery of Art: East Building*, by R.B.D. McLanathan. Washington, D.C.: National Gallery of Art.

Brown, N. O. (1959). *Life against Death: The Psychoanalytical Meaning of History*. New York: Random House, Vintage Books.

Brown, W. S. (1975). Left brain, right brain. *Harper's* 254(1497).

Bryson, L. (1954). *Reason and Discontent: The Task of Liberal Adult Education*. Pasadena, Calif.: Fund for Adult Education.

Bühler, C. F. (1960). *The Fifteenth Century Book: The Scribes, the Printers, the Decorators*. Philadelphia: University of Pennsylvania Press.

Byers, P. (1977). A personal view of nonverbal communication. *Theory into Practice* 16(3):140.

Carpenter, E. (1957). The new languages. In Edmund Carpenter and Marshall McLuhan (eds.), *Explorations: Studies in Culture and Communication*, vol. 7, pp. 1-21. Toronto: University of Toronto Press.

——— (1959). *Eskimo*. With sketches by F. Varley and photographs from the collection of R. Flaherty. No. 9 in the *Explorations* series. Toronto: University of Toronto Press.

——— (1974). *Oh, What a Blow That Phantom Gave Me!* New York: Bantam Books.

―――― (1975). The tribal terror of self-awareness. In P. Hockings (ed.), *Principles of Visual Anthropology*, pp. 451-461. The Hague: Mouton Publishers.

Chapple, E. (1970). *Culture and Biological Man: Explorations in Behavioral Anthropology*. New York: Holt, Rinehart and Winston.

Cherry, C. (1966). The communication of information. In A. G. Smith (ed.), *Communication and Culture: Readings in the Codes of Human Interaction*. New York: Holt, Rinehart and Winston.

Cherry, L. (1977). A new vision of dreams. *New York Times Magazine*, July 3.

Chiera, E. (1966). *They Wrote on Clay*, edited by G. Cameron. Chicago: University of Chicago Press.

Clarke, A. C. (1977). *The View from Serendip*. New York: Random House.

Collier, J., Jr. (1967). *Visual Anthropology: Photography as a Research Method*. New York: Holt, Rinehart and Winston.

Comstock, G. (1978). The impact of television on American institutions. *Journal of Communication* 28(2):12-28.

Cowen, R. C. (1977). Should biologists redesign organic life? *Christian Science Monitor*, February 3, p. 13.

Craig, C. G. (1979). Jacaltec: field work in Guatemala. In T. Shopen (ed.), *Languages and Their Speakers*, pp. 3-57. Cambridge, Mass.: Winthrop.

Dale, L. A., and R. A. White (1977). Glossary of terms found in the literature of psychical research and parapsychology. In B. B. Wolman (ed.), *Handbook of Parapsychology*. New York: Von Nostrand Reinhold.

Davis, F. (1975). *Inside Intuition: What We Know about Nonverbal Communication*. New York: New American Library, Signet Books.

―――― (1978). *Eloquent Animals: A Study in Animal Communication*. New York: Coward, McCann & Geoghegan.

Davison, W. P., J. Boylan, and F.R.C. Yu (1976). *Mass Media: Systems and Effects*. New York: Praeger.

Dillard, J. L. (1973). *Black English: Its History and Usage in the United States*. New York: Random House, Vintage Books.

Dubos, R. (1968). *So Human an Animal*. New York: Charles Scribner's Sons.

Edgerton, R. (1976). *Deviance: A Cross-Cultural Perspective*. Menlo Park, Calif.: Cummings.

Fantel, H. (1977). How Edison stumbled on his phonograph. *New York Times*, April 24, p. D31.

Ferris, C. D. (1978). Information power—you must help control it. *Christian Science Monitor*, August 2, p. 22.

Fincher, J. (1976). *Human Intelligence*. New York: G. P. Putnam's Sons.

Forsdale, J., and L. Forsdale (1966). Film literacy. *Teachers College Record* 67(8):608-617.

Forsdale, L. (1974). *Nonverbal Communication*. New York: Harcourt Brace Jovanovich.

Gardner, S. (1968). *Blake*. New York: Arco.

Gerbner, G. (1972). Communication and the social environment. *Scientific American* 227(3):153-160.

Goffman, E. (1976). *Gender Advertisements*. New York: Harper & Row.

Gombrich, E. H. (1972). The visual image. *Scientific American* 227(3)82-96.

Gould, J. (1979). Do honeybees know what they are doing? *Natural History* 88(6):66-75.

Gove, P. B. (1962). A letter to the editor of Life Magazine. In J. Sledd and W. R. Ebbitt (eds.), *Dictionaries and That Dictionary: A Casebook on the Aims of Lexicographers and the Targets of Reviewers*. Glenview, Ill.: Scott, Foresman.

Griffin, D. R. (1976). *The Question of Animal Awareness: Evolutionary Continuity of Mental Experience*. New York: Rockefeller University Press.

——— (1977). Expanding horizons in animal communication behavior. In T. A. Sebeok (ed.), *How Animals Communicate*, pp. 26-32. Bloomington: Indiana University Press.

Gurdjieff, G. (1969). *Meetings with Remarkable Men*. New York: E. P. Dutton.

Haas, M. R. (1964). *Thai-English Student's Dictionary*. Stanford, Calif.: Stanford University Press.

Hall, E. T. (1959). *The Silent Language*. Garden City, N.Y.: Doubleday.

——— (1966). *The Hidden Dimension*. Garden City, N.Y.: Doubleday.

——— (1976). *Beyond Culture*. Garden City, N.Y.: Doubleday, Anchor Books.

Harrington, R. (1952). *The Face of the Arctic*. New York: Henry Schuman.

Hayakawa, S. (1963). *Symbol, Status and Personality*. New York: Harcourt, Brace, and World.

Herbert, F. (1965). *Dune*. Radnor, Pa.: Chilton Book Co.

Hoebel, E. A. (1960). *The Cheyennes: Indians of the Great Plains*. New York: Holt, Rinehart and Winston.

Hogben, H. (1949). *From Cave Painting to Comic Strip: A Kaleidoscope of Human Communication*. New York: Chanticleer Press.

Hooke, S. H. (1954). Recording and writing. In C. Singer, E. J. Holmyard, and A. R. Hall (eds.), *A History of Technology: From Early Times to Fall of Ancient Empires*, vol. 1. New York and London: Oxford University Press.

Hovland, C. J., I. L. Janus, and H. H. Kelley (1953). *Communication and Persuasion*. New Haven, Conn.: Yale University Press.

Huxley, A. (1970). *The Doors of Perception*. New York: Harper & Row, Perennial Library.

Ivins, M. (1974). Ed who? *New York Times Magazine*, June 30.

Janovy, J., Jr. (1978). *Keith County Journal*. New York: St. Martin's Press.

Jaynes, J. (1977). *The Origin of Consciousness in the Breakdown of the Bicameral Mind*. Boston: Houghton Mifflin.

Jourard, S. M. (1971). *The Transparent Self*. 2nd ed. New York: Van Nostrand Reinhold.

Jowett, J. (trans.) (1952). *The Dialogues of Plato*. No. 7. *Great Books of the Western World*. Chicago: Encyclopaedia Britannica.

Kluckhohn, C., and D. Leighton. (1946). *The Navaho*. Cambridge, Mass.: Harvard University Press.

Kochman, T. (ed.) (1972). *Rappin' and Stylin' Out: Communication in Urban Black America*. Urbana: University of Illinois Press.

Korzybski, A. (1941). *Science and Sanity: An Introduction to Non-Aristotelian Systems and General Semantics*. 2nd ed. Lancaster, Pa.: Science Press Printing Co.

Kuhn, T. S. (1959). *The Copernican Revolution: Planetary Astronomy in the Development of Western Thought*. New York: Random House, Vintage Books.

LaBarre, W. (1964). Paralinguistics, kinesics, and cultural anthropology. In T. Sebeok, A. Hayes, and M. Bateson (eds.), *Approaches to Semiotics*. The Hague: Mouton Publishers.

Langer, S. (1948). *Philosophy in a New Key: A Study in the Symbolism of Reason, Rite, and Art*. New York: American Library, Mentor Books.

Lasswell, H. (1948). The structure and function of communication in society. In L. Bryson (ed.), *The Communication of Ideas*. New York: Harper & Brothers.

LeBoyer, F. (1976). *Loving Hands*. New York: Knopf.

Lilly, J. C. (1978). *Communication between Man and Dolphin: The Possibilities of Talking with Other Species*. New York: Crown.

Linden, E. (1975). *Apes, Men, and Language*. New York: E. P. Dutton.

Linehan, E. (1979). The trouble with dolphins. *National Geographic* 155:506-545.

Luce, G. B. (1971). *Body Time: Physiological Rhythms and Social Stress*. New York: Pantheon Books.

MacCurdy, E. (1958). *The Notebooks of Leonardo da Vinci*, vol. 1. New York: George Braziller.

Magee, B. (1979). *Men of Ideas*. New York: Viking Press.

May, R. (1977). Gregory Bateson and humanistic psychology. In J. Brockman (ed.), *About Bateson*. New York: E. P. Dutton.

McLuhan, M. (1962). *The Gutenberg Galaxy: The Making of Typographic Man*. Toronto: University of Toronto Press.

——— (1964). *Understanding Media: The Extensions of Man*. New York: McGraw-Hill.

McLuhan, M., and Q. Fiore (1967). *The Medium Is the Massage: An Inventory of Effects*. New York: Bantam Books.

——— (1968). *War and Peace in the Global Village*. New York: Bantam Books.

Mehrabian, A. (1976). *Public Places and Private Spaces: The Psychology of Work, Play, and Living Environments.* New York: Basic Books.

Merle, R. (1969). *The Day of the Dolphin,* translated by Helen Weaver. New York: Simon and Schuster.

Miller, G. A. (1975). *The Psychology of Communication.* New York: Basic Books.

Miller, G. R., and H. E. Nicholson (1976). *Communication Inquiry: A Perspective on a Process.* Reading, Mass.: Addison-Wesley.

Montagu, A. (1977). *Touching: The Human Significance of the Skin.* 2nd ed. New York: Harper & Row.

Monteux, P. (1957). My early years. On record jacket of Stravinsky, *The Rite of Spring,* Radio Corporation of America, LM-2085.

Moore, C. (1978). The impetus to build: forms and feeling. *Christian Science Monitor,* February 16, pp. 24-25.

Morris, C. (1946). *Signs, Language, and Behavior.* Englewood Cliffs, N.J.: Prentice-Hall.

Murphy, G. (1973). Introduction to *Dream Telepathy,* by M. Ullman and S. Drippner, with A. Vaughn. New York: Macmillan.

Nance, J. (1975). *The Gentle Tasaday: A Stone Age People in the Philippine Rain Forest.* New York: Harcourt Brace Jovanovich.

Navajo war code was unbroken (1979). *New York Times,* January 7, p. 41.

Olson, D. R. (1977). Oral and written language and the cognitive processes of children. *Journal of Communication* 27(3):10-26.

Ornstein, R. E. (1977). *The Psychology of Consciousness.* 2nd ed. San Francisco: W. H. Freeman.

Patai, R. (1976). *The Arab Mind.* New York: Charles Scribner's Sons.

Popper, K. (1968). *The Logic of Scientific Discovery.* New York: Harper & Row, Harper Torchbooks.

Premack, A. J., and D. Premack (1972). Teaching language to an ape. *Scientific American* 227(4):92-99.

Premack, D. (1976). *Intelligence in Ape and Man.* Hillsdale, N.J.: Lawrence Erlbaum.

Pursell, C. W., Jr. (1971). Samuel F. B. Morse. In R. L. Breeden (ed.), *Those Inventive Americans.* Washington, D.C.: National Geographic Society.

Read, P. P. (1974). *Alive: The Story of the Andes Survivors.* Philadelphia: J. B. Lippincott.

Reif, R. (1978). Gutenberg Bible brings $1.8 million. *New York Times,* March 10, p. C30.

Rensberger, B. (1974). "Talking" chimpanzee asks for names of things now. *New York Times,* December 4, p. 45.

Rogers, E. M., and R. A. Rogers (1976). *Communication in Organizations*. New York: Free Press.

Ruben, B. D. (1975). Intrapersonal, interpersonal, and mass communication processes in individual and multi-person systems. In B. D. Ruben and J. Y. Kim (eds.), *General Systems Theory and Human Communication*. Rochelle Park, N.J.: Hayden Book Co.

Ruesch, J., and W. Kees (1956). *Nonverbal Communication: Notes on the Visual Perception of Human Relations*. Berkeley and Los Angeles: University of California Press.

Safire, W. (1979a). On language. *New York Times Magazine*, May 20, pp. 10-12.

——— (1979b). On language. *New York Times Magazine*, June 17, pp. 9-10.

——— (1979c). On language. *New York Times Magazine*, June 24, pp. 9-10.

——— (1979d). On language. *New York Times Magazine*, July 1, pp. 6-8.

Sagan, C. (1976). Quoted in Dear spaceman, this is our world . . . *To the Point International*, June 14, p. 41.

——— (1977). *The Dragons of Eden: Speculations on the Evolution of Human Intelligence*. New York: Random House.

Samples, B. (1976). *The Metaphoric Mind: A Celebration of Creative Consciousness*. Reading, Mass.: Addison-Wesley.

Sandburg, C. (1949). *Lincoln Collector: The Story of Oliver R. Barrett's Great Private Collection*. New York: Harcourt, Brace.

Sapir, E. (1929). The status of linguistics as a science. *Language* 5:207-214.

Satir, V. (1976). *Making Contact*. Millbrae, Calif.: Celestial Arts.

Schmandt-Besserat, D. (1977). The earliest precursor of writing. *Scientific American* 238(6):50-59.

Scholderer, V. (1970). *Johann Gutenberg: The Inventor of Printing*. 2nd rev. ed. Oxford: Oxford University Press.

Schramm, W. (1977). Some notes on research, theory, and production in instructional television. Background paper for the Essential Learning Skills Television Project. Bloomington, Ind.: Agency for Instructional Television.

Scientists in Hawaii to resume project halted by dophins' release (1977). *New York Times*, December 16, p. A19.

Schwartz, T. (1974). *The Responsive Chord*. Garden City, N.Y.: Doubleday, Anchor Books.

Shannon, C., and W. Weaver (1949). *The Mathematical Theory of Communication*. Urbana: University of Illinois Press.

Shorey, H. H. (1977). Pheromones. In T. A. Sebeok (ed.), *How Animals Communicate*, pp. 137-163. Bloomington: Indiana University Press.

Shepard, R. F. (1976). Holography takes roots in SoHo in museum devoted to future. *New York Times*, December 29, p. 16.

Slater, P. (1974). *Earthwalk*. New York: Bantam Books.

Smith, A. G. (1979. Anthropology. In B. Budd and B. Ruben (eds.), *Interdisciplinary Approaches to Human Communication*, pp. 57-70. Rochelle Park, N.J.: Hayden Book Co.

Smith, R. L. (1972). *The Wired Nation: Cable TV: The Electronic Communications Highway*. New York: Harper & Row, Harper Colophon Books.

Stegner, W. (1979). My name is Tsoai-talee. A review of *The Names: A Memoir*, by N. S. Momaday. *New York Times Book Review*, March 6, p. 7.

Steinbeck, J., and E. F. Ricketts (1951). *The Log from the Sea of Cortez*. (The narrative portion of the book *Sea of Cortez*, 1941, reissued with a profile "About Ed Ricketts.") New York: Viking Press.

Tart, C. T. (1977). Putting the pieces together: a conceptual framework for understanding discrete states of consciousness. In N. E. Zinberg (ed.), *Alternate States of Consciousness*. New York: Free Press.

Terry, W. (1977). Nureyev leaps into films as Valentino. *Saturday Review*, April 30.

Thomas, L. (1974). *The Lives of a Cell: Notes of a Biology Watcher*. New York: Bantam Books.

────── (1979). *The Medusa and the Snail: More Notes of a Biology Watcher*. New York: Viking Press.

Thorpe, W. H. (1974). *Animal Nature and Human Nature*. Garden City, N.Y.: Doubleday.

Trotter, R. J. (1976). The other hemisphere. *Science News* 109:218-220.

Turner, W. (1977). Two men, facing trial for releasing dolphins, say the creatures have a right to be free. *New York Times*, July 5, p. 23.

von Frisch, K. (1953). *Dancing Bees: An Account of the Life and Senses of the Honey Bee*. New York: Harcourt, Brace, and World.

Wallace, A. F. C. (1972). *The Death and Rebirth of the Seneca*. With the assistance of Sheila C. Steen. New York: Random House, Vintage Books.

Warde, B. (1955). Foreword to *Five Hundred Years of Printing*, by S. H. Steinberg. Baltimore: Penguin Books.

Watzlawick, P. (1977). *How Real Is Real? Confusion, Disinformation, Communication*. New York: Random House, Vintage Books.

Weaver, W. (1949). Recent contributions to the mathematical theory of communication. In C. Shannon and W. Weaver, *The Mathematical Theory of Communication*. Urbana: University of Illinois Press.

Webb, E., D. Campbell, R. Schwartz, and L. Sechrest (1966). *Unobtrusive Measures: Nonreactive Research in the Social Sciences*. Chicago: Rand McNally.

Weizenbaum, J. (1976). *Computer Power and Human Reason: From Judgment to Calculation*. San Francisco: W. H. Freeman.

Wilson, E. O. (1975). *Sociobiology: The New Synthesis.* Cambridge, Mass.: Harvard University Press, Belknap Press.

Wilson, J. (1963). *Thinking with Concepts.* Cambridge: At the University Press.

Wilson, M. (1954). *American Science and Invention.* New York: Simon and Schuster.

Winger, H. W. (1955). Historial perspectives on the role of the book in society. *Library Quarterly* 25(4).

Winter, R. (1976). *The Smell Book: Scents, Sex, and Society.* New York: J. B. Lippincott.

Name Index

Addams, Chas., 122
Ailey, Alvin, American Dance Theater, 163, 164
Ali, Muhammad, 21
Andrae, Christopher, 225
Anouilh, Jean, 100
Arden, Harvey, 78
Arieti, Silvano, 147
Aristotle, 70, 71
Arnheim, Rudolf, 173, 178
Astaire, Fred, 166
Atwood, Margaret, 138

Bannister, Roger, 126
Barna, La Ray M., 93
Barnlund, Dean C., 29, il. 30, il. 33, 34, 35, 40, 41
Bartenieff, Irmgard, 196
Baryshnikov, Mikhail, 166
Bataille, Georges, 44
Bates, Marston, 253
Bateson, Eric, 94-98
Bateson, Gregory, 94, 109, 111, 123, 130, 138, 149, 175, 177
Baugh, John, 81
Beatles, 166
Bee Gees, 166

Beethoven, Ludwig von, 83, 158-159, 166
Bell, Alexander Graham, 64
Benedict, Ruth, 75-76
Berlo, David K., 41
Bertalanffy, Ludwig von, 38, 39
Birdwhistell, Ray, 182, 188, 202
Blake, William, 124
Blakemore, Colin, 150
Bogen, Joseph E., 148-149
Boulding, Elise, 265
Boulding, Kenneth E., 111, 112, 133
Boulle, Pierre, 226
Boylan, James, 113-114, 133
Bridgman, P. W., 111, 123
Broad, C. D., 116
Broca, Pierre-Paul, 138
Brockman, John, 46
Bronowski, J., 38, 141
Brooks, John, 64
Brown, J. Carter, 193
Brown, Norman O., 213
Brown, Warren, 141
Bryant, William Cullen, 63
Bryson, Lyman, 43, 44, 62
Buddha, 47
Bühler, Curt F., 51
Byers, Paul, 140

291

NAME INDEX

Calder, Alexander, 194
Campbell, Donald T., 270
Carpenter, Edmund, 22, 117, 144-146, 256
Carr, Gerry, 125
Carroll, Lewis, 7
Carter, Thomas Francis, 72
Castaneda, Carlos, 133
Chan, Sister Joanna, 98-102
Chapple, Eliot D., 174
Cherry, Colin, 11
Cherry, Laurence, 141
Chiera, Edward, 51
Churchill, Winston, 193
Cicero, 70-71
Clarke, Arthur C., 69
Coleman, Ronald, 118
Collier, John, Jr., 252
Comstock, George, 218
Condon, John C., 105
Condon, William, 175
Corinth, Lovis, 142
Cowen, Robert C., 155
Craig, Colette Grinevald, 250, 254
Cross, Lloyd, 66

Daguerre, Louis, 63
Dance, Frank E. X., 14, 41
da Vinci, Leonardo, 63
Davis, Flora, 175, 196, 232-233, 242
Davison, W. Phillips, 113-114, 133
Descartes, René, 152
Dillard, J. L., 107
Donne, John, 91, 273-274
Doty, Roy, 140
Dubos, René, 111

Edgerton, Robert B., 87-89
Edison, Thomas, 64-65
Einstein, Albert, 21, 173
Eisenhower, Dwight D., 119
Ekman, Paul, 202
Elizalade, Manuel, Jr., 77
Ellinghaus, W. M., 268
Ellington, Duke, 153, 154
Escher, M. C., 166

Fantel, Hans, 65
Ferris, Charles D., 69
Fessenden, R. A., 65

Fincher, Jack, 142, 148, 150
Fiore, Quentin, 73, 209, 212, 221
Flaherty, Robert, 145
Forsdale, Joan, 165, 166
Forsdale, Louis, 28, 83, 165, 166
Fouts, Roger, 235, il, 236, 244-245
Freud, Sigmund, 181
Friesen, Wallace V., 202
Frings, Hubert, 243
Frings, Mabel, 243

Gabor, Dennis, 65
Gallagher, William M., 119-120
Gardner, Beatrice, 232, 233
Gardner, R. Allen, 232, 233
Gibson, Ed, 123
Gerbner, George, 218
Goffman, Erving, 189, 271
Gombrich, E. H., 23
Gould, Gordon, 65
Gould, James L., 239
Gove, Philip B., 6
Griffin, Donald R., 172, 224, 231
Gurdjieff, G. I., 56
Gutenberg, Johann, 51, 58-62, 72, 208, 216

Haas, Mary R., 171
Hall, Edward T., 17, 46, 89, 105, 137, 142, 175, 184, 193, 195, 200
Handsome Lake, 47
Harrington, Richard, 21
Harper, Nancy, 72
Hawes, Leonard C., 41
Hayakawa, S. I., 113
Heisenberg, Werner, 134
Herbert, Frank, 121
Hess, Eckhard, 190
Hocking, Paul, 269
Hoebel, E. Adamson, 89
Hogben, Lancelot, 72
Holmes, Sherlock, 270
Hooke, S. H., 51-52
Hovland, Carl I., 8
Humphrey, John, 165-166
Hutchon, Kathryn, 270
Huxley, Aldous, 116

Ivins, William M., Jr., 73

James, William, 115
Jamison, Judith, 163, il. 164, 166
Janis, Irving L., 8
Janovy, John, Jr., 226
Jaynes, Julian, 146-147, 151
Jourard, Sidney M., 183

Katz, Solomon H., 143-144
Kees, Weldon, 154, 156
Kelley, Harold H., 8
King, Martin Luther, Jr., 21
Kluckhohn, Clyde, 170
Knapp, Mark L., 203
Kochman, Thomas, 107
Koko (gorilla), 233
Korzybski, Alfred, 18
Kozinski, Jerzy, 220-221
Kuhn, Thomas S., 18

La Barre, Weston, 87
Lana (chimpanzee), 235
Langbauer, William, 238
Langer, Susanne, 166-167
Larson, Carl E., 14
Lasswell, Harold, 19, 40, 41, 42
Le Boyer, Frederick, 183
Leigh, Vivian, 118
Leighton, Dorothea, 170
Lilly, John C., 235-236, 238-239, 243
Lincoln, Abraham, 54
Linden, Eugene, 232, 236, 243
Linehan, Edward J., 238
Lipton, James, 15
Lucas, George, 121
Luce, Gay Baer, 200
Lucy (chimpanzee), 235, il. 236

McAuliffe, Anthony C., 21
McLuhan, Eric, 270
McLuhan, Marshall, 21, 65, 66, 68, 73, 205, 206-207, 208, 209, 211, 212, 217, 220, 221, 240, 270
Magee, Bryan, 249
Marconi, Guglielmo, 65
May, Rollo, 138
Mehrabian, Albert, 192
Mendel, Gregor, 155
Merle, Robert, 226, 244
Miller, George A., 216
Miller, Gerald R., 248, 251, 270

Mitchell, Jack, 164
Momaday, N. Scott, 106
Montagu, Ashley, 183
Moore, Charles, 167
Morris, Charles, 11
Morris, Desmond, 203
Morse, Samuel F. B., 63
Mortenson, C. David, 41
Murphy, Gardner, 128
Murray, Sir James, 15
Murray, K. M. Elizabeth, 15

Nance, John, 77-78, 105
Newton, Sir Isaac, 123
Nicholson, Henry E., 248, 251, 270
Niépce, Nicéphore, 63
Nureyev, Rudolph, 186

Olson, David R., 57
Ornstein, Robert E., 139-141

Pasteur, Louis, 121
Patai, Raphael, 76
Pei, I. M., 194
Plato, 56, 70
Popper, Karl R., 251, 269
Porter, Richard E., 106
Premack, Ann James, 233-235, 238
Premack, David, 233-235, 238, 241
Pribram, Karl, 140
Pursell, Carroll W., Jr., 63

Quintilian, 71

Räderscheldt, Anton, 142
Ravel, Maurice, 142
Read, P. P., 124
Reif, Rita, 58
Rembrandt, 166
Rensberger, B., 235
Richter, 152
Ricketts, E. F., 13
Rogers, Everett M., 36, 37, 40
Rogers, Rekhas Agarwala, 36, 37, 40
Rorschach, Hermann, 134
Ruben, Brent D., 110
Ruesch, Jurgen, 154, 156
Rumbaugh, Duane M., 235
Russell, Bertrand, 5, 8

NAME INDEX

Safire, William, 268-269
Sagan, Carl, 163, 233, 240
Samovar, Larry A., 106
Samples, Bob, 149, 150
Samuels, Mike, 178
Samuels, Nancy, 178
Sapir, Edward, 168-172, 206-207
Sarah (chimpanzee), 233-235, il. 234
Satir, Virginia, 111
Scheflen, Albert, 28, 82-83
Schmandt-Besserat, Denise, 50
Scholderer, Victor, 62
Schramm, Wilbur, 143, 173
Schulze, Johann Heinrich, 63
Schwartz, Richard D., 270
Schwartz, Tony, 132
Sechrest, Lee, 270
Sereno, Kenneth K., 41
Shakespeare, William, 14, 20
Shannon, Claude, 24-28, il. 24, 32, 40, 42
Shepard, R. F., 66
Sholes, C. L., 64
Shopen, Timothy, 178
Shorey, Harry H., 184
Slater, Philip, 220
Smith, Alfred G., 253, 256
Smith, Ralph Lee, 268
Socrates, 56, 57, 61, 70, 213
Sommer, Robert, 203
Soumaoro, Bourama, 102-105
Sperry, Roger, 148
Spiegel, Laurie, 214
Spielberg, Steven, 121
Stegner, Wallace, 106
Steinbeck, John, 13
Stevenson, Adlai E., 119-120, il. 119
Stravinsky, Igor, 134
Sutton, George, 145

Tart, Charles T., 125
Terry, Walter, 186
Thomas, Lewis, 2, 36, 155, 219, 239

Thoreau, Henry David, 73-74
Thorpe, W. H., 231
Trotter, Robert J., 144, 146
Twain, Mark, 64

Vail, 63
Varley, Frederick, 145
Voltaire, 19
von Frisch, Karl, 226-227, 232

Wallace, Anthony F. C., 47
Warde, Beatrice, 61-62
Washoe (chimpanzee), 232, 235, 239, 244-245
Watzlawick, Paul, 132, 133, 241
Weaver, Warren, 9, 24
Webb, Eugene J., 270
Weiner, Norbert, 219
Weizenbaum, Joseph, 214-215, 216, 221
Wernicke, Karl, 139
White, Rhea A., 127
Whorf, Benjamin Lee, 168-172, 206-207
William of Occam, 15
Wilson, Edward O., 9, 227, 228, 238, 243
Wilson, John, 7
Wilson, John, 165
Wilson, Mitchell, 64
Winger, Howard W., 46, 50
Winn, Marie, 221
Winter, Ruth, 184
Winters, Shelley, 118-119
Wiser, Charlotte, 92
Wiser, William, 92
Witkin, Robert, 152
Wyeth, Andrew, 166

Yousef, Fathi E., 105
Yu, Frederick T. C., 113, 114, 133

Zinberg, Norman E., 134
Zworkin, Vladimir, 65

Subject Index

Alphabet
 Ameslan, 159, 232
 history of, 54, 70
 of the deaf of North America, 159, il. 160
 phonetic, 49, 209
Alternate States of Consciousness: Multiple Perspectives on the Study of Communication (Zinberg), 134
American Sign Language for the deaf (ASL), 159, il. 160, 233
Ameslan, 159, 232
Amish, 78, 79
Andes plane crash, 124-125
Animal Communication (Frings and Frings), 243
Animals. *See* Nonhuman creatures; specific species, e.g., Dogs and Dolphins
Anthropology, 77-78, 253-254, 269, 270
Apes, 241, 243
Apes, Men and Language (Linden), 236, 243
Arabs, 76, 184
Artistic abilities, 139, 140, 141, 143, 144-145, 149, 181
Architecture, 167, 193
Artists, 166
 perceptions, 120-121, il. 122
Ashokh (bard), 56
Asians, 186
Astronauts, 123-124
Athletes, 86-87, 127, 184, 189
Attention, selective, 113, 114-117, 119, 129, 130, 132
 to environment, 114-115
 to media, 115
Audience, 20-21, 22, 23, 33, 132

Bali, 94-98, 127
Bangladesh, 84
Bees, 224, 225
 See also Honeybees
Behavior, 82-83, 109, 111, 113, 253-254
 rules of, 83, 85, 87, 89, 90, 126
 shifts in, 81, 83-84, 265-266
Behavior as communication, 6, 8, 11
Being There (Kozinski), 220-221
Beliefs, personal, 117-120, 132
Beliefs, religious, 125, 126-127

SUBJECT INDEX

Berlin Wall, 82
Beyond Culture (Hall), 105
Bicameral mind, 146
Bicultural, 89-90
Biological communication, 10
Birds, 184, 226, 229, 243
Black Americans, 78, 79, 81
Black English, 79, 106-107
Body color, 188
Body language. *See* Nonverbal communication
Body movements, 156, 186-188, 194-197, 202
   See also Nonverbal communication
Body Time: Physiological Rhythms and Stress (Luce), 203
Books, styles and techniques, 263-265
Brain, 25-26, 45, 116, 130, 137-152
   asymmetry, 139
   bilaterality, 137, 138-139, il. 140, 149
   left hemisphere, 138, 139, 140, 141, 142, 143, 146
   of Cetacea (whales, etc.), 139
   right hemisphere, 139-141, 142, 143-146, 148, 157
Brain-damaged individuals, 142
Broca's area (brain), 138
Buddhist culture, 47, 244

Casablanca (film), 121
Caste system, 92, 94, 95, 96
Cats, 224, 225
Cause-effect relationships, 23-24, 38-39, 113, 169
Caught in a Web of Words (Murray), 15
Cave paintings, 43, 44, il. 45, 70
Cetacea, 235, 237-239
Change, impact of, 60, 63, 67, 68, 71, 210, 216, 265-268
Chemical changes, 126, 127
   See also Smell
Chemical notation, 158
Chemical signaling, 29
Chicanos, 78, 79, 183
Chickens' pecking order, 230
Chimpanzees, cross-species communication studies, 232-235, il. 234, il. 236, 240, 244-245
China, 49, 58, 87, 98-102, 169
Chinatown (New York), 101
Chinese ideograms, 49, 101
Chinese immigrants, 99-100
Circular causality, 39-40, il. 39, 41
City as Classroom: Understanding Language as Media (McLuhan, Hutchon, and McLuhan), 270
Clay tablets, 50, 51
Clocks, 163
Close Encounters of the Third Kind (film), 121, 244
Code, Marine Corps, 80-81
Code of Handsome Lake (Handsome Lake), 47
Codes, 153-179, 254
Codification, 153, 154
   analogic, 156-157, 160-163, 165-167, 172, 176, 177
   biological, 154
   cultural, 154, 156
   digital, 156, 157-160, 172, 177
   genetic, 154-156
   illiteracy, 163, 165-166
   rhythm, 174, 175
   synchrony, 174-175
Communicator, 20, 132, 247, 248, 274
Communication, 113, 128, 130, 132, 133, 137, 153, 154, 174, 175-177, 216, 248
   as extension beyond body, 46, 205, 218, 219, 220
   as process, 8, 12, 17, 18, 20, 28
   as system, 24-29, il. 24, 40
   definitions of, 1, 2, 5, 6, 8, 17, 32, 166
   importance of, 43-44, 70, 273
   intercultural barriers to, 93-94, 150
   internal body, 8
   interpersonal, 25, 26, 27-28, 33-35, 40, 130, 150
   intrapersonal, 12, 29-32, 33, 34, 35, 40, 130
   intraspecies, 225, 235, 238, 240
   machine-interposed, 25, 26, 27-28

models of, 17-41
nonhuman, 8, 11, 82, 223-245
within cultural context, 75-76, 91, 92, 105, 100-110
See also Behavior as communication; Biological communication; Communication technology; Cross-cultural communication; Cross-species communication; Environmental communication; Extraterrestrial communication; Genetic communication; Group communication; Nonverbal communication
Communication Between Man and Dolphin (Lilly), 239, 243
Communication Inquiry: A Perspective on Process (Miller and Nicholson), 230
Communication mode. See Medium
Communication skills, 4, 247-256, 263
Communication technology, 59-60, 63-66, 67-68, 213, 214-216, 218, 220, 266-268, 270
Computer Power and Human Reason: From Judgment to Calculation (Weizenbaum), 221
Computers, 65, 67, 159, 214-216, 219, 267, 268
Consciousness, 9, 12, 140, 146, 147
Continuity theory, 225
Corpus callosum (brain), 139
Cross-cultural communication, 91-104, 105, 106, 150
Cross-species communication, 10, 13, 225, 240, 242, 244-245, 267
chimpanzees and humans, 232-235, 236
Cetacea and humans, 235, 237-239
Cues. See Stimuli
Cultural relativism, 90-91
Culture, 75-106, 109, 125, 128
as system, 82, 90-91
definitions of, 76-82, 104, 126
dominant, 82, 90-91
See also specific cultures, e.g., Islamic; Cultures, variations in; Oral cultures; Print cultures
Culture-bound, 76
Culture exchanges, 104
Culture shock, 91-104, 123-125
Cultures, variations in, 76, 78, 84, 87-89 93-104, 137, 142-143, 144, 147, 165-166, 169-171, 183, 187, 189-190, 191, 197, 200-201, 210, 258-260
Cuneiform, 52, il. 54

DNA (deoxyribonucleic acid), 155
Dancers, 86-87, 163, il. 164, 186
Dancing Bees (von Frisch), 227
Day of the Dolphin (Merle), 226, 244
Deaf, 159, 160
Decoding, 26, 32, 80, 154, 233
Deer, 224
Dictionaries, 6, 8, 15, 157, 248
Discontinuity theory. See Great Gap theory
Dogs, 184, 224, 225
Dolphins, 10, 224, 226, 235, 237, 238, 240, 243, 244
Dreams, 129, 141, 149
Dune (Herbert), 121

Education, 101-102, 130, 142-143, 148-149, 189, 193
Electronic media. See Communication technology
Eloquent Animals: A Study in Animal Communication (Davis), 242
Empirical method, 249, 250, 253-254, 269
examples of, 256-263
Encoding, 25-26, 32, 154, 155
ELIZA, 215-216
English language, 16, 49, 157-158, 169-170
Environment, 37-38, 40, 110, 114-115, 117, 123, 144, 170, 218-219, 220, 240, 252
Environmental communication, 192-194, 207, 213, 252
Eskimo (Carpenter, Varley, and Flaherty), 144-146

298 SUBJECT INDEX

Eskimos, 21, 171, 184, 211
  Inuits, 144-146, 148
Ethics, 255
Ethics (Aristotle), 70
Ethnocentrism, 90-91
Evolution, 146, 147, 218, 225
An Exaltation of Larks or, The Venereal Game (Lipton), 15
The Exorcist (film), 117-118
Experiences, 109, 111, 113, 132, 148
Extrasensory perception, 127, 128
Extraterrestrial communication, 241-242, 244
Eye contact, 174, 176, 187, 188-190, 204
Eye pupil size, 190-191

Faces, mirror opposites, il. 151
Feedback loop. *See* Circular causality
Field theory. *See* General System Theory
Feelings, 82, 166-167, 177, 185
Fifth Symphony (Beethoven), 83, 158-159
Fish, 184, 224, 225, 229
Flint Journal (newspaper), 119-120
Form as opposed to content, 206
Foundations of Communication Theory (Sereno and Mortenson), 41
From Cave Painting to Comic Strip: A Kaleidescope of Human Communication (Hogben), 72
The Functions of Human Communication (Dance and Larson), 14

Gender Advertisements (Goffman), 27
Gender signals, 197, il. 198, 271
General System Theory, 35-41
  definition, 36
Generalization, 247, 251
Genetic communication, 9, 11, 12, 13, 154-156, 181
The Gentle Tasaday: A Stone Age People in the Philippines (Nance), 105-106
Gestalts, 139, 144
Global village idea, 65, 68-69, 72, 105, 211-212, 217, 220
God and Golem, Inc. (Weiner), 219

Gorilla, 233
Great Gap theory, 225, 229, 230, 232, 239, 241, 243
Greek, 55, 70-71
Group communication, 20, 130
Gutenberg Bible, 51, 58, il. 59, 60, 62

Hamlet (Shakespeare), 20
Hand holding, 184, il. 186
Haptics. *See* Touch
Hausa (African) language, 171
Hearing, 173, 209, 210, 211
Heinsenberg principle, 134
The Hidden Dimension (Hall), 105
Hieroglyphs, 52-53, 54, il. 55
History, 18, 43-73, 146-147, 218, 266
Holograms, 65, il. 66, 67, 267
Homo erectus, 45
Homo sapiens, 10, 150, 225, 241
Honeybees, 9, 13, 227
  dance of, 227-228, 230, 231-232
How Real Is Real? Confusion, Disinformation, Communication (Watzlawick), 133
Human Communication Theory: The History of a Paradigm (Harper), 72
Human Intelligence (Fincher), 142
Human superiority questioned, 225, 229, 230, 232, 239-240, 241
Hypnosis, 127, 215
Hypothesizing, 251, 252, 258-259, 260, 262-263, 269, 272

Illiteracy, analogic and digital, 163, 165-166, 177
The Image (Boulding), 11, 133
Image, as knowledge, 111-113, 132, 207
Imitation, 93, 100
In-awareness, 86-87, 154, 187
India, 84
Indians, 78, 79, 106, 126
  Cheyennes, 89
  Iroquois, 47
  Navajo, 80-81, 170-171
Individual differences, 22, 92, 93, 109, 133, 148

Individuality, 76, 109-113, 126, 132, 137, 156, 209
Informants, 254-255, 272
Information explosion, 62, 68-69, 110, 211, 212, 267-268
Information, metabolizing, 110, 111, 113
Information processing, 137, 139-141, 142
Information, stored, 132
Inputs, 39, 82, 110, 141
Insanity, 89, 177
Insects, 224, 243
Inside Intuition: What We Know about Nonverbal Communication (Davis), 196, 202
Institute for Primate Studies, Norman, OK, 235
Intelligence in Ape and Man (Premack), 241
The Intelligence of Feeling (Witkin), 152
Intercultural communication. *See* Cross-cultural communication
Intercultural Communication: A Reader (Samovar and Porter), 106
Internal body system, 29, 36, 37
Interpersonal space, 191, il. 192
Interpersonal communication. *See* Communication, interpersonal
Interspecies communication. *See* Cross-species communication
Intrapersonal communication. *See* Communication, intrapersonal
Intraspecies communication. *See* Communication, intraspecies
An Introduction to Intercultural Communication (Condon and Yousef), 105
The Invention of Print with Movable Type in China and Its Spread Westward (Carter), 72
Islamic cultures, 47, 84, 167, il. 168, 184, 187, 199
Italians, 187

JANUS, 238-239
Jews, 78, 79

Journey to Ixtlan: The Lessons of Don Juan (Castaneda), 133

Kewala Basin Marine Research Facility, Hawaii, 244
Kinesics and Context: Essays on Body Motion Communication (Birdwhistell), 202
Kinesics. *See* Body movements
King Kong (film), 122
Knowledge, 141
  subjective, 111-113, 130
Koran, 47, 84
Korea, 58

Language, 6, 8-9, 45, 46, 82, 84, 93, 139, 140, 146, 154, 156, 157-158, 169-172, 178, 206, 207, 225, 229, 248-249, 254
  changing usage, 268-269
  qualities necessary for, 231
  use by chimpanzees, 232-235, il. 236
Languages and Their Speakers (Shopen), 178
The Lark (Anouilh), 100
Laser beams, 69
Le Sacre du Printemps (Stravinsky), 134
Leaf-cutter ants, 224
Learning, 82-87, 138
Left handedness, 141, 150, il. 151
Left hemisphere. *See* Brain
Lexicography, 6
Light bulbs, 207
Logic (Aristotle), 70

Machine-to-machine communication, 10
Mali, Republic of, 102-104
Maps, 145, 161-163
Mass media, 66-68, 130, 205
  as change agents, 205-206
Mass Media: Systems and Effects (Davison, Boylan, and Yu), 133
Mathematics, 101, 139, 140, 156, 222
Mechanics of the Mind (Blakemore), 150
Media, 22-23, 43, 270
  development of new, 44, 67-68, 71, 72,

73
Media, private, 68, 208-209
Meditation, 126
Medium, 22-23
The Medium Is the Massage: An Inventory of Effects (McLuhan and Fiore), 221
"Medium is the message" idea, 206, 221
The Metaphoric Mind: A Celebration of Creative Consciousness (Samples), 150
"Meditation XVII" (Donne), 91
Memorization, 47, 56, 100
Memory, selective, 113, 128-130, il. 131, 132
Manwatching: A Field Guide to Human Behavior (Morris), 203
Metacommunication, 176-177, 231
Micro cultures, 79-80
Monkeys, 224
Morse code, 155, 156, 158
Motion pictures, 65, 67, 84, 165-166, 206, 220
Motor activity (body), 139
Multicultural, 89-90
Multilingual, 84
Multiple messages, 175
Music, 121, 134, 158-159, 167, 173

National Gallery of Art, Washington, D.C., il. 194
Navajo war code, 80-81
Nervous system, 29, 116, 211
New Guinea, 87-89
Newspapers, 60
"No man is an island" idea, 91, 273-274
Noise interference, 26-28, 193
Nonhuman communication. *See* Communication, nonhuman
Nonhuman creatures, 182, 184
  communication with humans, 10, 13, 225-226, 232-235, 236-239, 242
  communication within species, 225, 235, 238, 240
  rights of, 244
Nonverbal aptitudes, 139

Nonverbal communication, 9, 31, 34, 44, 45, 82, 94, 172, 174, 181-204
  definition, 181-182
Nonverbal Communication in Human Interaction (Knapp), 203

Objects as communicators, 197, 199-200
Observation, naturalistic, 247-248, 249-254, 269
  four examples, 256-263
  of printed materials, 263-265
Occam's Razor, 15
Oculisics. *See* Eye contact
Odor. *See* Smell
Olfaction. *See* Smell
Oral cultures, 46-47, 56, 57, 208, 209, 210, 211, 212
The Origin of Consciousness in the Breakdown of the Bicameral Mind (Jaynes), 146
Out-of-awareness, 85-86, 154
Outputs, 39, 82, 110
Oxford English Dictionary, 15

Pakistan, 84
Paralanguage, 176
Papyrus, 50-51, 52
Perception, selective, 113, 117-128, 129, 130, 132
Perceptions, 139, 209, 210
Perceptual states, different, 126-128
Personal Space: The Behavioral Basis of Design (Sommer), 203
Personality, 111, 113
Pheromones, 184, 186
Philippines, 77-78
Phonograph, 64-65
Photography, 62, 161, 255-256
  history of, 63
The Plug-In Drug: Television, Children, and the Family (Winn), 221
Poetics (Aristotle), 70
Ping-pong theory, 28
A Place in the Sun (film), 118
Planet of the Apes (film), 226
Pollution, 121

SUBJECT INDEX

Postal systems, automated, 266-267
Posture, 196-197
Pragmatics of Analoguing: Theory and Model Construction in Communication (Hawes), 41
Preliterate cultures. *See* Oral cultures
Primates, 10
Principles of Visual Anthropology (Hocking), 269-270
Print cultures, 62, 67, 208-210, 211
Printing with movable type, 44, 58-60, 61, 62, 71, 72, 206, 208-210
Prints and Visual Communication (Ivins), 73
Privacy, 68, 208-209
The Process of Communication: An Introduction to Theory and Practice (Berlo), 41
Proxemics. *See* Interpersonal space
Psi, 127-128
Psychokinesis, 127
Psychology, 109, 111, 128, 146
Psychotherapy, 127, 215-216
Puerto Ricans, 79, 183, 189-190

Radio, 65, 66-67, 217, 222
The Random House Dictionary, 16
Reading, 208, 209-210, 233
Read-out instruments, digital, 160, il. 161
Reinforcement, 113-114, 201
Religion, 83, 146, 149
Repression, 129
Research, 249, 253-54, 255-256, 269, 270
 field, 250
 laboratory, 250
 use of recording equipment, 255-256
Retention. *See* Memory
Rhetoric, 70-71, 72
Rhetoric (Aristotle), 70
Rhythm, 174, 200, 203
Right handedness, 141, 150, il. 151
Right hemisphere. *See* Brain
Robin and Marian (film), 61
Rodents, 224
Role, defined, 99-100
Roman Catholics, 98-102, 118, 125

Rorschach test, 134
Rosetta stone, 53, il. 55

Sapir-Whorf hypothesis, 168-172, 205, 206-207
Satellites, 65, 68, 161-163, 211, 266
Science, 140, 142, 239
Scientific method, 250-252, 253-254
Scientists, 241, 253
 perceptions, 121, 123
Scribes, il. 48, 60-61, 62, 208, 209
The Sea of Cortez (Steinbeck and Ricketts), 13-14
The Second Ring of Power (Castaneda), 133
Seeing, 208, 209, 210
Seeing with the Mind's Eye: The History, Techniques and Uses of Visualization (Samuels and Samuels), 178
Selection processes, 113-132
Senses, 207, 208
 See also Hearing; Sight; Smell; Touch
Sensory activity (body), 139, 173
Sensory perceptions, 209, 210, 224
A Separate Reality: Further Conversations with Don Juan (Castaneda), 133
Sexism, 16, 265, 271
Sight, 173, 178
Signaling systems, 8, 9, 10, 11, 12, 13, 26, 153, 154, 156, 175-176, 181, 201-202, 224
 See also Codes; Codification
The Silent Language (Hall), 105, 200
Signs, 6, 49, 154, 172, 173, 230, 231
 bus stop, 256-258
Sign language. *See* American Sign Language of the deaf; Ameslan
Sinister People: The Looking Glass World of the Left Hander (Fincher), 150
Skateboarder, il. 88
Skepticism, 275
Skin, 183
Smell, 184, 186, 224
Sociobiology: The New Synthesis (Wilson), 243

The Sorcerer (painting, Cave of Trois Frères, France), 45
Sound, 224
Source credibility, 20
Southampton Island, maps, 145
Soviet Union, 82
Spatial relationships, 139, 141, 146, 207, 211, 224
Speech, 44, 45, 46, 50, 138, 139, 141, 223
Spiders, 224
Star Wars (film), 121
Stimuli, 8, 10, 29-31, 34, 117, 132
A Streetcar Named Desire (film), 118
Subcultures, 78-81, 82, 83
Suicide, 87-89
Sumerian pictographs, 51-52, 54
Superstition, 258-260
Surfacing (Atwood), 138
Symbols, 6, 172, 230, 231, 233, 234
Synchrony, 174-175, 196-197, 274
System. *See* General System theory

Tacesics. *See* Touch
Tape recorders, 255-256
Tasaday, 77-78, 105-106
The Teachings of Don Juan: A Yaqui Way of Knowledge (Castaneda), 133
Telegraph, 63, 64-65
Telephone, 64, 206, il. 212, 267
Television, il. 48, 65, 67, 71, 218, 221, 266, 267, 268
Thai-English Student's Dictionary (Haas), 171
Thai language, 171-172
Thinking, 19, 29, 57, 123, 140, 144, 168, 172-173
Through the Looking Glass (Carroll), 7
Throughputs, 40, 82, 110
Time, 100, 200-201, 207, 211
Touch, 27-28, 183-184, il. 185, 224
Touching (Montagu), 183
Typewriter, 64

Unconsciousness, 9, 10, 25, 85-86, 87, 248
Understanding Media: The Extensions of Man (McLuhan), 221
Unmasking the Face: A Guide to Recognizing Emotions from Facial Expressions (Ekman and Friesen), 202
Unobtrusive Measures: Nonreactive Research in the Social Sciences (Webb et al.), 270
Uses and gratification, 114

Valence, 31
Variable factors, 18
Video discs and tapes, 256, 266
Visual Thinking (Arnheim), 178
"Voices of the gods" theory, 146

Walden (Thoreau), 73
Walking, 85-87
War and Peace in the Global Village (McLuhan and Fiore), 73
Wernicke's area (brain), 139
Whales, 224, 225, 237, 238, 240, 243
  song of the humpback, 238
Wolves, 224
Writing, 44, 240, 263-265
  advantages of, 57
  as analytical tool, 57
  Chinese, 49
  cuneiform, 52
  hieroglyphs, 52-53, il. 55
  history of, 51-55, 58, 62, 71
  ideograms, 49, 53
  opposition to, 56-57
  pictographs, 51-52, 53
  sign, 49
  sound, 49
  Sumerian, 51-52
  surfaces, 50-51, 57, 62, 71
  See also Scribes

Yerkes Regional Primate Research Center, Atlanta, 233, 235